Best of
Baseball

PAUL ADOMITES
SAUL WISNIA

CONSULTANT
DAVID NEMEC

PUBLICATIONS INTERNATIONAL, LTD.

Paul Adomites (chapters 2-6) was the author of *October's Game*, was co-author of *Babe Ruth: His Life and Times*, and was a contributing writer for *Treasury of Baseball*, *Total Baseball*, and *Encyclopedia of Baseball Team Histories*. He served as publications director for the Society of American Baseball Research (SABR) and founded and edited *SABR Review of Books*, as well as its successor, the *Cooperstown Review*. He is a frequent contributor to *Pirates Magazine* and *In Pittsburgh*.

Saul Wisnia (chapter 1) is a former sports writer for *The Washington Post* and feature writer for the *Boston Herald*. He was co-author of *Babe Ruth: His Life and Times* and contributing writer to *Raging Bulls!*, *Baseball: More Than 150 Years*, and *Treasury of Baseball*. He has been an archivist for the New England Sports Museum and co-hosted a Boston-area sports radio talk show, and his work has appeared in *Sports Illustrated* and *The Boston Globe*.

David Nemec is a baseball historian who has authored and co-authored numerous baseball history, quiz, and memorabilia books, including the *Beer & Whisky League*, *Great Baseball Feats, Facts & Firsts*, *The Ultimate Baseball Book*, and *20th Century Baseball Chronicle*. He has consulted on such books as *Greatest Baseball Players of All Time* and *Baseball: More Than 150 Years*.

Ballpark Illustrations: Paul Pearson

Photo credits:

Front cover: **Focus on Sports; National Baseball Library & Archive, Cooperstown, NY.; Photofile.**

Interior: **Archive Photos:** 223; **Bettmann:** 15; Bettmann/Corbis: 117, 181, 265; **National Baseball Library & Archive, Cooperstown, NY:** 139.

CONTENTS

INTRODUCTION • 6

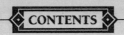

CONTENTS

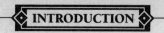

SELECTING THE BEST

WILLIE MAYS OR MICKEY MANTLE? Ty Cobb or Babe Ruth? The '27 Yankees or the '75 Reds? Major League Baseball has been attracting fanatical followers since its birth well over a century ago, and from the start these faithful onlookers have waged debate over the comparative merit of the players and teams making up America's pastime. This slew of never-ending arguments is a tradition passed down from one generation to the next, and while the names have changed through the years, one thing is certain: The emotion accompanying the dialogue is as strong as ever.

In an attempt to help readers ponder the unanswerable, writers and editors for *Best of Baseball* have studied, squabbled, and studied some more to produce lists of the game's greatest performers in a variety of areas. These alphabetically (sometimes chronologically) arranged selections should not be viewed as etched in stone; like the names regularly thrown about in barrooms throughout the country, they are open to debate. They should, however, provide readers with a better sense of the different elements that go into making a player great— everything from power, speed, and defense to craftiness, grit, and personality.

The first and largest analysis focuses on the 50 greatest baseball players of all time. Coming up with such a list was an excruciating task—more than 100 Hall of Famers had to be eliminated—and those players picked in the end received the nod for a variety of reasons. The more obvious selections were men whose legendary status put them in a class by themselves (e.g., Babe Ruth, Ted Williams, Cy Young), but many others in the Top 50 had statistics that actually fell short of many others who were *not* included. The explanation for such blasphemy is simple: There is more to baseball than mere numbers.

Take, for instance, the case of Dave Kingman. Some crazed Wrigley Field bleacher bums might protest that their hero had more home runs than many players on the list, but finding room for "Kong" and his 442 dingers at the expense of a Tris Speaker or Roberto Clemente would be ridiculous. Speaker and Clemente had fewer homers combined (357) than Kingman, but both were exceptional outfielders who exhibited power, speed, and leadership while regularly hitting above .320. The graceless Kingman hit just .236 over his career, was often laughable in the field, and struck out 1,816 times—nearly once per game. Then there is Ozzie Smith. Slugging shortstops like Vern Stephens and Al Dark produced far more runs per season, but it is likely no player in baseball history ever prevented more runs from scoring *against* his team than the slick-fielding Smith. The acrobatic "Wizard of Oz" may have hit just 28 homers over 19 seasons, but a far more important number has earned the

stalwart of three pennant-winning Cardinal clubs a spot on the list—his 13 Gold Gloves.

Failing to combine excellence with longevity was a crucial element in many players not cracking the Top 50. Hall of Famers Ralph Kiner, Hack Wilson, and Roy Campanella were all dominating performers over short periods of time, but none had careers long enough to warrant consideration. In contrast, Carl Yastrzemski was a Gold Glove outfielder who still ranks high on many all-time offensive charts—yet too many of *his* monumental numbers were amassed over two decades of solid seasons peppered with just a few truly outstanding campaigns. Yaz gave perhaps the best clutch performance in history during his Triple Crown run of 1967, but for more than 16 years following it, he was rarely even the best hitter on his own team.

Consistency alone is not enough; only with consistent *greatness* could a player expect to join this elite fraternity. The Top 50 includes 10 members of the 500-home run club, eight 300-game winners, and 21 position players (out of 38 picked) with lifetime averages of .310 or higher. How tough was the competition? Only four current players—Smith, Cal Ripken, Ryne Sandberg, and Rickey Henderson—made the grade; Ozzie for his sterling defense, Ripken for his all-around play and incredible conquest of Lou Gehrig's "unbreakable" record of 2,130 consecutive games played, Sandberg for his complete package of skills at second base, and

Henderson for his awesome blend of power and speed. Fellows like Barry Bonds, Ken Griffey Jr., Frank Thomas, and Greg Maddux may eventually have arguments for inclusion, but for now they fall short in tenure.

There are a few notable exceptions to such thinking. Dodger left-hander Sandy Koufax won only 165 games in his career, but after going 36-40 in his first six major-league seasons, he was 129-47 with five ERA titles, four no-hitters, and three Cy Young Awards in his last six—a flash of brilliance so outstanding that it earned him first-ballot induction as the youngest (36 years old) Hall of Famer ever and inclusion among the Top 50's staff of 12 pitchers. Joe Jackson is another for whom a short stretch of greatness was enough; "Shoeless Joe" played just nine full seasons before being banished at age 31 with seven teammates in the Black Sox scandal, but the illiterate outfielder's .356 career average still trails only Cobb's and Rogers Hornsby's on the all-time charts.

Negro Leaguers Satchel Paige and Josh Gibson made it in primarily on reputation. Few of their Black Ball exploits were recorded in scorebooks or newspapers, and we can only speculate on how many homers Gibson might have hit and how many games Paige might have won were they allowed into the big leagues during their prime. Jackie Robinson, his .311 lifetime big-league average notwithstanding, is in simply for being who he

was—the single most important American figure of the last half-century.

Following a biography/analysis of each Top 50 player, a series of all-time "best" lists looks at a variety of specific categories. Here, especially in departments such as "10 Best Team Leaders," "10 Grittiest Players," and "10 Best Personalities," insight gained from old players and old stories carries as much or more weight than statistics. Anyone who faced Pete Rose or watched his head-first slides knows that "Charlie Hustle" belongs on the grit list. Negro League teammate Satchel Paige said Cool Papa Bell was so fast he could "shut out the light switch and be in bed before the room got dark," a tale the staff had in mind when Bell was selected among the fastest players of all time.

Every conceivable batting and pitching category has been covered. There are lists devoted to the strongest sluggers (e.g., Jimmie "The Beast" Foxx and Harmon "Killer" Killebrew), best bunters (Richie Ashburn, Brett Butler), craftiest hurlers (Luis Tiant, Juan Marichal), and hardest throwers (Nolan Ryan, Bob Feller). And along with the familiar names are a few surprises. Beside Ryan and Feller on the list of the greatest speedballers is Steve Dalkowski, an Orioles farmhand who broke backstops with his wild 110-mph fastballs and had 1,396 strikeouts and 1,354 walks over 995 minor-league innings—the highest ratios for both departments in pro history. Ted Williams once took a

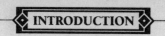

pitch from Steve during a pregame warmup and claimed it was the fastest he had ever seen, and although a sore arm prevented Dalkowski from ever reaching the big leagues, his place in history is preserved here.

Selections for the best games in history offer wonderful memories for some and horrific nightmares for others. For sheer drama, there are the final games of the 1912, 1924, and 1960 World Series—all decided in the bottom of the last inning—as well as the sixth contest of the '75 Series won by the Red Sox 7-6 on Carlton Fisk's 12th-inning homer off the Fenway Park foul pole. Dodger followers will lament the inclusion of the 1950 and '51 regular-season finales in which pennants were lost on the last day to the Phillies and Giants respectively, while Red Sox diehards will try and survive reminders of a more contemporary letdown—the sixth game of the '86 World Series in which Boston blew a two-run lead with two outs in the 10th and lost 6-5 when Mookie Wilson's grounder went through first baseman Bill Buckner's legs.

The evolution of the game was taken into account throughout the evaluations. Rabbit Maranville may have made 711 career errors (including a seasonal high of 53) while playing mostly shortstop from 1912-35, but his name stands on the all-time defensive list right alongside modern stars Smith and Luis Aparicio—who made far fewer miscues with well-groomed fields and bigger gloves to aid their efforts. Charlie Comiskey's Browns had just four regular pitchers and 20 homers as a team one season in the midst of winning four straight American Association titles from 1885-88; when the 1975-76 Reds took back-to-back world championships, they used a 10-man staff and had four different *players* hit 20 or more homers. Dramatically different in makeup, both of these clubs are listed among the best of all time.

The lists will undoubtedly prove educational to many fans. The careers of Hall of Fame managers Walter Alston and Casey Stengel are well documented, but how about Frank Selee, who compiled a lifetime winning percentage of .598 (fourth highest all time) and led the Boston Beaneaters to five National League championships during the 1890s? Cardinal/Dodger president Branch Rickey is heralded as the man who engineered the first major-league farm system and brought Jackie Robinson to the majors, but Rube Foster was just as significant a figure in black baseball as founder and president of the Negro National League—the circuit from which Robinson and most early black big-leaguers eventually came.

It's all here—from *The Boys of Summer* (listed in "10 Best Books") and *Bull Durham* ("10 Best Films") to Tom Boswell ("10 Best Writers") and Ernie Harwell ("10 Best Broadcasters"). Left-handers Babe Ruth and Bill Lee pitched for the Red Sox

60 years apart, but the fun-loving "Bambino" and philosophical "Spaceman" both show up in one of the more winsome categories—"Best Personalities." Super fans such as Ebbets Field cowbell-clanger Hilda Chester receive mention, and even umpires get their due—with Hall of Fame arbiters such as Billy Evans and Bill Klem serving as proof that men in blue can be rock-tough symbols of class and not mere punching bags for disgruntled fans and players.

So enjoy your journey through *Best of Baseball*. You may never find the answer to Mays vs. Mantle, but chances are you'll have more ammunition with which to make your argument—along with plenty of additional insights on the national pastime to help spark new debates.

CHAPTER 1

50 Best Players

O F THE 10,000 men who have slipped on major-league jerseys over the last 120 years, 50 extraordinary individuals stand out among the rest. More than just All-Stars, greater than the average Hall of Famer, these are the 50 greatest baseball players of all time.

Mickey Mantle (left) and Willie Mays

HANK AARON

HE NEVER HIT 60 HOME RUNS IN A SEASON—or even 50. Henry Aaron became the all-time Homer King and accumulated his considerable cache of records not by pumping out statistics that jumped off the paper, but rather with a career of steady and unheralded consistency. From 1955-74, Hank Aaron averaged *36 home runs a year for 20 full seasons.*

How could production like this go unnoticed? The former Negro Leaguer had a fine rookie season with the Milwaukee Braves in 1954 (.280 with 13 homers), yet even as he blossomed into one of the National League's top hitters, the slim, shy Alabaman with the quick and powerful wrists was overshadowed by sluggers the likes of Willie Mays, Mickey Mantle, and Duke Snider.

A batting title in '56 (.328) and a World Series win and MVP season the following year (.322, 44, 132) garnered Aaron some notoriety, but when talk turned to someone breaking Babe Ruth's season homer mark (60) or career homer mark (714), Hank's name was rarely mentioned. The heir to Babe's throne would be a muscle-bound masher like Mays or Mantle, not a skinny line-drive hitter whose drives happened to find the outfield fence with regularity. Over the next several years, Aaron garnered a second batting title (.355 in 1959) and three Gold Gloves for his outfield play, but still he remained in the shadows.

Then in the mid-1960s, Willie and Mickey began slowing down, and after the Braves moved their franchise to the homer-friendly climate of Atlanta, Aaron began heating up. He led the NL with 39 and 44 home runs his first two Southern summers and clubbed his 500th homer in 1968. Aaron slugged 44 more in 1969, became the ninth major-leaguer to reach 3,000 hits in 1970, and slammed home run No. 600 off Gaylord Perry of the Giants in '71 en route to a career-high 47-homer year at age 36.

When "Hammerin' Hank" passed Mays with his 649th clout in June 1972, the race to catch Ruth began—a race against age, time, and bigotry. Aaron received 930,000 pieces of mail in 1973, including racial slurs, death threats, and plots to kidnap his children. He survived that pressure and rallied to hit 40 homers in just 392 at-bats, finishing the '73 season one home run short of Ruth.

Aaron tied the Babe on Opening Day the following year, then passed him with a shot into the Braves' bullpen off Al Downing of the Dodgers on April 8, 1974, in Atlanta. Hank finished up two years later with 755 homers, 2,297 RBI (also a record), 3,771 hits (third all time), and 2,174 runs—second all time, and the same number accumulated by a guy named Ruth. Asked about this tie for eternity, Aaron said he kind of liked it that way.

MAJOR LEAGUE TOTALS

BA	G	AB	R	H	2B	3B	HR	RBI	SB
.305	3,298	12,364	2,174	3,771	624	98	755	2,297	240

GROVER CLEVELAND ALEXANDER

NAMED AFTER A FORMER PRESIDENT of the United States, Grover Cleveland Alexander later had a future U.S. president (Ronald Reagan) portray him in the motion-picture depiction of his life. But while the right-handed ace set National League records for victories (373, tied with Christy Mathewson) and shutouts (90) over his long career, his life off the mound was anything but an American success story.

As a rookie, Alexander went 28-13 in 1911 while baffling hitters with his strange three-quarter-arm motion and leading the NL in victories (a 20th-century rookie record), shutouts (seven), complete games (31), and innings (367) for fourth-place Philadelphia. In 1914, Alexander went 27-15 while leading the senior circuit in wins, strikeouts (214), complete games (32), and innings (355).

The Phillies reached their first World Series in 1915, and Alexander led the charge—going 31-10 and pacing the league in wins, ERA (1.22), strikeouts (241), complete games (36), innings (376), and shutouts (12) while walking a mere 64. It was the first of three straight years in which he paced the league with 30 or more wins, a stretch in which he went 94-35 with a 1.54 ERA, 608 strikeouts, and just 170 walks over an incredible 1,152 innings. He completed 108 of 131 starts over the span, including 36 shutouts—16 of them in 1916 alone to set a major-league record.

Traded to the Cubs following the 1917 season, Pete spent most of the next year overseas fighting in World War I. The shelling he encountered there left him partially deaf and may have led to the seizures and alcohol problems that began surfacing around the time he went 16-11 with a league-best 1.72 ERA and nine shutouts for Chicago in 1919. His last great season—27-14 with league-best wins, ERA (1.91), and strikeouts (173)—followed, but his fastball was gone and he never struck out more than 77 in a season again.

Guile helped him go 138-94 over the last 10 years of his career. After his drinking had prompted the Cubs to dump him off to St. Louis in '26, Alexander's most legendary moment came while pitching relief in the World Series that fall—a strikeout of Yankee slugger Tony Lazzeri with the bases loaded in the seventh inning of the final game. His career numbers showed what he was able to achieve despite his troubles, but in the end he was perhaps the most famous American to die broke and alone in a hotel room.

MAJOR LEAGUE TOTALS									
W	L	ERA	G	CG	IP	H	ER	BB	SO
373	208	2.56	696	438	5,189.1	4,868	1,474	953	2,199

LUKE APPLING

HE HOMERED OVER the RFK Stadium fence at the age of 75 in the first Cracker Jack Old-Timer's Game in 1982, but Luke Appling was anything but a slugger in his stellar 20-year career with the Chicago White Sox. The steady shortstop was a hitter few could match for patience, perseverance, and production—just the man to have leading off your lineup for the better part of two decades.

A baseball and football star at Oglethorpe University in his hometown of Atlanta, Appling was with the Atlanta Crackers when he caught the eye of both the Cubs and White Sox. The South Side got him, and the 23-year-old debuted in the fall of 1930 with a .308 mark in 26 at-bats. He struggled the next year (.232 in 96 games), improved steadily in '32 (.274 as the starting shortstop), and broke through in '33, hitting .322—the first of nine straight years and 15 times overall Appling topped the .300 mark.

Appling was a fine example of a player far more common in his day than now—a scrappy, nonflashy leadoff man who could always be counted on to give a good effort at the plate. This might mean ripping a single or double, working the pitcher for a walk, or sacrificing the runner—but it rarely meant a wasted plate appearance. There are tales of his fouling off as many as 23 pitches in a single at-bat, and nobody seemed to mind that he had only

45 homers in 2,422 games. A .310 lifetime hitter, he averaged 80 walks, 81 runs, and just 31 strike-outs in his 15 years of playing 100 or more games. Were it not for World War II, Luke would have likely reached 3,000 hits.

Appling's many fine seasons were peppered with a few outstanding ones. In 1936, he led the AL with a career-high .388 average and also recorded personal bests with 204 hits, 128 RBI, and 111 runs—all the more amazing considering his six home runs. He also led the AL with a .328 batting mark in '43, when he again showed his ability to get more with less by notching 80 RBI, 27 steals, and 90 walks despite only three homers.

Appling was known as "Old Aches and Pains" because of his endless complaints about his own health or the conditions of the Comiskey Park infield. In actuality he was quite durable, a swift and steady fielder who ranks high on the all-time lists with 2,218 games played at short, 4,398 putouts, 7,218 assists, and 1,424 double plays. In almost every category, he trails Luis Aparicio, who came to the White Sox six years after Luke's retirement to give the team nearly two more decades of Hall of Fame work at short—40 years during which they won only one pennant (1959).

MAJOR LEAGUE TOTALS									
BA	G	AB	R	H	2B	3B	HR	RBI	SB
.310	2,422	8,856	1,319	2,749	440	102	45	1,116	179

Ernie Banks

Among the greatest sluggers in National League history and one of baseball's premier goodwill ambassadors, Ernie Banks forged his spot in history the first seven years of his career.

He set a season record for homers by a shortstop (47), belted 40 dingers or more five times in six years, and became both the first MVP winner from a losing team and the first NL player to win the award two consecutive seasons. He never reached such heights again, but he stuck around smiling for 11 more years despite nagging injuries and under-achieving teams to earn distinction as perhaps the most popular player of his era.

The first black player in Chicago Cub history, Banks hit .275 with 19 homers and 79 RBI in 1954, his first full year after being plucked from the Negro League Kansas City Monarchs. In '55, he had his first spectacular season, hitting .295 with 44 homers, 117 RBI, and a league-best fielding average of .972 while belting an NL-record five grand slams and setting a homer mark for shortstops he would later top twice. Fans had never seen such power at his position, and the modest right-handed Banks matched his pop with grace in the field and a classy demeanor.

Banks may well have been the most valuable player in baseball from 1955-60. His 248 home runs over the span topped the majors, and his seasonal averages of 41 homers, 116 RBI, 28 doubles, and eight triples were accompanied by three fielding titles. In 1958, his .313 average and league-leading 47 homers, 129 RBI, and .614 slugging mark earned him his first MVP Award despite Chicago's 72-82 finish. A year later, he copped the honor again with a .304 average, 45 dingers, an NL-best 145 RBI, and an ML-record .985 fielding mark at short for a 74-80 team. In 1960, he led the majors with 41 homers.

Following a 37-homer year in 1962, Banks would never again be as strong an offensive or defensive force. An ailing knee ended his 717-game playing streak in 1961 and prompted a shift to first base the following year, where he was a reliable 25-homer, 85-RBI player the rest of the decade. Even with less prodigious stats, his cheery disposition and fabled sunny-day refrain "let's play two" kept his popularity growing.

"Mr. Cub" had never played in the postseason entering 1969, but Chicago opened a 9½-game NL East lead over the upstart New York Mets in August. A dramatic fold doomed the Cubs to second place, but Ernie's 106 RBI matched his best total since '60 and earned the 38-year-old his last of 11 All-Star selections.

MAJOR LEAGUE TOTALS									
BA	G	AB	R	H	2B	3B	HR	RBI	SB
.274	2,528	9,421	1,305	2,583	407	90	512	1,636	50

JOHNNY BENCH

DURABILITY, GRACE, AND GLAMOUR are not attributes usually associated with catchers. Johnny Bench had movie-star looks, a gift for gab, and for many years an affinity for donning tuxedos and hitting the stage—but he also had a glove, arm, and bat that made him the best catcher in baseball.

Picked by Cincinnati in 1965's major-league draft, the 6′1″, 208-pound Oklahoman tore up the minors and made the Reds for good in '68. The 20-year-old receiver didn't disappoint, catching a rookie-record 154 games and setting a new mark for all NL catchers with 40 doubles. His 15 homers, 82 RBI, and .275 average earned him Rookie of the Year honors, along with his first of 13 straight selections to the All-Star team. Taking immediate leadership of the Reds' pitching staff, he used a then-unorthodox one-handed catching style to routinely nab enemy basestealers.

In '69, Bench and the team matured, Johnny raising his offensive numbers to .293, 26, 90 and adding a Gold Glove (the first of 10 straight) while the Reds improved to an 89-73 finish. More growth was expected in 1970, but what transpired was astonishing: Bench burst to the top of the majors in homers and RBI by midseason, and by year's end he was still in front with 45 dingers and 148 RBI. Cincinnati won the pennant with a 102-60 record, and Bench was named MVP. A dismal '71 season for

Johnny (.238, 27, 61) and the Reds (79-83) followed, but in '72 both rebounded as Bench was tops in the majors again with 40 homers and 125 RBI, and the Reds took another pennant.

Now a regular on television variety shows and commercials, Bench kept himself in the lights by averaging 29 homers and 114 RBI from 1973 through 1975—when the "Big Red Machine" of Bench, Joe Morgan, Pete Rose, Tony Perez, and company went 108-54, won its third pennant in six years, and finally went all the way with a World Series triumph over Boston. A second consecutive pennant followed in 1976, and Bench was named MVP of a World Series sweep over the Yankees after batting .533.

Johnny slowed down a bit following a 31-homer, 109-RBI year in '77 (when he also won his final Gold Glove), but he remained a power threat (his 1,013 RBI led all players in the '70s) until age and injuries prompted his move to first base in 1981. Two more years playing third followed, and when Bench retired in '83, his final numbers of 389 homers (including a then-record 327 catching) and 1,376 RBI assured him a spot among the all-time greats.

MAJOR LEAGUE TOTALS									
BA	G	AB	R	H	2B	3B	HR	RBI	SB
.267	2,158	7,658	1,091	2,048	381	24	389	1,376	68

YOGI BERRA

A SQUAT, FUNNY-LOOKING KID from a St. Louis neighborhood known as "Dago Hill," Lawrence Peter Berra developed a reputation for being uncouth and unworldly and saying things that made no sense. In reality this man, whose appearance and disposition earned him the nickname "Yogi," was a shrewd and successful businessman, one of the most popular Americans of the 20th century, and the most consistently superb catcher in the history of major-league baseball.

In 14 full seasons from 1948-61, the 5′8″ receiver with the infectious grin averaged 23 homers and 94 RBI, led American League catchers in games caught and total chances eight times each, and from 1957-59 went a stretch of 148 games and 950 chances without an error. Not coincidentally, he played on 14 pennant-winners and 10 World Series championship clubs in his 19-year career, setting records for Series games, hits, and doubles along the way.

Berra reached the majors late in 1946 after a stint in the Navy and time spent in the cavernous Yankee farm system. Over the next two years, he split time as a backup catcher and outfielder. Red Sox owner Tom Yawkey asked Yankee counterpart Dan Topping to "throw in that kid you've got in left field" to sweeten the pot in a proposed Ted Williams-for-Joe DiMaggio swap in '47, but Topping held off, and the following year Berra was the Yankees' starting catcher and a .305 hitter with 14 homers and 98 RBI.

So began over a decade of sustained brilliance. Beginning in '49, Berra had at least 20 homers and 82 RBI for 10 straight years, reaching heights of 30 homers twice (then an American League record for catchers), 125 RBI, and a top batting average of .322 in 1950. A great guess hitter who performed best in the clutch, Berra was named MVP in 1951, '54, and '55, yet was so consistent that his award-winning years were indistinguishable from the rest of his career. Berra's expert handling of pitchers, achieved by focusing on their varying personalities, was part of his own brand of genius.

Yes, genius. Berra may have said things like "nobody goes to that restaurant anymore; it's too crowded" and "a nickel ain't worth a dime anymore," but the Hall of Famer usually got his point across—along with a laugh. Yogi was probably the most popular ballplayer of his generation, and his personality translated well to managing. He was just the second manager to win pennants in both leagues, turning the trick with both the Yankees (1964) and Mets (1973). Some may still think him a clown; in reality, he is a true American success story.

MAJOR LEAGUE TOTALS									
BA	G	AB	R	H	2B	3B	HR	RBI	SB
.285	2,120	7,555	1,175	2,150	321	49	358	1,430	30

DAN BROUTHERS

NAME THE HALL OF FAME SLUGGER who started his big-league career as a pitcher and eventually wound up a .342 lifetime hitter. Babe Ruth? Yes, that's right—but there's more than one correct answer. You have to go back to 1879 to find him on the Troy Trojans, where, after 35 hits allowed in 21 innings, management realized that he might be better suited for a different position. Dan Brouthers was thereby moved to first base, where he developed into a five-time batting champ.

A very large man (6'2", 207 pounds) for his day, "Big Dan" hit .274 his rookie season—good enough to lead Troy but apparently not enough to offset 34 errors in 39 games (in his defense, he then played first bare-handed). Up with the Buffalo Bisons in 1881 after more semipro work, Brouthers blossomed as the National League's homer (eight) and slugging (.541) leader while batting .319 in the 83-game season. Thus began a string of six consecutive seasons in which he led the NL in slugging, hit a combined .351, and won a pair of batting titles.

Baseball was evolving, but as the pitching distance, number of balls required for a walk, and schedule length changed, Brouthers always adapted. One thing he couldn't control was the growing pains the game underwent during his career; when Buffalo nearly went bankrupt in 1885, Dan was part of the "Big Four" players sold to the Detroit

Wolverines for $7,500. NL President Nick Young, believing the move would unfairly affect the pennant race, banned the four from playing for Detroit the remaining three weeks of the season.

Making up for lost time quickly, Brouthers led the league in doubles from 1886-88 (averaging 36 in a season), in runs during '87 (153) and '88 (118), and in homers in '86 (11). Big Dan moved on again, this time to spend three years on three different teams in three different leagues in the same city. He won a third batting crown (.373) with the NL's Boston Beaneaters in '89 (his overall average of .348 during the '80s led the majors), hit .330 with the Players' League's Boston Reds in '90, and hit a league-high .350 with the American Association's Boston Reds in '91.

He won a final batting crown (.335) with Brooklyn in 1892 (when he also led the NL with 124 RBI and 197 hits). Dan next journeyed to Baltimore, Louisville, and Philadelphia—hitting .300 at every stop before heading back to the minors after the 1896 season. Old friend and New York Giants manager John McGraw signed the 46-year-old Brouthers for a pair of games in 1904 (he went 0-for-5 but became a rare four-decade player), and Dan later served as a Giants scout and press-box custodian at the Polo Grounds.

MAJOR LEAGUE TOTALS									
BA	G	AB	R	H	2B	3B	HR	RBI	SB9
.342	1,673	6,711	1,523	2,296	460	205	106	1,296	256

STEVE CARLTON

WHETHER HE WAS A YOUNGSTER on a championship club, the lone bright spot on a dismal team, or the ageless hero of another champion, Steve Carlton could always be counted on to do one thing: win games. Carlton earned 329 victories—second only to Warren Spahn among left-handers.

An early big-league advocate of weight training, 20-year-old Steve built up enough of a fastball from conditioning to make the '65 Cardinals. A regular member of the rotation two years later, he went 14-9 with a 2.98 ERA to help St. Louis to the '67 world championship. He made his first of 10 All-Star teams for the '68 pennant-winners (going 13-11), and after adding a strong curve and slider in 1969, he posted a 17-11 mark with a 2.17 ERA (second in the NL) and 210 strikeouts.

Carlton had an "off" year in 1970, going 10-19 while embroiled in a salary dispute, but he followed with his first 20-win season (20-9) in '71. More money squabbles prompted St. Louis to suddenly trade him to Philadelphia for righty Rick Wise—a rash decision the Cards would regret. Pitching in 1972 for a last-place Phillies team that went 59-97, Steve earned his first Cy Young Award with a phenomenal 27-10 record. He led the NL in wins, ERA (1.97), strikeouts (310), innings (346), and complete games (30) while totalling 46 percent of all Philadelphia victories.

Just 44-47 the following three seasons while hampered with elbow problems, Carlton bounced back to a 20-7 mark for the 1976 NL East Division champs. Another Cy Young Award came in '77, when he topped the majors in wins with a 23-10 slate, but Philly lost in the playoffs for the second of three straight years. Bothered by the occasional negative story, Steve was no longer talking to the press by 1980, but he gave reporters plenty to write about by leading Philadelphia's first pennant-winner in 30 years with a 24-9 mark, 286 K's, and a 2.34 ERA. He was even better in the postseason—going 3-0 to help the club to its first-ever world championship—and became the fourth three-time Cy Young Award winner.

"Silent Steve" copped his record fourth Cy Young honor in '82 after going 23-11 and leading the NL in wins, strikeouts (286), and shutouts (six). A final strikeout crown (275) for the '83 pennant-winners pushed his career whiff total near 4,000, and he won his 300th game late that year. When he finally quit in 1988 after playing out the string with four teams, he had a 329-244 record to rank among baseball's winningest pitchers, and his 4,136 strikeouts remained second only to Nolan Ryan.

MAJOR LEAGUE TOTALS									
W	L	ERA	G	CG	IP	H	ER	BB	SO
329	244	3.22	741	254	5,217.1	4,672	1,867	1,833	4,136

ROBERTO CLEMENTE

THE GREATEST ATHLETE in Puerto Rican history, Roberto Clemente was also just the second baseball player—following Jackie Robinson—to have his picture on a U.S. postage stamp. The first Latin American elected to the Hall of Fame was so revered in his homeland that his untimely death in 1972 plunged the country into a state of shock.

Clemente suffered a back injury in a car accident just before his 1955 rookie season that plagued him throughout his career, but the 21-year-old was still an instant success for the last-place Pirates as a rifle-armed right fielder—and a .311 hitter his second season. Pittsburgh was a pennant-winning club by 1960, and Clemente helped lead the way with a .314 average, 16 homers, and 94 RBI, then hit .310 in a World Series triumph over the Yankees.

The Pirates slipped to sixth in '61, but Clemente claimed his first batting title (.351) and his first of 12 consecutive Gold Gloves with 27 assists. Possessing brilliant range and a spectacular arm, he routinely made throws to third base on the fly from the deepest right-field corners, and he eventually paced the NL in assists five times. On the basepaths, the 12-time All-Star was aggressive and daring, and as a dark-skinned Latin he was never afraid to speak his mind against racism.

After .312 and .320 averages in 1962 and '63, Roberto took his second batting crown with a .339

mark in '64 and a third title (.329) the following
season. Although he slipped to fifth (.317) in the
race in '66, he had his finest power season, bashing
29 homers and driving in 119 runs en route to the
MVP Award. The proud Clemente maintained that
his '67 season (a league-leading .357 average, 23
homers, and 110 RBI) was even better, but despite
averaging .328 with 188 hits, 18 homers, and 86
RBI during the 1960s, Roberto was constantly overshadowed by NL outfielders Mays and Aaron.

Hitting .352 and .341 during an injury-plagued
1970-71, Clemente finally received national attention in the fall of the latter year. The Pirates faced
the Orioles in the World Series, and Roberto was
the star of a seven-game Pittsburgh win with a .414
average, 12 hits, two homers, and spectacular play
in right field. He hit .312 the following year and
lashed a double on the season's final day to become
the 11th player with 3,000 hits. But he would never
get a chance to add to the total. The 38-year-old
star was killed on a humanitarian mission to earth-
quake-ravaged Nicaragua when his plane crashed
just after takeoff that New Year's Eve. The Hall of
Fame waived its traditional waiting period to let
the .317 lifetime hitter in that summer.

MAJOR LEAGUE TOTALS

BA	G	AB	R	H	2B	3B	HR	RBI	SB
.317	2,433	9,454	1,416	3,000	440	166	240	1,305	83

TY COBB

A MOVIE ON THE LIFE OF BABE RUTH drew hordes to the theaters despite being a critical flop a few years back, but when a similar picture on Ty Cobb debuted a while later, it was gone in a matter of weeks—most folks showing little interest in paying tribute to the greatest hitter for average (.366) in major-league history. Nearly 70 years after his career, the reputation of "The Georgia Peach" apparently hasn't changed much. He might have hit and run better than anyone else in baseball, but this was still one mean son of a bitch.

Cobb's vicious streak seemed at times to engulf him. Harassed as a scrawny 18-year-old with the Tigers in 1905, he quickly added weight and muscle along with a philosophy of playing hard and trusting no one. He never hit below .316 after his rookie season, and in 1907, at the age of 20, he became the youngest player in history to win a batting title with his .350 mark, leading the American League with 116 RBI, 212 hits, a .473 slugging mark, and 49 stolen bases to boot.

The left-hander with the split-handed grip could bash line drives and bunt with equal skill. In the field, he used his fine speed and a solid arm to cut down runners, and he registered 20 or more assists on 10 occasions.

But what he did best was hit—and run the bases. His 1907 batting title was the first of nine straight and 12 overall (although two of the batting titles are disputed). Cobb led the Tigers to three straight pennants, from 1907-09, and remained the key to Detroit's attack for 20 years. Perennially among American League leaders in slugging and steals (he won six stolen base crowns), he was also the team's most reliable RBI man for many years—averaging 109 a season from 1907-12 en route to 1,937 for his career. As a runner, he felt no shame in sliding with his spikes high, and he often poised himself on dugout steps sharpening them to intimidate foes.

Ty won the Triple Crown in 1909 with nine homers, 107 RBI, and a .377 average, and two years later he had perhaps his finest season with a career-high .420 average and league-leading totals in hits (248), doubles (47), triples (24), runs (147), RBI (127), and steals (83). In 1915, he set a stolen base record of 96 that held for nearly 50 years, and in 1922 he hit .400 for the third and last time at the age of 35. Serving as player/manager his final six years with the Tigers, he joined Connie Mack's Athletics in '27 to finish his career before retiring rich from wise investments but virtually devoid of friends. His major-league records for hits (4,189) and steals (891) have since been topped, but the .366 mark will likely endure—along with the sordid reputation of the man who achieved it.

MAJOR LEAGUE TOTALS

BA	G	AB	R	H	2B	3B	HR	RBI	SB
.366	3,035	11,434	2,246	4,189	724	295	117	1,937	891

MICKEY COCHRANE

NO MAJOR-LEAGUE CATCHER ever compiled a higher career batting average than Gordon Stanley "Mickey" Cochrane—and few players at any position were such strong-minded leaders. A .320 lifetime hitter over 13 seasons, he led the A's and Tigers to five pennants—doubling as manager for the two flags won with the Tigers—and made such an impression on semipro player Mutt Mantle that when Mantle's first son was born just after the '31 World Series, he named him Mickey.

Cochrane was so impressive at minor-league Portland in 1924 that Philadelphia owner/manager Connie Mack bought the team for $200,000 to secure Mickey's rights, then sold it shortly thereafter. Joining the A's the following year, the 22-year-old left-handed batter hit .331 as a rookie and slugged three of his six season homers in the same May game. Never possessing tremendous power (he hit 20 homers just once), Cochrane was an excellent contact hitter and runner who never struck out more than 26 times in a season.

A durable catcher in an era when receivers seldom caught over 100 games, he topped the figure easily his first 11 seasons and was consistently among American League batting leaders. Cochrane hit .338 in 1927 and averaged .345 with 90 RBI from 1929-31, when he helped the A's to three consecutive pennants and two world championships.

Mack called him the most important factor in those titles. One legend of "Black Mike's" fiery leadership had him screaming that his teammates were "yellow-bellied buzzards" during a shellacking by the Yankees, then promptly stroking a base hit to start a game-winning rally. Cochrane hit just .245 in 31 World Series games, but few matched his bite and influence as a postseason bench jockey.

After his finest power year in 1932 (35 doubles, 23 homers, 112 RBI) and a .322 mark in '33, Cochrane was one of the first A's sold off by Mr. Mack in his second franchise fire sale—fetching $100,000 and fringe catcher Johnny Pasek from Detroit. Named player/manager of the Tigers, Mickey hit .320 and won the pennant in '34. He came back to hit .319 and lead another pennant-winning club the following year, then scored the championship-clinching run in a six-game World Series victory over the Cubs.

Reduced to part-time duty in '36, Cochrane's career ended in May of the following season when his skull was fractured by a Bump Hadley pitch, leaving him near death and in and out of consciousness for 10 days. He managed another season and later became a scout, coach, and general manager, but he never displayed the same vigor of old.

MAJOR LEAGUE TOTALS									
BA	G	AB	R	H	2B	3B	HR	RBI	SB
.320	1,482	5,169	1,041	1,652	333	64	119	832	64

EDDIE COLLINS

CONSIDERED ONE OF THE SMARTEST MEN in baseball history, Eddie Collins was also among the game's most efficient gentlemen. The Hall of Famer collected 1,300 RBI and scored 1,821 runs over his 25-year career despite hitting just 47 homers. The second baseman twice stole six bases in the same game en route to 744 lifetime thefts, and he averaged .333. Later, in his only scouting trip as general manager of the Red Sox, he signed Bobby Doerr and inked the rights to Ted Williams.

A Columbia graduate, Collins joined the Philadelphia A's following his 1906 graduation and became Connie Mack's regular second baseman three years later. He hit .346 in 1909 and swiped 67 bases, then led the AL with 81 steals while batting .322 the following year as the A's advanced to the World Series. When the Mackmen topped the Cubs in five games, Collins was the leading batter with a .429 mark.

Teaming with Stuffy McInnis, Jack Barry, and Frank "Home Run" Baker in Philadelphia's famed $100,000 infield—so called for the total salaries paid the four men—Collins helped the A's to four pennants and three world championships from 1910-14. He averaged .344 over the five-year span with 59 steals and 111 runs a season despite just 11 homers. He led the league in runs from 1912-14 and hit .347 over 20 World Series games. His lone batting title in 1914 (.344) earned Collins a new Chalmers automobile as the AL MVP, but when Mack broke up the team the following winter, Eddie was sold for $50,000 to the White Sox.

An immediate star in the Windy City, Collins batted .332 his first season and helped the White Sox to a world championship in 1917 with a .409 World Series mark against the Giants. His .319 average and league-best 33 steals helped the Sox win the 1919 pennant, but upon discovering later that eight of his teammates had thrown that fall's World Series to the Reds, Collins was appalled. He had his best season ever in 1920 (batting .372 with 224 hits) but never forgave the accused players.

Player/manager for much of his last three years (1924-26) in Chicago, 40-year-old Collins returned to the A's in '27 and hit .336 in 226 at-bats. He was a bit player in his final three seasons, and following his 1-for-2 swan song in 1930 could claim the unique distinction of having hit .340 or higher in four different decades. His consistency, longevity, and nine fielding titles supported Mack's claim that Collins was "the greatest second baseman I ever saw." Eddie stayed in the game the rest of his life, helping the Red Sox as a front-office man from 1933 until his death in 1951.

MAJOR LEAGUE TOTALS

BA	G	AB	R	H	2B	3B	HR	RBI	SB
.333	2,826	9,949	1,821	3,312	438	186	47	1,300	744

JOE DIMAGGIO

H E WAS THE MOST REGAL of performers during his career with the New York Yankees, and the quiet, somewhat mysterious way he has carried himself for 45 years since has only added to the sense of elegance surrounding Joe DiMaggio. Upon first coming to the Yankees in 1936, DiMaggio was no early candidate for nobility. This poor son of an Italian fisherman had what reporters called "squirrel teeth" and the naïveté to believe a quote was some kind of soft drink. Asked for plenty of "drinks" after hitting .323 with 44 doubles, 15 triples, 29 home runs, and 125 RBI his rookie season, he outdid even the great Lou Gehrig his second year, leading the league with 46 homers and 151 runs while batting .346.

One of three DiMaggio brothers (along with Vince and Dom) to play in the majors, Joe appeared to have no weaknesses as a ballplayer. A right-handed batter who almost always made contact—never striking out more than 39 times in a season—he was hurt by the 457-foot "Death Valley" in left-center field of Yankee Stadium but still managed to hit .315 there over his career. As a center fielder, he was fast and graceful but never flashy, making great plays look easy and always delivering strong throws to the right man. He was seldom called upon to steal bases (he stole 30 in 39 career attempts), but nobody doubted he was one of the fastest players of his generation. Though quiet, he was a leader in the Yankee clubhouse.

After winning batting titles in '39 (when his .381 mark earned him the MVP Award) and '40 (.352), DiMaggio captured the attention of the entire country in 1941. Beginning with a single on May 15, Joe compiled a major-league-record 56-game hitting streak—during which he hit .408 with 15 homers. He was the subject of songs, prompted contests and endless media coverage, and beat out Ted Williams (a .406 batter on the *season*) for his second MVP trophy.

World War II intervened in 1943, and 31-year-old Joe came back three years later slightly below his previous form. His average and power numbers were down (he won a third MVP Award with subpar .315, 20, 97 totals in 1947), but he still had a flair for the dramatic: After missing the first 65 games of the '49 season with a heel injury, he returned to hit four homers in three games—sparking the Yankees to the seventh of nine world championships they would win in his 13-year career.

Age and injuries hampered Joe's effectiveness, and he retired after a final World Series win in 1951 to go about marrying Marilyn Monroe, peddling Mr. Coffee, and simply being Joe DiMaggio.

MAJOR LEAGUE TOTALS									
BA	G	AB	R	H	2B	3B	HR	RBI	SB
.325	1,736	6,821	1,390	2,214	389	131	361	1,537	30

Bob Feller

The story of Bob Feller's rise to major-league pitching stardom seems too corny to be true. A farm boy groomed to be a ballplayer by his dad, Feller honed his skills on a field carved out of his old man's wheat acreage. He was still in high school when he amazed the baseball world with 15 strikeouts in his first big-league start. Plenty of whiffs and 266 wins later, "Rapid Robert" had become one of the game's greatest success stories.

Signed by the Indians at age 17, Feller tied Dizzy Dean's ML record of 17 strikeouts in one 1936 start before returning to Iowa at season's end to finish high school. Feller struggled with control throughout much of his career, but even while walking 361 over his first 488 innings, the 6'0" right-hander proved he could win. He went 9-7 in 1937, then improved to 17-11 in '38 with a league-high 240 strikeouts—including 18 on the season's final day—to set a new big-league record.

The following year, Feller began a string of three straight outstanding seasons, going 24-9, 27-11, and 25-13 through 1941 while leading the majors in victories and strikeouts each year and adding an ERA title (2.61) and Opening Day no-hitter in 1940. Possessing a devastating fastball he claimed was speedier than its clocked 98.6 mph, he also had a fine curve and slider in his arsenal.

Just 22 at the end of the '41 campaign, Feller

already had a 107-54 record with 1,233 strikeouts. But for nearly four years, he was unable to add to the totals while serving as a gun crew chief on the battleship *Alabama*. A late-season return in '45 produced a 5-3 record, but there was fear Feller might not excel again over a full season after such a long layoff. Bob stopped the talk with a 26-15 record in '46 that included a 2.18 ERA, his second no-hitter, and league-leading totals in wins, strikeouts (a then-ML-record 348), and shutouts (10).

A 20-11 record and 196 strikeouts in '47 marked his fifth consecutive full season leading the AL in both wins and whiffs, but Feller's days as a speed-baller were over. He struggled to a 19-15 mark for the world champs of 1948 (losing a 1-0 two-hitter in the World Series), then went just 15-14 with 108 strikeouts in '49. A third no-hitter and 22-8 mark in 1951 marked Bob's last great season, and he was a 35-year-old spot starter when his 13-3 mark helped the Indians to another pennant in '54. By the time of his retirement two years later, he had thrown 12 one-hitters and notched 2,581 strikeouts en route to a 266-162 career mark. Knowing his time overseas had likely cost him a shot at 350 wins, the sports writers made him a first-ballot Hall of Famer.

MAJOR LEAGUE TOTALS									
W	L	ERA	G	CG	IP	H	ER	BB	SO
266	162	3.25	570	279	3,827	3,271	1,384	1,764	2,581

JIMMIE FOXX

HE WAS CALLED "THE RIGHT-HANDED RUTH" in his heyday, and few nicknames ever rang so true. James Emory Foxx was a Maryland boy just like the Babe, another good-natured giant who slugged prodigious home runs, enjoyed the fast life, and picked up checks wherever he went. While Ruth began his career as a pitcher, Jimmie prolonged his by taking to the mound. Both also died young, yet while Ruth has remained a household name, ol' "Double X" has lost some of his luster—a shame even if his name has moved down a bit in the record books.

A catcher in the minors, Foxx joined the Athletics as a 17-year-old in 1925 and spent time at several positions before becoming the club's regular first baseman (where he would later win three fielding titles) in 1929. He hit .354 while smashing 33 homers and notching 118 RBI that year, and he was a major catalyst as the A's won three straight American League pennants through 1931—averaging .327 with 33 homers and 131 RBI over the span, along with a .344 mark in World Series play. The A's fell to second in '32, but Foxx was better than ever, winning his first MVP Award by waging a summer-long assault on Ruth's record of 60 homers and finishing just short with 58 to accompany a .364 average and league-leading 169 RBI, 151 runs, and .749 slugging percentage. When Jimmie followed up with a Triple Crown/MVP year in '33 (.356, 48, 163), he had folks forgetting about Ruth.

Repeating the purging process he had made following his 1910-14 dynasty, Mack began disassembling the team. After a .334, 44, 130 performance in 1934 and a .346, 36, 115 year in '35—including his third home run title—Foxx was sent to the Red Sox for a pair of players and $150,000 of Tom Yawkey's cash. Jimmie loved the friendly left-field wall at Fenway Park and hit off and over it with regularity the next several years. Included was a third MVP season in '38, when he slugged 50 homers (35 at home) and led the league with 175 RBI, a .349 average, and a .704 slugging mark to silence writers who said he was slipping. His 415 homers during the '30s topped all players.

A bad sinus condition and years of downing Scotch eventually ended Foxx's string of 12 straight 30-homer, 100-RBI seasons, and in '42 the Sox waived the 34-year-old to the Cubs, where he spent parts of two lackluster seasons. Jimmie returned to Philadelphia—this time with the Phillies—and hit .268 in his 1945 finale while even managing to pitch in nine games. His 1.59 ERA notwithstanding, it was his .325 lifetime average, 534 homers, 1,922 RBI, and .609 slugging percentage that made Foxx a first-ballot Hall of Famer.

MAJOR LEAGUE TOTALS									
BA	G	AB	R	H	2B	3B	HR	RBI	SB
.325	2,317	8,134	1,751	2,646	458	125	534	1,922	87

LOU GEHRIG

NOW THAT HIS INCREDIBLE STREAK of 2,130 consecutive games played has been topped by Cal Ripken, there is a new opportunity to examine the career of Lou Gehrig. What Gehrig accomplished in the seasons comprising his string remains a remarkable achievement—and only his own Yankee teammate Babe Ruth can claim a more prodigious level of sustained offensive excellence.

It seems fitting that a player of Ripken's disposition toppled Gehrig's mark; Gehrig was himself a wise and modest man who drew far more solace from family than nightclubs. A native New Yorker and left-handed slugger at Columbia University, the sturdy six-footer joined the Yanks at age 20 in 1923 and saw limited duty behind star first baseman Wally Pipp for two seasons. Gehrig's first game of his streak came as a pinch-hitter on May 31, 1925, and when he started the next day after Pipp complained of a headache, nobody thought much of it. In the end, Pipp was out of a job as Gehrig played the final 126, finishing at .295 with 20 homers.

Cleanup hitter on the Yankee pennant-winners of 1926, Lou paced the American League with 20 triples while adding 47 doubles, 16 homers, and 112 RBI. He also hit .348 in a World Series loss to St. Louis, but Ruth remained the main man with 47 homers and four more in the Series. "The Iron Horse" lessened the gap in '27, running neck-and-neck with Babe much of the season before finishing with 47 dingers. Ruth set the world afire by smashing a record 60 for the world champs, but Gehrig was AL MVP with astounding totals of 218 hits, a .373 average, a league-best 175 RBI, and 52 doubles, 18 triples, and a .765 slugging percentage never topped by anyone not named Babe.

Lou upped his average to .374 in '28, leading the league with 47 doubles and 142 RBI. Similar stats followed each of the next nine years, and over 11 full seasons from 1927-37 Lou averaged .350 with 39 homers and 153 RBI (including an AL-record 184 in '31) while playing on four world champions. His numbers fell off to .295, 29, 114 when the Yanks took their third straight Series in '38, and some said the streak was getting to him. In fact, the problem was a rare and incurable disease called amyotrophic lateral sclerosis—now known as Lou Gehrig's Disease—that was eating away at his body.

The suddenly sluggish and feeble-footed star took himself out of the lineup May 2, 1939, with a .143 average, and upon learning his fate shortly thereafter never played again. A July 4 "day" at Yankee Stadium honored a classy man who told the hushed crowd, "I have an awful lot to live for," but less than two years later he was dead at age 37.

MAJOR LEAGUE TOTALS

BA	G	AB	R	H	2B	3B	HR	RBI	SB
.340	2,164	8,001	1,888	2,721	534	163	493	1,995	102

CHARLIE GEHRINGER

SELDOM HAS ANYONE accomplished so much with as little animation as Charlie Gehringer. Starting second baseman on the Detroit Tigers for 16 years, he was so unflappable in character and so unwavering in his consistent excellence that he became known as "The Mechanical Man." Manager Mickey Cochrane once said of the bachelor who lived with his mother until he was 43: "He says hello on Opening Day and goodbye on Closing Day, and in between he hits .350."

A football and baseball man at the University of Michigan, Gehringer signed with the Tigers in 1924 and made the majors to stay in '26. A .277 hitter as a rookie, the left-handed contact man went up over .300 (.317) his second campaign and failed to top the magic mark just once (.298 in '32) over the next 14 years. A smooth and sure-handed fielder who made exceptional plays look routine, he topped American League second basemen in fielding average and assists seven times each.

Charlie improved the longer he played, raising his average to .320 in '28 and .339 in 1929, when he also led the AL in runs (131), hits (215), doubles (45), triples (19), and steals (27) while driving in 106 runs. His steady batting stroke assured he would seldom strike out—his 42 whiffs as a rookie were his ML high—and in time he also added more power, bashing as many as 20 homers.

The Tigers won the pennant in 1934 and '35, and Gehringer was a key force in both championships. He led the AL with 134 runs and 214 hits in '34 while placing second in doubles (50) and batting (.356) and fifth in RBI (127), then hit .379 during a seven-game World Series loss to St. Louis. In '35, he was nearly as superb—hitting .330 (fifth in the league) with 123 runs (second) and 108 RBI, followed by a .375 World Series mark as Detroit topped the Cubs. Adding another doubles title (60 in 1936) and a batting crown (.371 in '37) to his honors, Gehringer played in each of the first six All-Star Games from 1933-38 and went 10-for-20. Overall during the '30s, he averaged .331, and collected 100 RBI and 200 hits six times each.

Helping Detroit to a third pennant at age 37 in 1940 (.313, 10, 81), Gehringer fell off sharply in '41 (.220) and retired a year later. After three years in the Navy and a stint in the auto industry, he returned to Detroit for two years as general manager (1951-53), then six more as VP. His .320 career average, 574 doubles, 1,774 runs, and 1,427 RBI earned him Hall of Fame recognition, along with a 1969 selection by Major League Baseball as its greatest living second baseman.

MAJOR LEAGUE TOTALS									
BA	G	AB	R	H	2B	3B	HR	RBI	SB8
.320	2,323	8,860	1,774	2,839	574	146	184	1,427	181

BOB GIBSON

HE DIDN'T SOCIALIZE much during his 17 years with the St. Louis Cardinals, even at All-Star Games. He was stone-silent through eight of 'em, for he knew getting chummy with the guy beside him could be a distraction the next time he went to brush back or strike out the bum.

This aggressiveness had helped Gibson overcome plenty on the way to stardom, including childhood bouts with asthma and a heart murmur. The hard-throwing right-hander starred in baseball and basketball at Creighton University, and after a one-year fling with the Harlem Globetrotters, he had little success his first two tries at cracking the Cardinal rotation (going 6-11). In 1961, though, "Gibby" went 13-12 with a 3.24 ERA.

Gibson's control problems (he walked a National League-high 119 in '61) improved over the next two years, and when the Cardinals won the '64 pennant, Bob was in the limelight at 19-12 with a 3.01 ERA, 245 strikeouts, and just 86 walks. After losing his first World Series start to the Yankees, the high-kicking hurler came back to win his next two, including the Game 7 clincher. Although Gibson's next two seasons each produced 20 wins with at least 200 strikeouts, he was overshadowed by Dodgers star Sandy Koufax.

Koufax's retirement in 1967 left the door open for a new NL ace to emerge, and Gibson (13-7) was fill-ing the void until a line drive broke his leg in mid-season. Gibson returned recharged for the World Series that fall, and the Boston Red Sox didn't have a chance. In three starts, he had three complete-game wins (including his second Series clincher), a 1.00 ERA, and 26 strikeouts.

This proved just a prelude for 1968, when Gibson's 22-9 record only hinted at one of the most incredible performances in major-league history: 13 shutouts, 268 strikeouts, just 62 walks and 198 hits allowed over 305 innings, 28 complete games in 34 starts, 15 straight wins, and an ERA of 1.12 that remains the lowest in the modern era. Two more complete-game World Series victories for the NL MVP and Cy Young winner that fall versus Detroit (including a record 17-strikeout gem in the opener) stretched his Series winning streak to seven.

A great all-around athlete who won nine straight Gold Gloves and hit 24 career homers, Gibby had several more outstanding seasons—grabbing another Cy Young when he went 23-7 with a 3.12 ERA in 1970—before injuries wore him down and finally out in '75. His 251-174 record, 2.91 ERA, and 3,117 strikeouts suggest a Hall of Fame career earned with great skill, but intimidation was just as strong a factor.

MAJOR LEAGUE TOTALS										
W	L	ERA	G	CG	IP	H	ER	BB	SO
251	174	2.91	528	255	3,884.1	3,279	1,258	1,336	3,117

JOSH GIBSON

THE STATISTICS ARE SKETCHY, the stories only hearsay. The Negro Leagues operated under constraints that made keeping close track of player performance an impossible task, but those who watched these banished stars usually agreed on one thing: None hit a baseball further and with greater frequency than catcher Josh Gibson.

Growing up in Pittsburgh, Gibson began playing semipro ball as a teenager and, as legend has it, was watching the Negro League Homestead Grays in action when he was pulled from the stands and put behind the plate after the Grays catcher hurt his finger. A star on the Grays within a year, the stocky, 6'2" right-handed batter moved on to the Pittsburgh Crawfords in 1934. There, he played alongside fellow future Hall of Famers Judy Johnson, Oscar Charleston, and Cool Papa Bell in Black Ball's version of "Murderer's Row" and on occasion formed half of the most intimidating battery in Black Ball history—catching Hall of Fame legend Satchel Paige.

Fun-loving and popular among his teammates, Gibson—known as "the black Babe Ruth"—drew high praise from players black and white for his abilities. Roy Campanella said Josh was "the greatest ballplayer I ever saw." Jimmy Powers of the *New York Daily News* wrote in 1939, "I am positive that if Josh Gibson were white, he would be a major league star," an argument Gibson supported by blasting three homers off Dizzy Dean in two exhibition matchups.

One set of partial Negro League statistics credits Gibson with 146 home runs and a .362 average in 501 games spread over 16 seasons, but in reality he may have slugged as many as 84 homers playing over 200 contests a year in winter (in the Puerto Rican League), spring, and summer. Sometimes the Crawfords or Homestead Grays (Josh's team his last five seasons) secured big-league ballparks for their games, and stories abound of Gibson belting homers to the deepest points of Comiskey Park and Yankee Stadium. One shot to the upper deck of the Stadium supposedly traveled 580 feet and would have gone 700 had it cleared the wall.

Pirates owner William Benswanger and Senators boss Clark Griffith both claimed an interest in bringing Josh to the majors, but the man with a reported 850-900 home runs was still blasting them for the Grays when Jackie Robinson signed with Brooklyn in 1945. Gibson might still have made the big leagues, but struggles with alcohol and illness shrouded his final years, and he died of a brain hemorrhage at age 35 in January 1947—three months before Robinson's debut with the Dodgers.

NEGRO LEAGUE TOTALS*							
BA	G	AB	H	2B	3B	HR	SB
.354	439	1,820	644	110	45	141	17

*Incomplete

HANK GREENBERG

WHEN JACKIE ROBINSON joined the Dodgers in 1947, one of the first opposing players to publicly show support toward the first black big-leaguer of the century was Hank Greenberg. It really should not have been surprising; if there was anybody in the majors who had the slightest idea what Robinson was going through, it was the greatest Jewish slugger in the game's history.

A regular first baseman in the majors at age 22, the 6'3" right-handed Greenberg hit .301 with 12 homers as a Detroit rookie in 1933, then fueled new manager Mickey Cochrane's pennant-winners the following year with a .339 average, 26 homers, 139 RBI, and an astounding 63 doubles. Tiger fans applauded his decision not to play on the Jewish holiday of Yom Kippur, but Greenberg was routinely the object of anti-Semitic insults from both opposing players and fans.

Ignoring the pressure as best he could, the gentle giant emerged as 1935 American League MVP after leading the league with 36 homers and 170 RBI while hitting .328 and pacing the Tigers to a world championship. A broken wrist sidelined him for all but 12 games in '36, but he returned with a vengeance in 1937, collecting an incredible 183 RBI while belting 40 homers and hitting .337. Hank loved knocking in runs; only Lou Gehrig and Hack Wilson ever topped his 183, and his career average of .92 RBI per game matched Lou's 20th-century record.

In 1938, "Hammerin' Hank" tallied 58 dingers to match Jimmie Foxx's right-handed record. A .312, 33, 112 year followed in '39, and in 1940 Greenberg proved doubly valuable, pacing the AL with 41 homers, 150 RBI, 50 doubles, and a .670 slugging mark while moving to the outfield to make room for teammate Rudy York at first. The Tigers won another pennant and Hank claimed his second MVP trophy.

Drafted into the Army and forced to miss the '41 season, Greenberg re-enlisted the day after Pearl Harbor and wound up serving more than four years. Back for the second half of the 1945 campaign, he had 60 RBI in 78 games and clinched the pennant with a grand slam on the season's final day. Another season atop the AL homer and RBI charts (44, 127) followed in '46, but a salary dispute prompted Detroit to waive the Hall of Famer out of the AL. Hank joined the Pirates as reportedly the National League's first $100,000 player, but he retired at age 36 after a disappointing season (.249, 25, 74).

Greenberg still stands as baseball's fifth-best slugger with a .605 lifetime mark.

MAJOR LEAGUE TOTALS									
BA	G	AB	R	H	2B	3B	HR	RBI	SB
.313	1,394	5,193	1,051	1,628	379	71	331	1,276	58

LEFTY GROVE

DEPENDING ON WHO'S DOING THE ANALYZING, Lefty Grove is either the greatest left-handed pitcher of his era, the greatest lefty ever, or simply the greatest pitcher period.

Starring on a Baltimore minor-league team where he went 109-36 over five seasons, Robert Moses Grove didn't reach the majors until Connie Mack was able to pry him away for $100,600 around Lefty's 25th birthday in 1925. The fiery 6'3" hurler had an American League-leading 116 strikeouts as an A's rookie, but his fastball drifted and he went just 10-12 with a 4.75 ERA and 131 walks. Taking a tip from A's catcher Cy Perkins to step off the mound and relax more between pitches, Lefty lowered his walks to 101 and went 13-13 with a league-best 194 whiffs and 2.51 ERA in '26, then registered a 20-13 mark in 1927.

Baseball was in an era of growing offensive power, but Grove used skill and aggressiveness to stay on top. Lefty's 20-win campaign of '27 was the first of seven consecutive—and eight total—for the temperamental hurler, a period in which he went an amazing 172-54 and helped the A's to three straight pennants and two world championships from 1929-31. During the stretch, he extended his string of consecutive seasons leading the AL in strikeouts to seven, won the league ERA title each year from 1929-32, and also hurled 19 shutouts.

Lefty's record in 1930-31 alone was 59-9, and his 31-4 MVP season of '31 featured a 16-game winning streak that ended in a 1-0 loss to St. Louis when A's left fielder Jim Moore (playing for the sick Al Simmons) misjudged a fly ball. Grove tore apart the locker room after that one, screaming at everyone—including the absent Simmons for having the nerve to miss the contest. Red Sox owner Tom Yawkey figured victories were worth the viciousness and forked over $125,000 and two players for the 34-year-old ace and two others following Grove's 24-8 year in '33.

A sore arm prompted a disastrous 8-8, 6.50 season during Lefty's first year in Boston, but Yawkey refused Mr. Mack's refund offer and stuck by Grove. Further developing his curveball and depending more on guile than smoke, "Ol' Mose" rebounded to go 20-12 with his sixth ERA title (2.70) in '35. Although he would never win 20 games again, Grove added three more ERA crowns (giving him an ML-record nine) while going 63-29 for the Red Sox the next four seasons. He stuck around a bit after his arm went south a final time, but his final record of 300-141 gave him a .680 winning percentage—the best of any 300-game winner.

MAJOR LEAGUE TOTALS									
W	L	ERA	G	CG	IP	H	ER	BB	SO
300	141	3.06	616	298	3,940.2	3,849	1,339	1,187	2,266

RICKEY HENDERSON

THERE ARE MANY WAYS to beat an opponent, and Rickey Henderson has mastered just about all of them. A solid .290 hitter with an eye for drawing walks and ever-dangerous power, he has led off a record 67 games with home runs. The top base-stealer of all time, he has swiped more than 1,100 bases. He's been a Gold Glove outfielder, a terrific postseason player, and a general pain in the butt for opponents through 18 big-league seasons.

An Oakland native, right-handed Rickey wasted no time making his presence felt upon joining his hometown team, batting .274 with a team-high 33 stolen bases in only 89 games during 1979. This was simply a warm-up for the 20-year-old; in 1980, Rickey hit .303 with 111 runs, and an ML-high 100 stolen bases. For the next six seasons and 11 of 12 overall, the "Style Dog" would remain atop the AL theft charts.

Henderson was the perfect catalyst for the A's under manager Billy Martin. Billy liked aggressive players who took chances, and Henderson enjoyed the challenge and thrill of being at the center of attention. Rickey's fantastic 1981 season was overshadowed by the major-league strike, but he still led the league with 135 hits, 89 runs, and 56 stolen bases while batting .319 and winning a Gold Glove. Second in MVP balloting, he helped the A's to the West Division title and hit .364 in an ALCS loss to the Yankees. Down to .267 the following season, he still scored 119 runs, thanks to a league-best 116 walks and an ML-record 130 stolen bases.

Following a 108-steal year in '83 and his best power display yet in '84 (16 homers in addition to 66 steals), the enigmatic igniter was sent to the Yankees in December 1984. Rickey reached new levels in New York, belting 24 homers with 80 steals and 146 runs during '85, and 28 homers and 87 steals the following year. Yankee pennant plans never materialized, however, and Rickey was sent back to the A's midway through the '89 campaign in time to help his old team to a World Series championship with a .441 average, three homers, and 11 steals in nine postseason games.

The 1990 season was his finest: a career-high .325 average (second in the AL), 28 homers, a .577 slugging mark (second), and a league-high 65 steals, 119 runs, and a .439 on-base percentage. A .313 hitter in the postseason this time, he was named AL MVP and finished the year just two behind Lou Brock's record of 938 stolen bases. The mark fell on May 1, 1991, and by the end of '96 the .287 career hitter was up to 1,186 steals, 1,829 runs scored, and 244 homers—a Hall of Fame combination that may never be matched.

MAJOR LEAGUE TOTALS									
BA	G	AB	R	H	2B	3B	HR	RBI	SB
.287	2,340	8,528	1,829	2,450	412	59	244	887	1,186

ROGERS HORNSBY

ROGERS HORNSBY'S batting performance from 1921-25 should be considered the greatest hitting stretch in major-league history. Through 696 games, 2,679 at-bats, and countless doubleheaders in the sweltering St. Louis sun, the Cardinals second baseman *averaged* a .402 batting mark.

The righty-hitting Texan hit .313 as a Cards rookie in 1916 before upping the mark to .327 (second in the National League) a year later. Not much of a power threat in those dead-ball days, Hornsby was moved to second base in 1920 and paced the NL in batting (.370), slugging (.559), RBI (94), hits (218), and doubles (44) despite just nine homers. It was the best offensive season by an NL second baseman in the 20th century, but it was only the beginning.

In 1921, the man called "Rajah" for his regal, hazel-eyed appearance upped his average to .397 with 44 doubles, 18 triples, 126 RBI, 131 runs, and 21 homers—leading the league in each department except the last while maintaining a hold on the NL batting, slugging (.639), and on-base-percentage (.458)—leads that would last four more years. His first .400 season (.401) followed, with Hornsby completing his full maturation as a slugger by belting 42 homers (then a record for second basemen), good for 152 RBI and the 1922 Triple Crown.

An aloof free-thinker nearly as despised as the

only man to compile a higher lifetime average—Ty Cobb—Hornsby outdid even the Georgia Peach during his infamous 1921-25 run. Limited by injury to 107 games in '23, he still averaged 216 hits, 123 runs, 41 doubles, 13 triples, 29 homers, and 120 RBI over the span—highlighted by the highest NL average of the 20th century (.424) in '24 and his second Triple Crown in 1925 (.403, 39, 143). Named player/manager of the underachieving Cards that same year, he led St. Louis to its first pennant and a stunning seven-game World Series upset of the Yankees in 1926 while batting .317.

As with Cobb, however, success couldn't calm Hornsby's bitter disposition. He routinely clashed with Cardinals owner Sam Breadon over money matters and, before the '27 season, was traded to the Giants. After more quarrels with New York ownership during his lone season there (.361), he passed through Boston (a seventh and final batting title at .387 with the '28 Braves) and Chicago (.380, 39, 149 totals a year later) before his production slipped. He eventually ended up back in St. Louis for part-time duty with the Cardinals and Browns, and his final .358 average, 301 homers, 1,584 RBI, and .577 slugging percentage earned him a Hall of Fame plaque—even if his attitude was anything but golden.

MAJOR LEAGUE TOTALS									
BA	G	AB	R	H	2B	3B	HR	RBI	SB
.358	2,259	8,173	1,579	2,930	541	169	301	1,584	135

JOE JACKSON

JOE JACKSON'S NAME DOES NOT ADORN a plaque at the Baseball Hall of Fame. He certainly has the qualifications—a .356 career average (third all time), and a penchant for graceful outfield play—but his legacy is not that of an outstanding athlete; only a fallen one. Jackson may or may not have taken part in the conspiracy by White Sox players to throw the 1919 World Series—he hit .375 and fielded flawlessly over the eight-game classic—but his banishment from the majors along with seven teammates more than a year later assured that his record would remain forever tainted.

An illiterate country boy and the pride of Brandon Village, South Carolina, Jackson acquired the nickname "Shoeless Joe" when a big-league scout saw him playing that way in a semipro game. Bench jockeys felt they could ride the sensitive, sullen left-handed batter from the game after an initial big-league trial with the Athletics had fizzled, but Jackson flourished upon joining the Cleveland Naps late in 1910. Never hitting below .360 from day one of the following season, the 22-year-old had reached .408 with 233 hits, 126 runs, 45 doubles, and 337 total bases by year's end. An incredible .420 performance by Ty Cobb doomed Jackson to second place in each aforementioned category, but after Joe followed up with a .395 season (again second to Cobb) and an American League-leading

226 hits and 26 triples in 1912, it was obvious that he would be sticking around.

Producing another fantastic year in 1913 (.373 with a league-high 197 hits, 39 doubles, and .551 slugging), Joe cooled off a bit at .338 and .308 in 1914-15—the latter season disrupted by a midseason trade from cash-poor Cleveland to the White Sox. Back up to .341 (third in the AL) with 202 hits (second), 40 doubles (third), 21 triples (first), and a .495 slugging average (second) in 1916, the speedy left fielder with the rifle arm and glove known as "the place triples go to die" hit just .301 the following season but was still a major cog in a Chicago world championship.

Quitting the team after 17 games in 1918 to work at a shipyard and avoid being drafted into World War I, Joe hit .351 with a career-high 96 RBI a year later to power the White Sox into another World Series—the tainted eight-game defeat to Cincinnati. A superb 1920 followed (.382 with 218 hits, 42 doubles, 20 triples, and 121 RBI) while news of the fix surfaced, and though acquitted in court, Joe was found guilty in the eyes of commissioner Kenesaw Mountain Landis. Banished from the game at age 31, Jackson maintained innocence until his death 30 years later.

MAJOR LEAGUE TOTALS									
BA	G	AB	R	H	2B	3B	HR	RBI	SB
.356	1,332	4,981	873	1,772	307	168	54	785	202

WALTER JOHNSON

THE CY YOUNG AWARD IS GIVEN ANNUALLY to the best pitcher in each league, which is ironic considering it isn't even named for the finest pitcher of all time. But while Cy's time was winding down around 1910, another hurler was just getting started with the old Washington Senators. And before he was through 21 years later, Walter Johnson would be heralded as one of the game's grandest gentlemen—and, in the eyes of most, the greatest pitcher of them all.

The quiet and ruggedly handsome son of Kansas farmers, Johnson was discovered playing for a semipro team in Idaho and was dispatched on a train to Washington—and the major leagues. A long-limbed right-hander with an easygoing sidearm motion, the 19-year-old could throw a 100-mph fastball but struggled to learn on the job, going 32-48 his first three years with teams that never rose above seventh place.

More comfortable with his role as Washington's ace by 1910, Johnson had his first spectacular season with a 25-17 record, 1.35 ERA, and 313 strikeouts for the seventh-place Senators. In a pattern that would repeat itself many times, the man nicknamed "Big Train" was a frequent victim of nonsupport from his light-hitting mates; he would eventually lock up a record 64 contests decided by a 1-0 score—winning 38.

The Senators showed dramatic improvement over the next few years, and Johnson anchored second-place finishes in 1912 and '13 with records of 33-12 and 36-7. The latter may have been the finest performance ever by a major-league hurler, as it included a 1.14 ERA, 11 shutouts, and five one-hitters. Johnson's work from 1912-16 included a 149-70 record, an ERA below 1.90 each season, 1,202 strikeouts, and just 326 walks. Eventually, he would pace the AL 12 times in strikeouts, six times in wins, and five times in ERA.

Washington slipped back to the second division as the years wore on, finishing with a winning record just four seasons from 1914-23. Walter still put together six straight 20-win campaigns, and then, in 1924, enjoyed the most satisfying year of his career—leading the league with a 23-7 record, 2.72 ERA, 158 strikeouts, and six shutouts and winning the seventh game of the World Series.

Two more seasons and another World Series appearance remained before a broken leg derailed Johnson's career, but by then he had racked up 417 wins (second only to Young), a 2.16 ERA, and 3,509 strikeouts (a record for over 50 years). Shutouts? The charter Hall of Famer had a record 110 of them, 34 more than a guy named Young.

MAJOR LEAGUE TOTALS

W	L	ERA	G	CG	IP	H	ER	BB	SO
417	279	2.16	802	531	5,923.2	4,914	1,422	1,363	3,509

SANDY KOUFAX

HE WAS A BONUS BABY GONE BAD, a player rushed to the majors with no bush-league experience who had taken the big bucks but failed to blossom. The demon-fast but erratic left-hander, Sandy Koufax, had a record of 36-40 through six disappointing seasons.

The concerns continued over the next six dazzling years, only now it was National League batters worrying how to hit the most dominating pitcher in history. It was an incredible turn of events, and it came with almost no warning. In 1954, the 19-year-old Brooklyn native had signed with his hometown team for a $14,000 bonus and $6,000 salary. Dodger bosses hoped a handsome, young Jewish star would boost attendance, but the hard thrower went just 9-10 his first three seasons.

Given more starts after the Dodgers' move west in '58, Sandy went 19-17 the next two years—but walked 197 in 312 innings. When he fell back to 8-13 in 1960, he received a salary cut. Then, during spring training the following year, a simple conversation turned everything around. Noticing the sheer force with which Koufax delivered each pitch, Dodger catcher backup Norm Sherry suggested Sandy ease up on his fastball and throw more changeups and curves.

The results were extraordinary: Koufax went 18-13 in '61, striking out a league-high 269 while walking just 96 in 256 innings. The best was yet to come; from 1962-66, Sandy was as masterful as any pitcher in history. In addition to leading the Dodgers to three pennants and two world championships with his 111-34 record, three Cy Young Awards, and 1963 MVP trophy earned over the five-year span, he also accomplished the following: led the NL a record five straight times in ERA (three times under 2.00), pitched a then-record four no-hitters (including a perfect game versus the Cubs), won four World Series games, tossed 33 shutouts (11 in '63 alone), and struck out 1,444 in 1,377 innings—highlighted by a then-record 382 in 1965.

Sandy's '62 season was cut short by a circulatory problem, and two years later a bad elbow developed into traumatic arthritis. He began taking cortisone shots regularly. He still went 26-8 in '65 and 27-9 in '66—leading the majors in victories, strikeouts, and ERA both years—but after the latter season he stunned the baseball world with this statement: "I don't regret for one minute the 12 years I've spent in baseball.... But I could regret one season too many." Sandy was calling it quits at age 30, and no one was surprised when six years later he became the youngest player ever inducted into the Baseball Hall of Fame.

MAJOR LEAGUE TOTALS									
W	L	ERA	G	CG	IP	H	ER	BB	SO
165	87	2.76	397	137	2,324.1	1,754	713	817	2,396

NAPOLEON LAJOIE

IT IS FITTING NAP LAJOIE was one of the first men honored with entry into the Baseball Hall of Fame, for he was in many ways essential to the survival and flourishing of the major leagues during their infancy. A standout in the pre-1900 National League, Lajoie was later a major selling point to fans for the upstart American League during the first years of this century.

After playing just three months in the minors during 1896, the graceful Lajoie was scooped up by the Phillies and hit .326 over 39 games. He did not dip below .300 for the next 10 seasons, batting .361 in '97 and leading the NL with a .569 slugging percentage. Moving from first to second base in 1898, "Larry" batted .324 and led the NL with 43 doubles and 127 RBI.

Seasons at .378 and .337 followed for the large (6'1", 195 pounds), right-handed slugger, but his league-maximum salary remained at $2,400 a year. When the American League set up shop in 1901, A's owner Connie Mack convinced Lajoie to stay in town but switch teams with a four-year, $24,000 contract. Nap responded by winning the Triple Crown for his new club with an incredible .426 average (highest this century) and a league-leading 14 homers, 125 RBI, 145 runs, 232 hits, 48 doubles, and .643 slugging mark—as well as a second straight year atop the second base fielding charts.

Upset over their star's betrayal, Phillies management received an injunction in 1901 forbidding Lajoie from playing in Philadelphia. Rather than face an uncertain trial, AL president Ban Johnson transferred Nap's contract to the Cleveland Blues. There he posted league-leading averages of .344 and .376 in 1903-04, paced second basemen in fielding from 1906-08, and managed from 1905-09. His .346 average for the century's first decade was second in the majors only to Honus Wagner, and as Cleveland rose to a contender, the team underwent an appropriate name change, becoming known from 1905-14 as the Naps.

So revered was Lajoie by fans, teammates, and opponents that when he dueled the despised Ty Cobb for the batting title down to the wire in 1910, Browns fielders allowed Nap to collect eight hits in a last-day doubleheader—six of them on safe bunts—in order to win. Lajoie *still* was a .385-.384 loser despite the performance. Finishing his major-league career back with Mack's A's in 1915-16, Lajoie retired with imposing numbers—3,242 hits, 1,504 runs, 1,599 RBI, and 657 doubles—then promptly went back to the minors and hit .380 at Toronto in '17. He probably figured that franchise needed some help as well.

MAJOR LEAGUE TOTALS									
BA	G	AB	R	H	2B	3B	HR	RBI	SB
.338	2,480	9,589	1,504	3,242	657	163	83	1,599	380

MICKEY MANTLE

To those who saw him play, Mickey Charles Mantle was something special: a combination of power, speed, and presence possessing so much natural talent that some viewed him as an underachiever despite his titanic accomplishments. A switch-hitter from the time his father pitched to him in the family's Commerce, Oklahoma, backyard, he overcame a bone disease known as osteomyelitis in his left leg to make the Yankees as a 19-year-old outfielder in the spring of 1951.

He was touted as the next Joe DiMaggio, and he recovered from a tough start to have a fine rookie year dimmed only by an injury to his good leg in New York's World Series win over Brooklyn. It was just the start of the health hazards that would plague Mantle's career, but as the starting center fielder on the most dominating team in baseball history, Mantle's star rose quickly. He batted .311 his second season, and he had already hit 121 homers by age 23 when he led the American League with 37 in 1955.

Superb defense, blistering power (as evidenced by his 565-foot shot at Washington), and annual totals of 100-plus runs and 90-100 RBI were not enough for some fans awaiting the next DiMaggio. Only after putting together an MVP/Triple Crown season in '56 (pacing the league with a .353 average, 52 homers, 130 RBI, 132 runs, and .705 slugging percentage) did Mantle win everyone over. He hit a career-high .365 with 34 home runs to cop a second straight MVP trophy in '57, and in 1961 he waged a season-long assault against Babe Ruth's record of 60 homers. He wound up six short when he was sidelined in September by a hip infection, and teammate Roger Maris broke the record with his 61st blast.

Mick had become the fan favorite, and when he recovered to win a third MVP prize in '62 (.321, 30, 89), it was still thought he might challenge Ruth's all-time record of 714 homers. But injuries (including surgery on one shoulder and both legs) and years of hard drinking had worn down his body, and after a strong year in '64 capped by three World Series home runs (his 18 homers in 12 Series broke Ruth's record), he and the Yankees began a rapid decline. He retired in 1968.

Mantle's 536 homers, 1,509 RBI, and leadership on seven World Series champions guaranteed him a Hall of Fame plaque, but his perseverance alone became legendary. When he struggled near death in 1995, baseball fans who came of age in the 1950s and '60s found themselves questioning their own mortality. If the great Mickey Mantle was vulnerable, they wondered, how safe are any of us?

MAJOR LEAGUE TOTALS									
BA	G	AB	R	H	2B	3B	HR	RBI	SB
.298	2,401	8,102	1,677	2,415	344	72	536	1,509	153

EDDIE MATHEWS

IF EVER A MAN WAS A FRANCHISE PLAYER, it was Eddie Mathews. He debuted at third base with the Braves during their last pitiful year in Boston (1952), moved with the club to Milwaukee for its 1950s glory days, then played and managed in the team's third home—Atlanta—during the '60s and '70s. Named a scout after his managerial career ended, Eddie was under contract to the Braves in some capacity or another for 30 years.

The muscular (6'1", 195 pounds), left-handed Mathews spent his first years in Atlanta as a slugger on its Southern League team (32 homers in '50), and by '52 Eddie was holding down third base in Boston as a 20-year-old. A dismal fielder at first, he showed promise at the plate (.242, 25, 58).

Like many Braves players, Eddie blossomed after the seventh-place club departed the empty stands of Boston for Milwaukee. He slugged a National League-leading 47 homers in 1953—then a record for third basemen—with 135 RBI (second) and a .627 slugging mark (second). Eddie's average jumped to .302, his strikeouts shrank from 115 to 83, and despite 30 errors he improved in the field as the team jumped to third place. Two more 40-homer seasons followed, and by '55 Eddie also led the league in assists at third.

The Braves finally caught the Dodgers and Giants to win the pennant in 1957, and Eddie did his part with 32 homers, 94 RBI, and an NL-best 299 assists before adding a homer and three doubles in the World Series triumph over the Yankees. Another solid year (31 homers, career-high 351 assists) followed in '58, but the Braves lost a rematch to the Yanks, and despite having topped 30 homers nine consecutive years (1953-61), Mathews was routinely overshadowed by teammate Hank Aaron—whom he out-homered only twice in their final 10 seasons together.

MVP runnerup in '59 (.306, 46, 114) when he captured his second NL homer title, Mathews already had 399 round-trippers by age 30 and was considered a threat to Babe Ruth's record of 714. But the slugger's best years were behind him; as Braves mania waned in Milwaukee, so did Eddie's homer output—from 39 to 29 to 23 in both '63 and '64. By the time the Braves got to Georgia in '66, he was good for only 16 dingers and a .250 average. By 1967, when he became the seventh member of the 500-homer club, Eddie was playing for Houston. Retiring with 512 home runs, 1,453 RBI, and a .509 slugging percentage, he managed the club from 1972-74 and watched old pal Aaron do what he couldn't—pass the Babe.

MAJOR LEAGUE TOTALS									
BA	G	AB	R	H	2B	3B	HR	RBI	SB
.271	2,391	8,537	1,509	2,315	354	72	512	1,453	68

CHRISTY MATHEWSON

IN THE ROUGH-AND-TUMBLE EARLY DAYS of baseball, players were viewed as dirty, violent thugs who spiked each other. But with the new century came a pitcher who would help change baseball's image—and garner a 373-188 record as one of the greatest, most popular players of all time.

Christy Mathewson grew up outside Factoryville, Pennsylvania, as the son of prominent farmers and was later president of his class and a baseball, basketball, and football star at Bucknell University. A 20-2 start in the Northern League prompted the right-hander's sale to the Giants in 1900, and after an 0-3 debut that summer he became a 20-game winner (20-17) with 221 strikeouts the following year. He dropped off to 14-17 but new manager John McGraw believed big things were ahead for the 6'1" screwballer.

In 1903, Matty began validating this confidence. Winning at least 30 games and leading the league in strikeouts each of the next three years, he went 94-34 with a cumulative ERA of 1.87 and 685 whiffs over 1,073 innings. The Giants won the pennant behind his 33-12 record in 1904, and Christy peaked the following year with a 31-9 mark that included a league-best 1.28 ERA and eight shutouts to lead another pennant run. Matty was fantastic in the World Series, setting a record with three shutouts to pace a five-game Giant victory over the

Athletics. Shy and often thought to be aloof, the blue-eyed hurler with the body resembling a Greek statue was worshiped nationwide from that point on and considered a fine example for a game that was cleaning up its image.

Mathewson improved on his personal bests with a 37-11, 11-shutout campaign in 1908 and showed his usual phenomenal control with 259 strikeouts and just 42 walks over 390 innings. He eventually won 20 or more games 12 consecutive seasons (including three more pennant-winners), going to the inside-curving screwball he called his "fade-away" more and more as his speed began to wane. Economical on the mound—he once needed just 67 pitches to complete a win—he was rumored to actually ease up in one-sided games, lacking concern for his personal stats.

Manager of the Reds for parts of three years after his career ended in 1916, Matty entered World War I as an Army captain and was gassed in a training exercise. Tuberculosis developed, and at his death in 1925, the 45-year-old charter Hall of Famer was mourned as no player would be until Lou Gehrig—as much for the improved perception of the game he helped create as for his 373 wins (tied for third all time), 79 shutouts (third), and 2.13 ERA (fifth).

MAJOR LEAGUE TOTALS

W	L	ERA	G	CG	IP	H	ER	BB	SO
373	188	2.13	635	434	4,780.2	2,502	1,132	844	2,502

WILLIE MAYS

THE NUMBER OF PEOPLE who saw Babe Ruth play are lessening each year, as are those who saw Ty Cobb perform. It is becoming increasingly difficult to judge players of days gone by against those of more recent vintage, but among careers still remembered by a great many fans, no ballplayer has been more glowingly praised than Willie Mays.

Mays, among the last Negro Leaguers to make the majors, was a strapping young Alabaman who could hit with power, run with style and speed, and catch anything struck in the direction of center field when he emerged as a 20-year-old New York Giant in 1951. Rookie of the Year (.274, 20 homers) on the National League champions, he missed most of the next two years fulfilling service obligations and returned in '54 rippling with new muscle and ready to wreak havoc on NL pitching. He didn't disappoint, hitting a career-high .345 to win his only batting title and ranking among league leaders with MVP totals of 41 homers, 119 runs, and 110 RBI.

In coming years, those types of numbers would seem almost commonplace, as from 1954-66 Mays accomplished the following for the Giants in New York and San Francisco: slugged at least 29 homers each season, averaging 40 a year; scored 100 or more runs 12 times, averaging 117; and notched 100 or more RBI on 10 occasions, averaging 109. He had four stolen base titles and he once swiped 58 of 68 over a two-year span.

Willie's over-the-shoulder catch of Vic Wertz's 430-foot smash to deep center in the '54 World Series has been called the greatest grab of all time, and it brought into national focus another key aspect of May's game: his defense. Willie won a Gold Glove each of the first seven years the trophy for fielding excellence was awarded, routinely turning in fantastic plays. He patented a flashy, one-handed basket catch, and—even with runners weary of testing his arm—recorded 12 or more assists on nine occasions.

For most of his career, Mays was viewed alongside Mantle as one of the two men most likely to break Ruth's all-time record of 714 home runs. After Willie slugged 52 to take home his second MVP Award in 1965, he had 505, and at age 34 appeared within striking distance. But by 1967, the man named Player of the Decade for the '60s had seemingly aged overnight. His flashes of brilliance grew less frequent, and by 1973 he was a slow-moving bench-warmer for the Mets. He never caught the Babe and was eventually passed by Hank Aaron, but 660 home runs, 2,062 runs, 1,903 RBI, a .302 average, and 338 steals isn't too shabby a legacy.

MAJOR LEAGUE TOTALS									
BA	G	AB	R	H	2B	3B	HR	RBI	SB
.302	2,992	10,881	2,062	3,283	523	140	660	1,903	338

JOE MORGAN

WILLIE MAYS GARNERED A REPUTATION as the most complete player of the last half-century, but one can make a strong argument that during the 1970s a 5'7", 160-pound second baseman was as big an offensive and defensive threat as any muscle-bound slugger since Mays. "Little Joe" Morgan combined blazing speed, great instincts, and an unwavering desire to win into a terrific package that sparked several teams to championships.

Morgan's career appeared to be on the fast track in 1965 when he hit .271 with 14 homers, 100 runs scored, and an NL-high 97 walks as a 21-year-old rookie for the Houston Astros. Then a fractured kneecap cut his power totals in '66, torn ligaments ruined his '68 season, and by 1969 he had slumped to .236 despite 49 stolen bases. The left-handed contact hitter with the trademark twitch in his elbow just before swinging was sent to Cincinnati following a .256 season in '71. Once out of the cavernous Astrodome, Joe began putting up the numbers his first season had foreshadowed.

Joe led the league in walks (115) and runs (122) his first year with the Reds, and he hit .292 with 16 homers and 58 steals for the '72 National League champs. It was the first of six straight years he would register at least 100 runs and 100 walks, a period over which he also averaged .301 with 22 homers, 84 RBI, and 60 stolen bases (in 72 attempts) per season. Not coincidentally, the Reds won four division titles, three pennants, and two world championships over the same span. And in a lineup featuring Pete Rose, Johnny Bench, George Foster, and Tony Perez, it was Little Joe who copped back-to-back MVP Awards for the World Series winners of 1975-76. He also teamed with Dave Concepcion to form a terrific double-play combination, and from 1973-77 Morgan won five straight Gold Gloves.

Known as a winner throughout baseball, Joe slipped back to .250 in 1979 before returning to the Astros as a free agent. He sparkplugged his old team to its first division title the following year, then nearly brought the San Francisco Giants a flag in '82 (.289 with 14 homers and 24 steals). Reunited with an aging Rose and Perez on Philadelphia's "Wheeze Kids" of '83, Morgan hit 16 homers before adding two more in a World Series loss to Baltimore.

His career totals of 1,865 walks, 689 steals, and an 81-percent steal success rate are among the best in history, and his 268 homers, 1,133 RBI, and 1,650 runs scored show the Hall of Famer's incredible all-around skills. When Morgan retired to begin a broadcasting career in 1984, only Eddie Collins had put in more time at second base.

MAJOR LEAGUE TOTALS									
BA	G	AB	R	H	2B	3B	HR	RBI	SB
.271	2,649	9,277	1,650	2,517	449	96	268	1,133	689

STAN MUSIAL

THE MINOR-LEAGUE LEFTY'S record stood at 18-5 on that August 1940 afternoon, but since he was a .300 hitter, his manager had him playing center field on a nonpitching day. Diving to make the catch on a line drive, the 19-year-old hurt the shoulder of his throwing arm upon hitting the ground. Forced to the outfield full-time when the injury failed to heal, Stanley Frank Musial still made the majors the very next summer—and retired 22 years later as a .331 lifetime hitter with 475 homers, 1,951 RBI, and 3,630 hits.

The 6'0", 175-pounder with the crouched batting stance that one writer said had him "appearing to be peering at the pitcher from around the corner" batted .315 with 10 homers and 72 RBI as a regular on the '42 World Series champs—the only full season he was not named an All-Star. There was no question of his star quality in 1943, as Stan led the NL with a .357 average, .562 slugging mark, 220 hits, 48 doubles, and 20 triples. The top producer (81 RBI, 108 runs) on a second straight pennant-winner, he was named NL MVP—the first of seven times he would finish first or second in the voting.

Another stellar season (.347, 12, 94 with a league-best 197 hits, 51 doubles, and .549 slugging mark) for the world champs of '44 followed, and after a year in the Navy, Musial copped his second MVP trophy in 1946, pacing the club to its third World Series title in five years while leading the NL with a .365 average, 124 runs, 228 hits, 50 doubles, and 20 triples. He hit so well versus the Dodgers that Ebbets Field fans nicknamed him "The Man."

Appendicitis slowed Stan in '47 (.312, 19, 95), but his 1948 season may have been the best by any NL hitter this century. Determined to add power and raise his salary toward the $100,000 Greenberg-Williams-DiMaggio level, Musial used a shorter grip and greater stride to smash 39 homers and finish tops in the NL in batting (a career-high .376), RBI (131), runs (135), hits (230), doubles (46), triples (18), and slugging (.702). Stan became the first NL player to win three MVP Awards for the effort.

Musial averaged 31 homers from 1948-57 (including five in a 1954 doubleheader) and added four more batting crowns—three straight from 1950-52 and his last (.351) in '57. Stan kept on hitting past his 40th birthday (.330 in 1962) before retiring as a grandpa in 1963. Owner or shared owner of 29 National League and 19 major-league records upon his retirement, he later helped St. Louis to another world championship as general manager in '67—a year before a statue was unveiled outside Busch Stadium to honor the greatest washed-up pitcher in Cardinals history

MAJOR LEAGUE TOTALS									
BA	G	AB	R	H	2B	3B	HR	RBI	SB
.331	3,026	10,972	1,949	3,630	725	177	475	1,951	78

SATCHEL PAIGE

JOE DIMAGGIO CALLED HIM "the best and the fastest pitcher I ever faced," but it wasn't until Leroy "Satchel" Paige was well past his 40th birthday that Joe could face him in a game that counted. Paige spent most of nearly 30 years of pitching relegated to the Negro Leagues, but through his heroics there and his barnstorming success versus major-leaguers, he created a legend that will long endure.

Paige always claimed he was born in 1906, although there were suspicions he was at least five years older. Whatever the case, the 6′3″, pencil-thin Mobile, Alabama, resident acquired his legendary nickname as a seven-year-old train porter, and by age 12 he was learning how to pitch in reform school after being caught for stealing. Signed by the semipro Mobile Tigers in 1924, he was with the Negro League Chattanooga Black Lookouts two years later.

Eventually playing on nearly a dozen different "Black Ball" clubs, Satchel blew his fastball by hitters and packed the stands wherever he went. Aside from his pitching prowess, part of Paige's appeal was his appearance on the mound. Curling his body up into a wild windmill-type delivery before throwing, he tossed a variety of pitches with pinpoint control. There were "Little Tom" and "Big Tom," his medium and speedy fastball; the "Two-

Hump Blooper," a moving changeup; and the "hesitation pitch," which included a complete stop in mid-rotation to throw off batters. *Total Baseball* credits Satch with 62 straight scoreless innings and a 31-4 record for the 1933 Pittsburgh Crawfords, but tales of his starting games off with nine consecutive strikeouts on demand and having his outfielders sit down with the bases loaded to frustrate batters were often more fun than the truth.

Earning an annual $40,000-plus income—far above that of most major-leaguers—Paige spent winters pitching in the Caribbean or Mexico and many autumns barnstorming with the "Satchel Paige All-Stars," playing against teams made up of white major-leaguers. He won four of six games against Dizzy Dean. Finally brought to the majors by Cleveland Indians owner Bill Veeck in 1948, Satchel drew record crowds wherever he pitched and contributed a 6-1 record, two shutouts, and a 2.48 ERA to help the Indians claim the World Series.

Later an All-Star reliever for Veeck on the St. Louis Browns, Satchel pitched in the minors well past his 50th birthday and made a three-inning stint for the A's in 1965—pitching shutout ball at age 59. Paige was the first man named to the Hall of Fame primarily for his Negro League play.

MAJOR LEAGUE TOTALS										
W	L	ERA	G	CG	IP	H	ER	BB	SO
28	31	3.29	179	7	476.0	429	174	183	290

CAL RIPKEN

WHILE IN THE MIDST of a 4-for-55 slump in 1982, rookie Cal Ripken Jr. worried that his major-league days were numbered. Thirteen years later, his days were indeed being numbered, only now it was immortality and not the minors that awaited him. Ripken reported for work on May 30, 1982, and just kept coming back, and when his attendance record reached 2,131 straight games on September 6, 1995, Cal passed Lou Gehrig to take hold of what was long considered the most "unbreakable" of all big-league records.

Son of longtime Orioles coach Cal Sr., the squeaky-clean right-handed workhorse debuted with Dad's team as a 20-year-old in 1981. Reaching a low point of .117 on May 1, 1982, he then caught fire, batting .281 to the end of the season and not missing a game after May 29 en route to a .264 average, 28 homers, 93 RBI, and the American League Rookie of the Year Award.

Having previously split time at shortstop and third, Cal was at short from day one in 1983. He wound up the AL MVP as he paced the Orioles to the world championship by leading the AL in runs (121), hits (211), and doubles (47). Defensively, he paced all AL shortstops in assists (534), a mark he raised to a league-record 583 the following year, when he also hit .304 with 27 homers, 86 RBI, and 103 runs. Top vote-getter for the AL All-Star team in '85 (.282, 26, 110) and '86, Cal fooled those who questioned whether a 6′4″ slowpoke could play short by annually placing among league leaders in total chances per game.

Cal Sr. was named Orioles manager for '87, and although Junior struggled to a career-low .252 average, he was given the treat of a new partner at second—his brother Billy. Cal's streak of 8,243 straight *innings* ended that summer, but as the fortunes of the club rose and fell wildly over the next three years, Cal was its lone constant, playing every day and continuing to provide great defense and 20-homer, 85-RBI power. In 1990, Cal made just three errors to set a major-league record for shortstops with a .996 fielding percentage.

In 1991, Cal had his best all-around season, setting career highs with a .323 average, 34 homers, and 114 RBI to win his second MVP Award along with his first Gold Glove. He passed old record-holder Ernie Banks with his 278th homer at short during the '93 season, and through 1996 had made 13 straight starts in the All-Star Game. He has increased his homer total to 353, and this—coupled with his 1,369 RBI, stellar defense, and the ongoing streak—assures Cal a spot in the Hall of Fame... provided he ever stops playing.

MAJOR LEAGUE TOTALS									
BA	G	AB	R	H	2B	3B	HR	RBI	SB
.277	2,381	9,217	1,366	2,549	487	43	353	1,369	35

BROOKS ROBINSON

HE CAME IN WITH EISENHOWER, went out with Carter, and in between ruled the highlight films as the finest third baseman of two generations. Brooks Robinson made the fantastic look routine and the impossible possible, and it is testimony to his defensive greatness that his 268 lifetime homers are merely an afterthought on his Hall of Fame plaque.

Appropriately, a player with a reputation as one of the game's true gentlemen was discovered playing in a church league. The Little Rock native debuted in 1955 with the Baltimore Orioles, and over the next five seasons he hit a forgettable .249 while often platooning at third.

Finally given the third base job for keeps in 1960, Robinson took his game to another level. Becoming a consistent .280 hitter with power for 20 home runs a season, he also won the first of his 16 consecutive Gold Gloves and made his first of 16 All-Star teams after raising his fielding average from .955 to a league-leading .977. Slow afoot, he based his defensive excellence on knowing the strengths and weaknesses of each batter. He looked stylish making even routine plays, and his uniform was usually dirty by game's end from dives into foul territory or the shortstop hole. For his ability to suck up everything hit his way, he was called "The Human Vacuum Cleaner" and "Hoover."

The Orioles had no luck catching the Yankees in the early '60s, but Brooks continued to shine—peaking with an MVP season in 1964 when he had an AL-best 118 RBI, hit a career-high 28 homers, and batted .300 for the only time in his career (.317, second in the league). An All-Star starter at third for 15 straight seasons, he was third in MVP voting in '65, and in '66 he finished second to brand-new teammate Frank Robinson—the pair combining with powerful first baseman Boog Powell to carry the Orioles to a World Series sweep of the Dodgers.

Three more pennants followed from 1969-71, Brooksie continuing as the defensive standout on a team that in two of those seasons fielded four Gold Glove winners. His shining moment came as MVP of the 1970 World Series, when he hit .429 with a pair of homers and made one incredible stop after another to thrill a national television audience and win the Series for the Orioles.

Robinson's offense slipped badly after 1970, but he continued to win Gold Gloves through his 38th birthday in 1975. When he finally retired two years later, he held records for third basemen in games (2,870), fielding average (.971), putouts (2,697), and assists (6,205). His Hall of Fame induction in 1983 drew one of the biggest crowds in history.

MAJOR LEAGUE TOTALS

BA	G	AB	R	H	2B	3B	HR	RBI	SB
.267	2,896	10,654	1,232	2,848	482	68	268	1,357	28

FRANK ROBINSON

HIS WAS A CAREER FULL OF FIRSTS: the first man to be named MVP in both leagues, the first player to hit 200 homers in both, the first (and only) black Triple Crown winner, and—perhaps most importantly—the first black manager in major-league history. Although not related to Jackie Robinson, Frank was a product of the new era Jackie had ushered in: a proud and outspoken black man not afraid to voice his opinions, able to make the big leagues and rise in the game based on skill alone—regardless of his skin color.

Robinson debuted with the Cincinnati Reds as a 20-year-old in 1956 and was named Rookie of the Year after batting .290 with 38 homers and a league-best 122 runs scored. The right-handed left fielder averaged 33 homers and 90 RBI his first five years (adding a Gold Glove in 1958), then copped his first MVP Award in '61 by hitting .323 with 37 homers, 124 RBI, 117 runs, 22 stolen bases, and a league-best .611 slugging percentage for the NL pennant-winners.

Robinson had an even better year in '62 (.342 with 39 homers, 136 RBI, and a league-leading 51 doubles, 134 runs, and .624 slugging mark), then put together three more seasons among the league leaders through 1965. A staunch civil rights advocate who had gotten in some trouble for carrying a gun, Robinson may have irked Cincinnati general manager Bill DeWitt; there seems no other explanation for DeWitt's trading outfielder Dick Simpson and Frank—whom he called "an old 30"—to the Baltimore Orioles for pitchers Milt Pappas and Jack Baldschun before the 1966 campaign.

Old Man Robinson didn't take long to prove DeWitt a fool. He won the AL Triple Crown and MVP Award in '66 with the Orioles, leading the league in batting (.316), homers (49), RBI (122), runs (122), and slugging (.637) before adding two more homers in a World Series sweep of the Dodgers—Baltimore's first world championship.

Injuries hampered Frank in both 1967 and '68, but beginning in 1969 he averaged 28 homers and 92 RBI to help the Orioles to three straight pennants and a second world championship. He then drifted from the Dodgers to the Angels (where he had his 11th and last 30-homer season) to the Indians, where in 1975 he crowned his historic debut as player/manager with a homer in his first at-bat. Subsequent stops produced Manager of the Year awards in San Francisco (1982) and Baltimore (1989). Today the Hall of Famer, whose 586 homers still stand as fourth all time, remains active in the game as assistant general manager in Baltimore. Jackie would have been proud.

MAJOR LEAGUE TOTALS									
BA	G	AB	R	H	2B	3B	HR	RBI	SB
.294	2,808	10,006	1,829	2,943	528	72	586	1,812	204

JACKIE ROBINSON

IT HAS BEEN SAID STATISTICS don't always do great players justice, but in Jackie Robinson's case no numbers would be impressive enough. Sure, Robinson was a lifetime .311 hitter who spearheaded six pennants and a world championship for the Brooklyn Dodgers, but it was as a crusader for his and all people that Jackie stood out.

Born in a shack on a Georgia cotton field, this grandson of a slave and son of sharecroppers was UCLA's first four-sport star before he enlisted in the Army during World War II. After his discharge, Robinson joined the Kansas City Monarchs of the Negro Leagues for the fine sum of $100 a week as debate over the major-league color ban increased. One of three players given a sham tryout by the Boston Red Sox in April 1945, Jackie received a far more sincere gesture from Dodger general manager Branch Rickey a few months later—a contract making him the first black player signed by a major-league organization in over a half-century.

Rickey saw in Jackie the blend of intelligence, character, and iron will needed to endure with quiet dignity the challenges ahead. After leading the International League in batting (.349) and runs scored (113) for minor-league Montreal in '46, Jackie made the Dodgers the following spring and began what became known as the "the most costly trial ever given a player." He was taunted verbally, spiked while playing first base, and thrown at on a regular basis while batting, but true to his word to Mr. Rickey, Robinson stayed calm and let his play do the talking.

It spoke loud and clear, as Robinson electrified Brooklyn crowds with his running (a league-high 29 steals) and production (.297 with 12 homers and 125 runs scored). The Dodgers won the pennant and set an NL attendance record, and Jackie was voted the first National League Rookie of the Year. Teammates who once considered passing a petition against his playing now defended him in on-field incidents, and Robinson grew into a leadership role on the finest clubs in Brooklyn history.

Jackie became an outstanding defensive second baseman who led the NL in double plays four straight years, and he had 19 career steals of home—once stealing his way around the bases to get there. By 1949, he finally felt comfortable fighting back against his tormentors, and the NL MVP supported his cause by leading the league in batting (.342) and steals (37) while scoring 122 runs and driving in 124. He averaged .329 with 108 runs and 93 RBI from 1949-53, and after his retirement three years later continued speaking out against injustice until diabetes cut him down in 1972, at age 53.

MAJOR LEAGUE TOTALS									
BA	G	AB	R	H	2B	3B	HR	RBI	SB
.311	1,382	4,877	947	1,518	273	54	137	734	197

PETE ROSE

THE HALL OF FAME WAS BUILT for guys like Pete Rose, yet Rose has been denied a place in this exclusive club. He is banished despite having never been proven guilty of gambling on baseball, but there's nothing the folks in Cooperstown can do about keeping his name out entirely. After all, they need someone to put atop their lists for all-time leader in hits (4,256) and games (3,562).

Son of a Cincinnati semipro football legend, Rose was a tough, crew-cutted kid who fought his way through the minors and into a spot as Reds starting second baseman in 1963. The 22-year-old switch-hitter was Rookie of the Year with a .273 average and 101 runs, and he also gained a reputation as a hot dog with his sprints to first base following walks. In '65, "Charlie Hustle" hit .312 and scored 117 runs with his first of 10 200-hit seasons.

Hitting .300 for 14 of 15 seasons, Pete claimed his first batting title with a .335 mark in '68 and his second with a .348 average in '69. Rose hit .316 with a loop-best 205 hits in helping the Reds to the 1970 NL pennant, and after hitting .304 in '71 and .307 for the '72 pennant-winners, he won his third and final batting title in 1973 with a .338 mark, 115 runs, 36 doubles, and a career-high 230 hits to garner his only MVP Award.

League leader in runs and doubles from 1974-76, Rose was the heart and soul of the "Big Red

Machine" that finally broke through with World Series wins in '75 and '76—Pete taking MVP honors in the '75 classic versus Boston with a .370 average. He topped off his first go-around in Cincinnati with his 3,000th hit and an NL-record 44-game hitting streak in 1978, then went to Philadelphia as a free agent and hit .331. Named Player of the Decade by *The Sporting News* for averaging .314 with more hits (2,045), runs (1,068), and doubles (394) than any player during the '70s, Rose celebrated with a .282 mark to help the Phillies to their first World Series title in 1980.

Piling up the hits more slowly after his 40th birthday came and went, Rose was back as player/manager with the Reds in 1985 when he stroked hit No. 4,192—a single to left-center off San Diego's Eric Show at Riverfront Stadium September 11 to pass Ty Cobb's seemingly unbreakable mark. The 17-time All-Star retired shortly thereafter with a .303 lifetime average, 2,165 runs (fourth all time), and 746 doubles (second). Pete managed the Reds until 1989, but when gambling allegations led to an investigation and subsequent banning of Rose by commissioner Bart Giamatti in '89, Pete's reserved spot in Cooperstown was taken away.

MAJOR LEAGUE TOTALS									
BA	G	AB	R	H	2B	3B	HR	RBI	SB
.303	3,562	14,053	2,165	4,256	746	135	160	1,314	198

BABE RUTH

IT WAS SAID WILLIE MAYS could "do it all," but not even Mays could match the achievements of the most well-rounded player of all time: George Herman "Babe" Ruth, pitcher *and* slugger extraordinare.

A kid of the streets who learned to play ball at St. Mary's Industrial School for Boys, 19-year-old George made the majors with the Boston Red Sox in 1914, and starting the next year went 78-40 with an ERA under 2.30 in helping the club to three World Series titles over four seasons. The left-hander completed a Series-record 29 consecutive scoreless innings in 1918, yet he was so successful a hitter that manager Ed Barrow began giving him outfield assignments on nonpitching days. The 6'2" giant liked the arrangement, and when he was allowed to roam the outfield almost exclusively in 1919, he hit an ML-record 29 home runs.

Theatrical producer and Red Sox owner Harry Frazee was not impressed. Needing money for his latest show, Frazee sold Babe to the New York Yankees in January 1920 for $125,000—plus a $300,000 loan on Fenway Park. Babe put his stamp of approval on the stupidest move in baseball history with a record-shattering 54 homers that year, and the fun was on. Fans wanted excitement after the hard realities of World War I and the Black Sox scandal, and Ruth supplied it—showing that one swing could accomplish what had previously taken a series of bunts, steals, and slides.

He was the quintessential hero of the Roaring '20s, a ham for the cameras who enjoyed having every move followed and could back up his bravado. Dominating as no player has before or since, he averaged 47 home runs and 133 RBI during the decade. Over his career, Ruth would lead the Yankees to seven pennants and four World Series championships (hitting 15 homers in Series play), despite regular indulgences in women, booze, and food. He drew screams and suspensions from his managers, and screams of delight from kids—to whom he always seemed to appeal to and relate best.

Even when his 94-46 pitching mark is not factored in, Ruth's records are remarkable. He slugged .847 in a single season (1920) and averaged a .690 slugging and .474 on-base percentage over his career. When the .342 lifetime hitter retired, his 714 home runs were about twice as many as his nearest competitor. That career total and Babe's season high of 60 homers in 1927 have both since been topped, but his impact on the game remains undisputed. He was baseball's most beloved performer—and its finest.

MAJOR LEAGUE TOTALS

BA	G	AB	R	H	2B	3B	HR	RBI	SB
.342	2,503	8,399	2,174	2,873	506	136	714	2,213	123

Ryne Sandberg

Ryne Sandberg has staked a claim to being one of the greatest second basemen in National League history during his 15 seasons with the Cubs. The perfect package, Sandberg has, in various seasons, hit over .300, smacked 40 homers, exceeded 50 stolen bases, and set major-league defensive records at the second sack.

A .300 hitter and smooth second baseman/shortstop in the Phillies minor-league system, Sandberg was included as a throw-in when the Phils and Cubs swapped shortstops (Ivan DeJesus for Larry Bowa) before the '82 season. The 22-year-old rookie promptly settled in at third base (a new position) for Chicago and hit .271 with 103 runs, 32 steals, and just 11 errors. The sturdy, 6'2", 185-pound right-handed batter quickly earned the nickname "Ryno" and respect around the National League for his tough, heads-up play.

Switched to second base in 1983, he earned a Gold Glove his first season there while batting .261 with 37 steals. In the '84 season, Sandberg proved himself to be the complete ballplayer every team dreams of. Hot from the start, the All-Star starter set career highs with a .314 average (fourth in the NL), 114 runs (first), 200 hits (second), 36 doubles (third), and 19 triples (first) while just missing becoming the first 200-20-20-20-20 man in major-league history. Crushing 19 homers en route to 84

RBI, he also collected another Gold Glove while making just six errors. His performance carried the Cubs to the NL East title (their first championship of any kind since 1945).

An All-Star each year thereafter, Ryno was a top performer in the field and at the plate over the next decade. In '85, he became the third major-leaguer with 25 homers and 50 steals in one season, and in 1988 he went the entire year without a throwing error. He belted 30 homers while going the final 90 games without a miscue of *any* kind in '89 (setting a major-league record), then in 1990 became the first second baseman to lead the NL in home runs (40) since Rogers Hornsby in 1925. Through it all, the Cubs added just one more division title (1989) and no pennants, and eventually the losing started to get to Ryne.

By 1994, he had won nine Gold Gloves, hit 240 homers, and made 10 All-Star teams (nine as a starter), but despite a .309 average, his '93 season was one of frustration amidst two hand injuries. When he began '94 batting .238 through 57 games for a struggling club, the future Hall of Famer decided to retire at age 34. However, after a year-and-a-half absence, Ryno returned to the Cubs in '96 and responded with 25 homers.

MAJOR LEAGUE TOTALS									
BA	G	AB	R	H	2B	3B	HR	RBI	SB
.286	2,029	7,938	1,264	2,268	377	76	270	997	337

MIKE SCHMIDT

JUST AS PEOPLE TEND TO forget the solid offensive numbers Brooks Robinson put up while dazzling fans with his glove, the defensive expertise of the man who became the game's best third baseman after Robinson's retirement is not always acknowledged. The slight is understandable. After all, Mike Schmidt did hit 548 home runs.

Schmidt earned 10 Gold Gloves to Robinson's 16, picking up a trophy each year from 1976-84 and again in 1986 after a year at first base. But Schmidt also topped 30 home runs 13 times and led the National League on eight occasions. As a rookie, the former Ohio University All-America shortstop hit a pitiful .196 with 136 strikeouts in just 367 at-bats for the '73 Phillies, but after spending the winter honing his swing in Puerto Rico, he doubled his home run output to a league-best 36 while batting .282 with 116 RBI and 23 stolen bases. It was the first of three straight seasons he would lead the league in homers, and his 404 assists at third set an NL record.

Schmidt continued his fence-busting with 38 round-trippers each season from 1975-77, along with leading the league in assists again. He dropped to a .251 average with 21 dingers in '78 and heard his share of booing from the fickle Philly fans when the club lost its third straight National League Championship Series that fall (Schmidt hit .200).

He rebounded to slug 45 homers in '79, but he wasn't given the chance to redeem himself in the postseason.

Mike won over the critics in 1980, setting career highs with 48 homers, 121 RBI, a .624 slugging percentage (he led the NL in all three categories), and a .286 batting average. The regular-season MVP then powered the Phils to their first world championship in 97 years, hitting .381 with two homers as MVP of the World Series triumph over Kansas City. His '81 encore would likely have been even better without a major-league strike, but the repeat MVP's 31 homers and 91 RBI in 102 games still led the league, and his .644 slugging mark and .316 average were new career highs.

After hitting "just" 35 homers in '82, Mike slugged 40 the following season to help the Phils to their second World Series in four years—a five-game loss to Baltimore. He remained one of baseball's biggest power sources and most respected performers as his 40th birthday neared, averaging 35 homers from 1984-87 and nabbing his third MVP Award in 1986 (.290, 37, 119). He retired early in the 1989 season when he felt his play slipping, but he was still named starting third baseman for the All-Star Game—a final tribute to the future Hall of Famer.

MAJOR LEAGUE TOTALS									
BA	G	AB	R	H	2B	3B	HR	RBI	SB
.267	2,404	8,352	1,506	2,234	408	59	548	1,595	174

TOM SEAVER

CERTAIN PLAYERS—no matter how long and successful their baseball careers—are destined to be remembered most for dramatic moments in which they played a part. Such it is with Tom Seaver. He won 311 games, struck out 3,640 batters, and posted a 2.86 ERA, but he continues to be recognized mostly for one thing: his presence on the Miracle Mets of 1969.

The Mets had been the laughingstock of baseball since 1962, and the 22-year-old right-hander stood out from the start when he joined them five years later. The NL Rookie of the Year went 16-13 with 170 strikeouts and a 2.76 ERA in '67 for a 61-101 club, then improved in every category (16-12, 205, 2.20) in '68 as New York finished 73-89—its first season with fewer than 95 losses. The Mets were improving, but nobody expected what came next.

The '69 club was competitive from the onset, but a slump put New York 9½ games behind the Cubs in August. However, Seaver won his last 10 decisions and the Mets finished first at 100-62—then beat the Braves and Orioles to claim their improbable world championship.

There were many heroes on the Miracle Mets, but "Tom Terrific" was the biggest. Seaver won the NL Cy Young Award, leading the league in wins at 25-7 while adding 208 strikeouts, five shutouts, and a 2.21 ERA. No miracles were forthcoming the next three years, but Seaver continued to dominate, going 59-34 and leading the league in ERA and whiffs in 1970 and '71. In 1970, he set a major-league record by striking out 10 straight Padres; he fanned 19 in the game.

Seaver won his second Cy Young (19-10 with a league-best 2.08 ERA and 251 strikeouts) for the '73 pennant-winners, his third two years later (22-9, 243, 2.38), and his last of five strikeout crowns and record ninth consecutive 200-plus strikeout year (235) in '76. Despite a 7-3 Seaver start in '77, Mets ownership did the unthinkable, trading him to the Reds for four youngsters. Tom hated to go but racked up a 14-3 mark the remainder of the year for Cincinnati and went 70-33 (including a league-best 14-2 in strike-shortened '81) over his first four-plus years there.

At age 37, Seaver slumped (5-13 in 1982) and found himself traded back to the Mets for one year, where he was 9-13. From there it was on to the White Sox—where a 16-11 record in '85 included his 300th win—and finally Boston where a sore arm kept him out of a World Series against the Mets in '86. A class act all the way, it was no miracle when he made the Hall of Fame in '92 by the greatest voting percentage in history.

MAJOR LEAGUE TOTALS										
W	L	ERA	G	CG	IP	H	ER	BB	SO
311	205	2.86	656	231	4,782.2	3,971	1,521	1,390	3,640

GEORGE SISLER

GEORGE SISLER WAS A PERFECTIONIST, which made playing on one of the worst teams in the American League tough to handle. The St. Louis Browns were never in much of a hunt for the pennant, so Sisler had to be content with pushing himself while also attempting to outdo the other heavy hitter in town—ornery Rogers Hornsby of the Cardinals. In the end, Sisler settled for statistical success: a .340 lifetime average and two .400 seasons.

Sisler was a star pitcher at the University of Michigan for coach Branch Rickey. Rickey moved on to the American League Browns as scout and then manager in 1913 before bringing George directly to the big leagues following his 1915 commencement. Compiling an ERA of 2.32 while beating the great Walter Johnson twice over his first 11 starts, Sisler showed promise as a left-hander but had such a sweet swing that Rickey decided to put him where he could play every day—first base.

A .305 hitter his first full year (1916) in the field, the 5'11", 170-pound dandy known as "Gorgeous George" was second only to Ty Cobb in batting (.353) and hits (190), then notched 37 steals the following campaign. Sisler possessed little power (21 total homers) his first five seasons, but in 1920 he and cross-town rival Hornsby both exploded to the next level. Hornsby checked in at .370, while Sisler was simply sizzling with a league-leading

.407 year in which he set a major-league record that still stands with 257 hits. He also notched 42 stolen bases, 49 doubles, 18 triples, and 19 homers en route to 137 runs and 122 RBI. Playing every inning of every Browns game, he went hitless in just 23 contests and wielded magic with his exceptional glove.

After hitting "only" .371 with an AL-best 18 triples and 35 steals in 1921, the genteel, cultured man Rickey considered the finest player he ever saw had another season for the ages in '22, batting .420 while also pacing the AL in hits (246), steals (51), triples (18), and runs (134). His 41-game hitting streak was the longest in the 20th century until Joe DiMaggio came along.

It would be his grandest moment. Poisonous sinusitis affecting Sisler's optic nerves resulted in double vision that sidelined him the entire '23 season, and he hit just .305 as player/manager upon his return. Another great year with the Browns (.345 in '25) and two more with the Boston Braves (.340 and .326 in 1928 and '29) remained, but by 1931 the future Hall of Famer was done as a player. Sons Dick and Dave followed him to the majors, and George kept in the thick of things himself as a scout for the Pirates until his death in 1973.

MAJOR LEAGUE TOTALS									
BA	G	AB	R	H	2B	3B	HR	RBI	SB
.340	2,055	8,267	1,284	2,812	425	164	102	1,175	375

OZZIE SMITH

Likely the best everyday player to compile a .231 average through four full major-league seasons, Ozzie Smith has improved mightily at the plate in the years since—and his glove has never needed tinkering. The finest fielding shortstop in history may well be the best pure defensive player the game has seen at *any* position, a diver and leaper whose acrobatic moves on the Astroturf of Busch Stadium and diamonds across the National League earned him the worthy nickname "Wizard of Oz."

Reaching the Padres after just 68 games in the minors, the 23-year-old switch-hitter hit .258 with 40 steals as a rookie in 1978. He dropped to a dismal .211 in '79 but led all NL shortstops in assists with 555. Ozzie's fielding was so amazing in 1980 that his 57 steals and improved .230 average were overshadowed; he won his first Gold Glove with an NL-record 621 assists and also led all NL shortstops with 288 putouts and 113 double plays.

Making his first All-Star appearance in 1981, when he led in assists for a third straight season and won his first fielding title (.976), Ozzie was back down to .222 as a hitter. The Padres then traded Smith to St. Louis for heavy-hitting shortstop Garry Templeton. The trade was one of the all-time blunders; Templeton's bat soured, and on a winning team Smith's skills became more apparent than ever. The Cards won the pennant in his first season with the team, and Ozzie contributed a .303 post-season average en route to the World Series title.

Cardinals manager Whitey Herzog once estimated that Ozzie saved the team 75 runs a year with his glove. Once he began adding increasingly improved offense to the equation, Smith became even more valuable. A .276 hitter by 1985, he helped the Cards to their second pennant that season and hit .435 in the playoffs against the Dodgers, including his first left-handed homer in 3,009 professional at-bats to win Game 5. In 1987, he was even better, as his .303 average, 104 runs, 75 RBI, and NL record-tying .987 fielding percentage earned him second place in MVP balloting and brought St. Louis another NL pennant. After that, a .270 average and 30-plus stolen bases became as routine for Smith as his stellar defense.

Ozzie's run of Gold Gloves ended at 13 straight in 1992, by which time he had led the league in assists eight times, fielding percentage seven times, and double plays on five occasions. His 8,213 assists through 1996 is a major-league record, and with a .277 average the past 12 years, the man who once struggled to stay afloat at the plate had become one of the better hitting shortstops in the league. As for fielding, he's in a league by himself.

MAJOR LEAGUE TOTALS									
BA	G	AB	R	H	2B	3B	HR	RBI	SB
.262	2,573	9,396	1,257	2,460	402	69	28	793	580

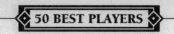

WARREN SPAHN

WARREN SPAHN of the Boston Braves was 25 when he recorded his first big-league victory. But by the time he was through, the lanky left-hander had 363 of them—a top mark for lefties that included *13 seasons* of 20 or more wins.

Spahn's late blooming was understandable; he was sent down by Braves manager Casey Stengel in 1942 for allegedly refusing to throw at Pee Wee Reese, then served three years in the Army where he was awarded the Purple Heart. Back with the Braves in '46, he went 8-5, then jumped to 21-10 his second full year while leading the NL in ERA (2.33) and shutouts (seven). Spahn developed an excellent screwball and slider to complement (and later compensate for) his fastball and curve, and his trademark high kick kept batters out of sync and baserunners guessing at when he'd spin around and attempt one of his frequent pickoffs.

In '48, Spahn (15-12, 3.71) and then-ace righty Johnny Sain (24-15) helped the Braves to their first pennant since 1914, and during one September stretch the duo started 11 of 16 games (going 9-2). "Spahn and Sain and pray for rain" was the rallying cry. Selfless Spahnie actually claimed 1948 was one of his *worst* seasons, and in '49 he bounced back to go 21-14 with a 3.07 ERA, leading the league in victories, innings (302), complete games (25), and strikeouts (151). It was the first of four straight years he would pace the National League in whiffs.

During the 1950s, Spahn was both consistent and commanding. He went 202-131 for the decade, leading the league in wins five times, strikeouts four times, shutouts twice, and ERA once. His ERA was never above 3.26, he won at least 20 games eight times, and he helped his own cause with 20 of his 35 lifetime homers. The Braves won pennants in 1957 and '58, took the World Series in '57, and finished second four other times.

One thing that eluded Spahn during the '50s was a no-hitter, so he threw two to start the new decade—one in September 1960 and another the following April, five days after his 40th birthday. He led the NL in wins and complete games both years (making it five consecutive times atop each category), and after dropping to 18-14 went 23-7 in 1963 at age 42—his final 20-win campaign. He wound up as he started, with Casey Stengel as his manager—this time with the hapless Mets—and only after a 7-16 season and a couple short stints in the minors would Spahn give up pitching. To nobody's surprise, the first-ballot Hall of Famer was one of the first to sign up for old-timer's games, where he was still high-kicking it into his 70s.

MAJOR LEAGUE TOTALS

W	L	ERA	G	CG	IP	H	ER	BB	SO
363	245	3.09	750	382	5,243.2	4,830	1,798	1,434	2,583

TRIS SPEAKER

HIS NAME HAS NOT MAINTAINED quite the luster of Babe Ruth and Ty Cobb, but for many years Tris Speaker was usually the third man mentioned in discussions surrounding the greatest outfielders of all time. One sentiment was undisputed: Nobody outshone Speaker in the field.

Learning to throw lefty as a teenager after breaking his right arm bronco-busting, the man whose prematurely graying hair would earn him the nickname "The Gray Eagle" hit .314 at minor-league Houston in 1907 before being bought by the Red Sox for around $800. It proved a wise investment, for after faltering in two brief Boston trials, the 21-year-old hit .309 with 35 steals as the club's starting center fielder in 1909. Working out with teammate Cy Young—who would hit the youngster flies with his fungo bat—speedy Speaker became adept at playing extremely shallow and registered an incredible 35 assists and 12 double plays during his first full season.

Joined by Harry Hooper and Duffy Lewis in 1910, Tris anchored baseball's greatest outfield for the next six years. He hit .340 with 20 assists (fewer runners were testing his arm) and 35 steals in 1910, and .334 with 26 more assists in 1911. The following year, the Red Sox claimed the world championship and Tris batted .383 with 222 hits, 12 triples, 90 RBI, 52 steals, and AL highs in doubles (53), homers (10), and assists (35) to claim the Chalmers Award and automobile the league's most valuable player.

The leader on an extremely close team, Speaker hit .363 and .338 the next two years. Dipping to .322 for the world champs of 1915, he was infuriated when owner Joe Lannin wanted to cut his salary to under $10,000 the next spring. Refusing to agree to the deal, he was traded to Cleveland in a move met with much displeasure throughout New England—especially after Tris led the AL in batting (.386), hits (211), doubles (41), and slugging (.502) his first year with the Indians.

A .354 hitter for Cleveland from 1916-26, Tris reached a height of .389 in '25. Named player/manager of the team in 1919, he took the club to a world championship the following year and averaged 52 doubles while leading the American League each season from 1920-23. Implicated along with Ty Cobb in a gambling scandal in 1926, Speaker was asked to "resign" his post as manager. This never-proved incident did little to tarnish his fine reputation. His .345 lifetime average, 3,514 hits, 792 doubles (the most ever), 1,882 runs, and 434 steals validate the Gray Eagle's spot in Cooperstown, and his 448 assists place him among the best defensive performers of all time.

MAJOR LEAGUE TOTALS

BA	G	AB	R	H	2B	3B	HR	RBI	SB
.345	2,789	10,195	1,882	3,514	792	222	117	1,529	434

HONUS WAGNER

MOST FAMOUS THESE DAYS as the guy whose 1910 baseball card could pay for a new house, John Peter Wagner also happened to be a .327 lifetime hitter with a National League-record eight batting titles and 722 stolen bases—as well as the greatest fielding shortstop this side of Ozzie Smith.

Supposedly discovered by Ed Barrow tossing coal chunks at a boxcar near his tiny Pennsylvania hometown, Honus demolished minor-league hurling for parts of three years before joining Louisville of the NL as an outfielder in 1897. Squat (5'11", 200 pounds) and bowlegged with a long, beaked nose, Wagner didn't look like a ballplayer—until he got on a field. Once there, the right-handed, barrel-chested slugger with deceptive speed hit .299 and .336 his first two full seasons, with over 100 RBI per year.

The Louisville franchise shifted to his hometown of Pittsburgh in 1900, and Wagner celebrated by collecting his first National League batting title with a career-high .381 mark while leading the NL in doubles (44), triples (22), and slugging (.573) despite just four homers. League leader in RBI (126 and 91) and stolen bases (49 and 42) each of the next two seasons, he hit .353 and .330 as the Pirates won back-to-back NL flags.

After playing as many as five positions in a season, Wagner thrived after being made Pittsburgh's starting shortstop in 1903. Becoming the game's best fielder at the spot, he developed a rifle arm and used his huge hands to scoop up everything hit near him. He also hit .350 with seven batting titles over the next nine seasons, earning the first in '03 when he hit .355 with 101 RBI, 46 steals, and a league-high 19 triples to power the Pirates to their third straight league championship.

Repeating as batting champ in 1904 at .349, Wagner was second at .363 the next year before winning four more crowns in a row. Never hitting more than 10 home runs, he paced the league in slugging six times as the classic dead-ball power hitter—leading the NL seven times in doubles, collecting 10 or more triples 13 times (with a high of 20 in 1912), and notching 100 or more RBI on nine occasions (five as league leader). Stolen-base king five times, he swiped 40 or more eight straight years and 20-plus for 18 consecutive seasons.

Retiring at age 43 in 1917 as NL leader in hits (3,415), runs (1,736), doubles (640), and triples (252); the charter Hall of Famer still ranks high on each list. He came back at age 59 from a disappointing post-baseball career to coach for the Pirates and stayed on 18 years, spinning many a yarn about the good ol' days.

MAJOR LEAGUE TOTALS									
BA	G	AB	R	H	2B	3B	HR	RBI	SB
.327	2,792	10,430	1,736	3,415	640	252	101	1,732	722

TED WILLIAMS

HE STRUCK OUT IN HIS FIRST major-league at-bat, homered in his last, and during the 21 years between made the art of hitting his personal quest. Ted Williams looked at the goal of wood meeting ball in a scientific way, and if grades were awarded instead of statistics, his achievements—a .344 lifetime average, 521 homers, and a slugging average (.634) second only to Babe Ruth—would rank him at the head of his class.

The lessons started early: swings taken before, after, and sometimes during school as a pencil-thin teen in San Diego. He and Pacific Coast League teammate Bobby Doerr both signed on with the Red Sox in the summer of 1937, and although Williams didn't make the big club the following spring, his parting shot to Boston's starting outfielders who had ridiculed him—"I'll be back and make more money than the three of you combined"—would prove dead on. A year later, he returned for good.

The rookie distinguished himself in 1939 with a .327 average, 31 homers, and a rookie-record 145 RBI. In '41, Joe DiMaggio captured the attention of the nation with a 56-game hitting streak, but Ted out-hit him .412 to .408 over the course of the streak and finished the season with 37 homers, 120 RBI, and a .406 batting mark. Sports writers awarded the MVP Award to DiMaggio in what turned out to be the first of many times the outspoken Williams (a two-time MVP winner) would be snubbed due to friction with the press.

Williams was a decent left fielder, but when he said he lived for his next at-bat it was no exaggeration. His goal was perfection at the plate; he sought the same from pitchers, and his careful eye enabled him to lead the American League in walks seven times in his first nine full seasons (each time with over 125). He was criticized for not swinging enough and not hitting in the clutch—this despite a .483 on-base percentage (the best in history) and a .359 lifetime average in September.

Winner of Triple Crowns in 1942 and '47 (he missed a third in 1949 by .0002 on his batting average), Ted led the American League nine times in slugging, seven times in batting, six times in runs scored, and four times in homers and RBI. The Player of the Decade for the 1950s hit .388 with 38 homers at age 39 in 1958, won his final batting title (.328) a year later, and slugged 29 long ones in just 310 at-bats in his swan-song season of '60. Despite missing nearly five full seasons as a Navy and Marine flyer and parts of two more to injury, he retired as third on the all-time homer list—and first in debates over the greatest hitter of all time

MAJOR LEAGUE TOTALS									
BA	G	AB	R	H	2B	3B	HR	RBI	SB
.344	2,292	7,706	1,798	2,654	525	71	521	1,839	24

CY YOUNG

A T ONE POINT, Lou Gehrig's 2,130 consecutive games were the career baseball record most predicted would never be broken. Now that Cal Ripken has put that thought to rest, the question arises anew: Five hundred and eleven wins? Twenty-five a year for over 20 years? Don't worry, Mr. Young, your mark appears safe.

Walter Johnson, Lefty Grove, and others have been lauded as the greatest pitcher of all time, but Denton True Young's 511 victories remain the benchmark for all hurlers—and far ahead of runnerup Johnson's 417. Pitching in an era when arms often burned out after a handful of 350-inning seasons, Young exceeded that total 11 times over a 14-year span and was a 20-game winner on a record 15 occasions. His 7,354 innings are more than 1,400 ahead of runnerup Pud Galvin.

Growing up just after the Civil War in Gilmore, Ohio, Young picked up his nickname (shortened from "Cyclone") from a catcher impressed by his speed. The hardy, 6′2″ farm boy reached the majors with the Cleveland Spiders in 1890, and after a 9-7 debut won 20 or more games each of the next nine seasons. Those early years were spent hurling from a pitcher's "box" some 50 feet from home plate, and when the distance was increased to 60′6″ with a mound added in 1893, the right-hander didn't seem to miss a beat.

The hard-throwing Young led the NL only once in wins, and he routinely gave up more hits than innings pitched (although that was the norm in the 1890s). Far from dominating in many of his first 11 seasons, his records grew instead through consistency and durability. His best NL years came in 1892 (36-12 with a league-leading nine shutouts and 1.93 ERA) and '95 (35-10), but it was after joining the Boston Pilgrims of the new American League in 1901 that Young had his most dominating campaigns. Leading the AL in victories his first three years with Boston (going 33-10, 32-11, and 28-9), he had a 1.95 ERA and walked just 127 in 1,098 innings over the span—topping it off in 1903 with two wins as Boston beat Pittsburgh in the first modern World Series.

Author of three no-hitters (including a 1904 perfect game), Young went 21-11 with a 1.26 ERA at age 41, and after his career ended in 1911 he lived well over 40 more years, attending old-timer's functions and tossing out the first ball at the 1953 World Series. Others may have been flashier, but when the two major leagues honor their best pitchers each season, they do so with a plaque named for the game's winningest hurler—Cy Young.

MAJOR LEAGUE TOTALS

W	L	ERA	G	CG	IP	H	ER	BB	SO
511	316	2.63	906	749	7,354.2	7,092	2,149	1,219	2,800

CHAPTER 2

10 BEST MANAGERS

THEY WERE SKILLED and respected leaders who led their teams to multiple flags. Yet their personalities ran the gamut, from quiet and dignified (Walter Alston) to raucous and surly (John McGraw). This assorted mix of characters comprises the 10 best managers of all time.

John McGraw

WALTER ALSTON

NO NICKNAME. No colorful habits. No temper tantrums or umpire baiting. Walter Alston, at first glance, seems to lack everything the other great managers of baseball had. But only one manager in the last half of the 20th century led his team to more victories than Walter Alston. In his 23 years as Dodger pilot, Alston's team finished in the second division just five times. His charges won seven league titles and four World Series.

Minor-league slugger Alston was hired by Branch Rickey to manage in the Dodgers' minor-league system, to immediate success. He won pennants and the Junior World Series for both St. Paul and Montreal, Brooklyn's top farm club.

The Alston era began in 1954, when Dodger skipper Charlie Dressen—feeling that his record of one second-place finish and two pennants in three years in Brooklyn merited a long-term contract—was rebuffed by penny-pinching Walter O'Malley. Alston accepted the one-year contract Dressen couldn't abide by, and he signed single-year deals for 22 more years.

Alston's career had its share of surprising bounces. After finishing second, first, first, and third his first four seasons, Alston's Dodgers plummeted to seventh in 1958, their first year in Los Angeles. But in '59, they rebounded behind the talented arms of young hurlers Sandy Koufax, Don

Drysdale, Johnny Podres, and Larry Sherry to win the National League flag in a playoff with Milwaukee and then dump the White Sox in the World Series.

After winning the 1963 pennant and sweeping the Yanks in that year's World Series, Alston's team tumbled to sixth place. So what happened the next year? The Dodgers won it all again. Then they took the pennant in 1966. In '67 and '68, they finished eighth and seventh in a 10-team league.

The Alston art of the comeback still had legs, however. With a new set of Dodger youngsters coming on board, they returned to the first division in 1970 and never left again as long as Alston was on the bench. Included was another World Series appearance in 1974.

Alston's even keel was the secret to his success. "Look at misfortune the same way you look at success: don't panic," he said. He never forced himself or his style on his players. Instead, he adapted to his team's strengths—the sluggers of Brooklyn, the young pitching aces of the '60s. When Mike Marshall proved in 1974 that he could perform the absolutely unique feat of pitching in nearly every game effectively, Alston let him do it—all the way to the World Series.

MAJOR LEAGUE RECORD				
W	**L**	**PCT**	**PEN**	**WC**
2,040	1,613	.558	7	4

LEO DUROCHER

L EO DUROCHER was a gambler—at the race track, at the poker table, and on the field. "Give me some scratching, diving, hungry ballplayers who want to kill you," was his managerial philosophy. In 24 years, Durocher sported a 2,008-1,709 record. Only six managers have ever won more games.

Durocher's first managerial job was with Brooklyn in 1939, where he also played shortstop. The Dodgers responded to his scrappy style and ended the season in third. Durocher, never much of a player but always a student of the game, let himself be replaced by Pee Wee Reese at short. By squeezing the maximum out of an aging pitching staff, Durocher and his 1940 Dodgers finished second.

The next year, everything worked. He explained, "They [the Dodgers] knew I had hunches all the time, that I did things that went against the book. Enough of them worked out so that over the last two months of the season, the kind of situation had developed that a manager dreams of and almost never gets—25 men who had absolute belief that any decision I made was the right one." Brooklyn took its first pennant in 21 years.

With the exception of war-decimated 1944, Durocher's Dodgers finished second or third every year for the next five. In 1942, they won 104 games but finished two behind the Cards. In 1946, a dead heat for first was broken when St. Louis swept two playoff games. Durocher's tongue-lashing of the Dodgers who tried to rebel against Branch Rickey's promotion of Jackie Robinson has gone down in baseball legend. But Leo, suspended by Happy Chandler for associating with gamblers, had to sit out Jackie's first season in 1947.

Fired in mid-1948, Durocher startled the borough of Brooklyn by joining the hated Giants. Featuring young Willie Mays, his 1951 team moved from 13½ games out of first to a first-place tie by the end of the season. Two Durocher moves were key: making outfielder Bobby Thomson a third baseman and moving Whitey Lockman to first base. And Thomson's stunning playoff homer capped it off.

In 1954, Durocher's Giants again took the pennant, then swept the Series from the powerful Indians. Dumped after finishing third in 1955, Durocher didn't manage until 1966, when he took over the woeful Cubs and finished 10th. But then he whipped them to five consecutive finishes in second or third.

Leo, though, didn't take to the new breed of cocky young players. The last chapter of his book *Nice Guys Finish Last* is called, "Whatever Happened to Sit Down, Shut Up, and Listen?"

MAJOR LEAGUE RECORD				
W	L	PCT	PEN	WC
2,008	1,709	.540	3	1

NED HANLON

NO MAN was more responsible for the way baseball was played in the 1890s than Ned Hanlon. As manager of the Baltimore Orioles, he led the roughest bunch of players ever to three league championships. In doing so, he created a style of baseball that people still referred to 60 years later: When a player got hurt on the field, someone was sure to say, "Rub dirt on it; take it like an Oriole."

Hanlon certainly didn't look the part of a back-street bully. He more resembled a high school English teacher. But his quick mind was always looking for the edge in everything he did. As a player, one of his favorite tricks was to fall to the ground, roll in apparent pain, and shout that the pitch had hit him. When the umpire would disagree, Hanlon would point to the red mark on his arm where he had been "hit" by the pitch. Of course, Hanlon had self-inflicted the mark by pinching himself.

The stories of Hanlon's Orioles using deceit and out-and-out cheating to win are many: Their third baseman would grab the belt of an opposing runner as he tried to tag from third on a fly; an Oriole runner would bypass third and run directly from second to home if the umpire wasn't looking; and Oriole bench men would use mirrors to reflect light into opposing batters' eyes.

But Hanlon's style wasn't just cheating. He helped create what became called "inside baseball," developing the hit-and-run to a fine art and training his fielders to back each other up. He was the first manager to hire a full-time groundskeeper and tailor his field to his team: The third base line slanted fair to help bunts; first was slightly downhill; the outfield grass was high to slow balls hit in the gaps; and the infield was rock-hard so his batters could hit down on the ball and beat out an infield hit—still known as the "Baltimore chop."

With Hanlon's astute eye for talent, he built his team through smart trades. Joe Kelley, Hugh Jennings, Willie Keeler, and Dan Brouthers were acquired in Hanlon deals. Well into the 20th century, until Babe Ruth changed things, the Hanlon/Oriole style was the dominant approach to the game. But perhaps the most significant Hanlon legacy is the number of highly successful managers who played (and learned) under him: John McGraw, Wilbert Robinson, Hugh Jennings, Kid Gleason, and Miller Huggins.

After Baltimore finished second in 1897 and '98, team ownership (which also held stock in Brooklyn) moved Hanlon and several of his players to the New York borough, where—while winning consecutive pennants in 1899 and 1900—they became known as "Hanlon's Superbas."

MAJOR LEAGUE RECORD				
W	L	PCT	PEN	WC
1,313	1,164	.530	5	0

TONY LaRUSSA

AFTER 18 YEARS of managing in the majors, Tony LaRussa's managerial record is among the top 20 of all time. His teams have reached league championship play six times; three times they have played in the World Series.

What sets LaRussa apart and earns him a place in the top 10 of all time is that he has created a new style of managing, one especially suited to baseball's latest era of sensitive, self-impressed, union-backed multimillionaire players. LaRussa is tough, but unlike McGraw, Weaver, and Durocher, he is no demon-possessed dictator. He is serious, but unlike Alston and McCarthy, he is no Corporate Citizen. He is intelligent, but unlike Stengel, he is no genius wearing clowns' clothes.

The LaRussa style, as detailed in George Will's book *Men At Work*, is "to find a way to find an edge in every situation." It involves much closer analysis of players and their skills—day-by-day, moment-by-moment—than managers did in the past. You can see it in LaRussa's eyes. He watches everything on the field with the same thin-lipped, intensely staring visage. Trained as a lawyer, LaRussa said, "I'd rather be riding busses managing in the minors than be practicing law."

A critical aspect of the LaRussa style is the coaches he hires. For many years, managers hired coaches as rewards for past lives together as teammates, often in the minors. As a result, the coaching-staff cronies seldom did much to help the manager win games. But LaRussa hired Jim Leyland as his third base coach, and Leyland went on to manage the Pirates to three consecutive National League East titles. Leyland hired Gene Lamont, who would manage the White Sox to two divisional titles, and Terry Collins, who became Houston's skipper.

LaRussa was just 34 years old when the White Sox hired him as their manager in 1979. He quickly became known as a hothead. The Sox steadily improved under his leadership, and in 1983 he took them to their first title (AL West) in 24 years. When he was fired by the Sox after a 26-38 start in 1986, his pride took a beating and his temper cooled.

Three weeks later, he took charge of an Oakland bunch in total disarray and turned a .373 team into a .570 team. Two years later, the A's were in the World Series. LaRussa's A's repeated as American League champions in 1989 and 1990 and won the 1989 "Earthquake" World Series over the cross-bay Giants. In 1996, he piloted St. Louis to a division title.

MAJOR LEAGUE RECORD				
W	L	PCT	PEN	WC
1,408	1,257	.528	3	1

JOE MCCARTHY

PERHAPS THE TERM "push-button manager" was invented to describe Joe McCarthy, but nothing could have been further from the truth. Completely dedicated to the game, with a voluminous memory and keen intelligence, McCarthy holds the highest winning percentage of any manager, .615. McCarthy and Casey Stengel share the record for most World Series titles (seven).

McCarthy summed up his attitude toward baseball: "So I eat, drink, and sleep baseball 24 hours a day. What's wrong with that? The idea of this game is to win and keep winning."

McCarthy began his managerial career in the minors at the age of 26. The Cubs hired him in 1926, and he gradually built a champion by adding sluggers Hack Wilson and Kiki Cuyler and maximizing a nondescript pitching staff. They won the 1929 National League pennant by 10½ games. But when the Cubs failed to repeat in 1930, McCarthy was ousted. It was the break of his life.

The New York Yankees—that battering, brawling collection of egos (led by Babe Ruth)—had finished third under friendly Bob Shawkey in 1930. Yankees ownership knew it was time for a change, and they hired McCarthy for the 1931 season. The Yanks didn't win in '31 but they did in '32, which made McCarthy the first manager to win pennants in both leagues. Their four-game drubbing of the

Cubs in that year's World Series was especially sweet revenge for McCarthy.

After his three consecutive second-place finishes, the New York press was calling McCarthy "Second-Place Joe." But then the Yank juggernaut caught fire. New York won four consecutive flags and took the World Series each of those years. After a third-place finish in 1940, the Yanks won three more consecutive league titles and two more Series. McCarthy made the Yankees *his* Yankees. Their style changed from Ruth's to Lou Gehrig's: quiet, powerful, proficient.

Wartime player losses caused McCarthy's minions to slip to third in 1944, fourth in 1945. GM Larry MacPhail forced McCarthy to resign 35 games into the 1946 season. The Red Sox brought McCarthy aboard for the 1948 campaign. That year and the next, McCarthy drove the Red Sox into fierce pennant chases only to lose on the last day of each season.

Two views of McCarthy's managerial style came from Joe Page and Joe DiMaggio. The former said in McCarthy's obituary, "I hate his guts, but there never was a better manager." Joe D. stated, "Never a day went by when you didn't learn something from McCarthy."

MAJOR LEAGUE RECORD				
W	L	PCT	PEN	WC
2,125	1,333	.615	9	7

John McGraw

JOHN MCGRAW was combative. Short and scrappy, he made his name as the toughest of Ned Hanlon's thugs, the old Orioles. Most experts agree he is probably the best player ever to become a great manager. And McGraw didn't just do battle with the players (his own and others) and umpires. He took on league presidents and team owners in wild verbal sparring matches, and he even punched out actor Bill Boyd (Hopalong Cassidy!) in a New York club. And as a manager, he won more games than anyone except Connie Mack.

"Sportsmanship and easygoing methods are all right, but it is the prospect of a hot fight that brings out the crowds," he once said. McGraw knew what it took to win and he made his prayers obey—or else. "With my team, I am an absolute czar. My men know it. I order plays and they obey." As a result, he was feared and he was hated, but he was never ignored.

After managing Baltimore in the last year of the National League club's existence in 1899, McGraw joined Ban Johnson's new American League in 1901 to manage the AL Baltimore club. But no league was large enough for two egos as outsized as his and Johnson's. McGraw jumped to the National League Giants in mid-1902. He was then 29 years old. For the next 30 years, his abrasive imperiousness dominated the news in the National League.

An offshoot of the 1903 peace agreement between the National League and American League was the Pirates/ Pilgrims best-of-nine World Series. But when McGraw's Giants took the NL flag the next year, he refused to acknowledge the validity of Johnson's league and wouldn't play the AL winners. Things changed for 1905, and when his Giants won again, they toppled Connie Mack's A's in just five quick games.

Three straight pennants from 1911-13 and another in 1917 were met by World Series defeats for McGraw and his men. But when his team took on the 1921 Yankees, newly bolstered by the arrival of Babe Ruth, McGraw took charge. He ordered his pitchers to throw the Babe nothing but "curveballs in the dirt." Ruth fanned eight times, hit only one homer, and the Giants prevailed, five games to three.

In the 1922 Series, with McGraw calling the pitches to Ruth, the Bambino batted just .118 and the Giants swept the Series in four games (excluding a tie). However, McGraw's Giants lost the World Series to the Yankees in 1923 and to the Senators in 1924 (in the last of the 12th of the seventh game on a bizarre bad hop over Fred Lindstrom). McGraw retired in 1932.

MAJOR LEAGUE RECORD				
W	L	PCT	PEN	WC
2,784	1,959	.587	10	3

FRANK SELEE

FRANK SELEE'S LEGACY as a great manager is assured with his lifetime winning percentage of .598, fourth best ever, and 1,284 wins. He managed in the majors for 16 years, five times capturing the National League title (with Boston), finishing second twice and third twice. In fact, no Selee-managed team ever finished lower than fifth place. A dozen men who played for him are in the Hall of Fame. But if Frank Selee hadn't come down with fatal tuberculosis at the age of 45, he certainly would be in the Hall of Fame himself, and many experts would be calling him the greatest manager of all time.

After 12 seasons with Boston, Selee moved to manage the Cubs, where he built one of the truly great dynasties of this century. Under Selee, the Chicagoans moved from fifth place to third, then to second in 1904. But Frank's health forced him to retire during the 1905 season. Under the leadership of his protégé, Frank Chance, the Cubs won pennants in 1906, '07, '08, and 1910—by a total of 51 games. Nearly all of the regulars on those teams were acquired by Selee.

Selee's team-building skills were apparent earlier in his career. He had won pennants as a minor-league skipper in Oshkosh in 1887 and Omaha in 1889. After the Players' League and American Association folded, Selee's reputation as a manager who treated his men like men, not children, attracted a load of adult-style talent. Boston took the league flag in 1891, '92, and '93. Their 1892 victory came in unique fashion. The 12-team league, in an attempt to boost lagging fan interest, played a split season. Selee's Beaneaters easily took the first half of the season and then rested during the second before whomping Cleveland in the championship playoff. Though the team stumbled the next three years, Selee resuscitated them, winning again in 1897 and 1898 and finishing second in 1899.

One of Selee's savviest skills was knowing what position best suited a player. Among his more famous (and successful) switches were: moving Frank Chance from the catcher's box to first base (a move Chance rebelled against initially, even threatening to quit the game), moving shortstop Johnny Evers to second, and shifting third sacker Joe Tinker to short, thereby creating the storied double-play combination Tinker to Evers to Chance.

Selee was a master of defensive strategy. He taught Chance the art of the 3-6-3 double play, developed a variety of positioning strategies, and devised complicated defensive signals to call plays and align his fielders.

MAJOR LEAGUE RECORD				
W	L	PCT	PEN	WC
1,284	862	.598	5	0

CASEY STENGEL

ALTHOUGH HIS NICKNAME came from his home town of Kansas City, Casey Stengel was meant for New York. "The Old Perfesser" hid his deep intelligence for the game behind a fanciful persona and a unique form of double-talk that came to be christened "Stengelese."

Stengel really had three managerial careers in the majors. From 1934 through 1943, he managed to finish higher than sixth only twice while skippering the Dodgers and Boston Bees and Braves. The last 3½ years, he headed up the legendarily awful Mets and never got out of 10th place.

But from 1949 through 1960, Casey did a superb job of managing a team whose performance has never been matched for such a long period of time. In those 12 years, he set more records than any other manager, winning 10 pennants, five in a row. He finished second and third once each. Seven times his Yankees won the world championship. He managed more World Series games than any other manager (63) and won more (37).

Despite Stengel's success as a minor-league manager in the late 1940s, most people thought the Yanks had hired the buffoon player who had once doffed his cap and let a bird fly out. But with his understanding of the game and his players, Stengel moved, manipulated, poked, and prodded his Yanks to victory after victory.

Having learned well the art of platooning from his former manager, John McGraw, Casey revivified the strategy and refined it to high art. His champions were built around three superstars—Mickey Mantle, Yogi Berra, and Whitey Ford. Everyone else was a role-player, to be used when and where the savvy Stengel decided. His pitchers seldom pitched in regular rotation; they were all "spot" starters. Even Ford was used selectively, where he was most likely to succeed. Casey knew something most managers didn't: "Most ballgames are lost, not won."

But when the Yankees were stunned by a terrifically lucky Pirate team in the 1960 World Series, Stengel was canned. The reason given? He was too old. Said Casey: "I'll never make the mistake of being 70 again."

Stengel ended his managerial career with a truly rotten team, the expansion Mets, and only his deft way with words kept the team interesting. Casey Stengel came to the majors with a puckish sense of humor, and he left the same way. But in between, he wheeled the greatest dynasty in baseball history. His grave marker quotes a perfect Stengelism: "There comes a time in every man's life and I've had plenty of them."

MAJOR LEAGUE RECORD				
W	L	PCT	PEN	WC
1,905	1,842	.508	10	7

EARL WEAVER

THE SIGHT of Earl Weaver embroiled in a loud, ugly argument with an umpire, kicking dirt and shoving his finger in the ump's face, made unappealing highlight films for years. Weaver was as feisty an umpire-baiter as any. He was tossed from nearly 100 games in his career (once while handing the lineup card to the umps before the game). His spats with buffoonish umpire Ron Luciano were especially unpleasant. But behind that cocky, noisy "kicker" was one of baseball's keenest minds.

Weaver ranks 10th all-time in winning percentage for managers. He made the Baltimore Orioles one of baseball's strongest teams during one of its strongest decades, the 1970s. And no manager ever had such an impressive debut. In his first three full years of managing (1969-71), the O's won 108, 101, and 109 games. In his first 10 years as Baltimore's skipper, Weaver's Orioles finished third once. Every other year they were first or second.

Weaver said his managerial philosophy was based on "pitching, defense, and the three-run homer." While some commentators have poked fun at that statement, it is actually brilliant. Baseball has been a game of big innings since Babe Ruth, and no one understood how to make it happen better than Weaver. The power of his lineups—at first anchored by Boog Powell and Frank Robinson, later by Lee May, Ken Singleton, and Eddie Murray—blasted those three-run clouts.

Weaver built a sensational pitching staff. Four of his starters won 20 games or more in 1971 (setting a record for a pennant-winner). Five other hurlers would reach 20 wins under Weaver. Seven times his staff had the league's lowest ERA. His defensive units were outstanding; his players won 35 Gold Gloves while he was managing them.

Even more important was the consistency in teaching the style that Weaver helped establish throughout the Oriole organization. Everyone trained as an Oriole was absolutely clear on the right way to execute fundamentals. Weaver and his minor-league managers made sure of it.

Weaver's 1982 Orioles finished second, one game back of the Brewers, and Earl decided to call it quits. Joe Altobelli replaced him and won the 1983 World Series with Earl's team. Weaver returned to manage the mediocre O's for the last 105 games of 1985, finishing fourth. But in 1986, his team stumbled to a dismal 73-89, last-place finish and Weaver hung it up for good. Never before had a Weaver-led team finished lower than fourth. His book, *Weaver on Strategy*, is a classic of the genre.

MAJOR LEAGUE RECORD				
W	L	PCT	PEN	WC
1,480	1,060	.583	4	1

HARRY WRIGHT

UPON HARRY WRIGHT'S DEATH in 1895, no less a legend than Henry Chadwick said, "There is no doubt that Harry Wright was the father of professional base ball playing."

When Harry Wright was a manager, the game was much different. Baseball was still growing noisily, still learning about itself. Wright's 1869 Cincinnati Red Stockings were the first openly all-professional team. Managers had more to worry about than when to change pitchers; baseball was rowdy, gamblers were everywhere. Managers had to schedule the games and serve as traveling secretaries and bookkeepers. Wright's total honesty in the face of such a difficult situation became the paradigm for the game's moral stance.

Harry and his brother George (the better player of the two) accompanied their cricket-playing father when he immigrated from England, but Harry fell in love with the American game and created the Red Stockings in 1866. The 1869-70 Reds were a juggernaut, winning 130 games in a row.

When the National Association was formed in 1871, Harry took many of his stars to Boston and won pennants in four of the five years of the NA. During that time, his teams won an astonishing 77 percent of their games; included was a remarkable 71-8 record in 1875. Wright's Bostons won two of the first three National League pennants. Although he managed for 15 more seasons, he never finished first again.

Wright's pioneering innovations were numerous; many have become baseball tradition. He introduced the idea of fielders backing up each other, and pitchers backing up bases. He instituted pregame batting practice and fungoes to outfielders. He invented hand signals, and he was the first manager to alter his defensive alignment to the styles of opposing hitters. The hidden-ball trick and double-steal were also Wright ideas. When he pitched, he changed speeds; no one had done that before. His catcher in 1870 was the first player to wear a glove.

Long before Bill James, Wright understood the vital importance of statistics to baseball. He devised his own special box scores and studied them late into the night, looking for angles to help his team win. His midnight-oil efforts even cost him his eyesight for a year. The *Cincinnati Enquirer* called him "a base ball Edison. He eats base ball, thinks base ball, and incorporates base ball in his players."

Because of his steadfast devotion to fair play (as outlined in cricket's tradition), his last job in baseball was as supervisor of league umpires.

MAJOR LEAGUE RECORD				
W	**L**	**PCT**	**PEN**	**WC**
1,225	885	.581	6	0

CHAPTER 3

10 BEST TEAMS

SOME PROVED THEIR DOMINANCE over several seasons (1949-53 Yankees); others came together for one glorious campaign (1954 Indians). Whatever the case, these teams were so utterly dominant that the races were often over by July. These 10 juggernauts are the greatest teams in baseball history.

Lou Gehrig (left) and Babe Ruth, New York Yankees

1885-88 ST. LOUIS BROWNS

WITH A HAUGHTY owner flamboyant enough to make George Steinbrenner look like a wallflower, and a sometimes ragtag collection of players, the 1885 St. Louis Browns seemed an unlikely club to win four straight pennants. But they had a nucleus of superstars—plus a drive to win inspired by a no-nonsense manager—that helped them establish the viability of the American Association (at least for a while) and earn a spot among the top teams of all time.

Their owner was Chris Von der Ahe, who spoke fractured English and handed out fines like Christmas cookies. Easy to ridicule, easy to hate, he still had an intuitive genius for entrepreneurship that boosted the Browns to success. First baseman and manager Charlie Comiskey believed in aggressive baseball and in total support from his players. He stressed "deft baserunning and heady play." (Years later, his dictatorial style spurred his 1919 White Sox to throw the World Series.)

In 1885, the Browns performed what might seem impossible. They won their league by 16 games without one batter in the top 10 in batting average, on-base percentage, slugging average, total bases, home runs, or hits. Their secret was a remarkable pitching pair that included Bob Caruthers and Dave Foutz. Between them, they hurled 890 innings with a 2.33 ERA and a 73-27 record. Caruthers had a deceptive delivery and a strong sense of a batter's weakness; Foutz was known for his calm demeanor.

That fall, they took on the NL's Chicago White Stockings, led by Cap Anson, in the second-ever World Series. Most folks saw it as just another post-season exhibition series, not the major event it has since become. After a Game 1 tie and a Game 2 forfeit to Chicago, the teams split the next four games and agreed that Game 7 would be a "winner-take-all" match. The Browns prevailed 13-4.

The next year, the Browns won the American Association by a dozen games. Their two best hitters were Caruthers the pitcher, who batted .334, and notoriously bad baserunner and fielder Tip O'Neill. The enterprising Von der Ahe had an idea: Let's promote this "World's Championship Series" into a major spectacle. His ploy worked, people took note, and the fans were treated to the first great World Series finish.

That '86 Series was won by the Browns in six games. They had to score three times in the last of the eighth to tie the final game. In the bottom of the 10th, St. Louis outfielder Curt Welch stormed across the plate with the winning run on a wild pitch, an event that went down in history as "the $15,000 slide," even though some accounts indicate he didn't slide, and the dollar amount was overstated too. (Von der Ahe took half of the series receipts; the players each received about $600.) But most historians agree that dramatic play was the high point of the AA's existence.

The Browns copped the 1887 pennant in easy fashion, winning by 14 games. It was O'Neill's year. Because of a rules change that counted walks as hits, he batted .492 (.435 if you exclude the walks). He also led the league in hits, runs, doubles, triples, homers, total bases, and slugging average—the only player ever to dominate a major league so completely. New pitcher Silver King was the top hurler, winning 32 games.

For some reason, the success of the 1886 World Series format was lost on the moguls of baseball, and they experimented with a new way to determine the champion: a 15-game, 10-city, 17-day tour. It was a mess. The Browns lost eight of their first 11 games, ending their Series chances. Von der Ahe, though, made them play the last four games anyway, then threatened not to pay them at all because they hadn't played "hard enough."

After three straight pennants and two World Series titles, the Browns looked solid for 1888, but strong-willed Comiskey felt he was losing control of his star players. So Von der Ahe put them up for sale. Before long, he had peddled or sold Caruthers, Foutz, Welch, star catcher Doc Bushong, and infielder Bill Gleason.

All the decimated Browns did was win again in '88. Even though their shortstop batted .175 and their center fielder .194, King was equal to the task.

He pitched in nearly half of his team's 137 games, totalling 585 innings with 45 wins and an ERA of 1.64—about half the league figure. O'Neill supplied the offense, once again winning the batting title and finishing second in on-base percentage and third in slugging. St. Louis, though, fell to the New York Giants in the World Series, six games to four.

1887 BROWNS
95 Wins 40 Losses

Pos	Player	AB	BA	HR
1B	C. Comiskey	538	.335	4
2B	Y. Robinson	430	.305	1
SS	B. Gleason	598	.288	0
3B	A. Latham	627	.316	2
RF	B. Caruthers	364	.357	8
CF	C. Welch	544	.278	3
LF	T. O'Neill	517	.435	14
C	J. Boyle	350	.189	2
OF/P	D. Foutz	423	.357	4
P	S. King	222	.207	0
C	D. Bushong	201	.254	0

Pitcher	IP	W	L	SV	ERA
S. King	390	32	12	1	3.78
B. Caruthers	341	29	9	0	3.30
D. Foutz	339	25	12	0	3.87

1902 PITTSBURGH PIRATES

OF THE THREE TEAMS from the first decade of this century that rank among the top 10 of all time, the 1902 Pittsburgh Pirates had the most interesting genesis. The National League, which had expanded to a bloated 12 teams after the 1892 collapse of the American Association, could see by 1899 that they had problems. The gap between first place and the middle of the pack was often 20 games by June. Not surprisingly, the fans of second-division teams stopped showing up soon afterward. The owners agreed to drop four of the poorest teams: Cleveland, Washington, Baltimore, and Louisville.

However, Louisville owner Barney Dreyfuss did not like that idea, so he engineered the most amazing trade in baseball history. Dreyfuss obtained half-interest in the Pittsburgh franchise. Pirate ownership paid him $25,000 (to settle debts remaining from the Louisville operation) and sent four Bucs to the as-yet-undissolved Colonels for 14 Louisville players, including stars Claude Ritchey, Tommy Leach, Deacon Phillippe, and Rube Waddell. But the key men were left fielder/manager Fred Clarke and Honus Wagner. Clarke would go on to make the Hall of Fame as a manager; Wagner would become the greatest shortstop of all time.

As of 1902, though, the 28-year-old Wagner did not even have a regular position. Part of the reason was his sheer abundance of natural talent; he could play anywhere well. Several baseball experts have said he could have been a Hall of Famer at any of four or five positions. In 1902, Wagner played in 136 of the 142 Pirate contests, appearing in the outfield, at shortstop, at third base, and at second. He even hurled five shutout innings, fanning five opponents, in one game.

This was a potent Pirate offense. They outscored the next-best team by 142 runs and also led the National League in hits, doubles, triples, batting average, on-base percentage, and slugging average and tied for the league lead in stolen bases. Their 103-36 record put them 27½ games ahead of second-place Brooklyn. Their .741 winning percentage is the second highest this century. (Over a 162-game schedule, that plays out to a 120-42 record.)

The Buc batting game was built around center fielder Ginger Beaumont, who led the league with a .357 average; .330 hitter Wagner; .316 batsman Clarke; and third baseman Leach, whose 22 triples tied for the league lead and whose awesome total of six homers led all NL blasters. He finished second to Wagner in RBI. Wagner led the league in runs, doubles, RBI, and slugging average. Clarke, Wagner, and Beaumont finished one-two three in "total average."

As was the custom of the era, only a handful of pitchers supplied nearly all of the Pirate innings. But unlike some other teams, the Pirates didn't rely on one man to carry all (or nearly all) the weight. Four Bucs pitched more than 200 innings; one threw 188. In comparison, four other NL teams had pitchers who threw more than 300 innings. Jack Chesbro led the Pirate staff and the league with 28 wins. (Two years later, he would set the 20th-century record with 41 wins as a New York Highlander.) Phillippe and Jesse Tannehill each won exactly 20.

Another reason for the success of the 1901, '02, and '03 Pirates (pennant-winners all, and the '03 group played in the first modern World Series) was Dreyfuss's personality. While other National League operations were being raided by Ban Johnson's upstart American League, Dreyfuss maintained a carrot-stick style to keep his team together. He treated his players well, but if anyone was rumored to be talking to American League scouts (and Dreyfuss had his spies hard at work), the miscreant was canned.

Player/manager Clarke was not just a solid hitter and superb fielder, but a true leader. Historian MacLean Kennedy, in his 1928 book *The Great Teams of Baseball*, stated, "Great players are born into the game once a decade, and great leaders come into the game once a decade, but great player/managers are born into the game once in two decades." Kennedy ranked Clarke with the best of all time: Cap Anson, Charlie Comiskey, and Frank Chance.

With the Wagner-Clarke-Leach nucleus, the Pirates never fell further back than fourth place from 1904 through 1909, when they won the pennant again and battled the Tigers through seven rugged games before winning their first World Series. In that Series, Ty Cobb and Wagner became the first two batting champions to oppose each other in the fall classic.

1902 PIRATES
103 Wins   36 Losses

Pos	Player	AB	BA	HR	RBI
1B	K. Bransfield	413	.305	0	69
2B	C. Ritchey	405	.277	2	55
SS	W. Conroy	365	.244	1	47
3B	T. Leach	514	.278	6	85
RF	L. Davis	232	.280	0	20
CF	G. Beaumont	541	.357	0	67
LF	F. Clarke	459	.316	2	53
C	H. Smith	185	.189	0	12
UT	H. Wagner	534	.330	3	91
UT	J. Burke	203	.296	0	26

Pitcher	IP	W	L	SV	ERA
J. Chesbro	286	28	6	1	2.17
D. Phillippe	272	20	9	0	2.05
J. Tannehill	231	20	6	0	1.95
E. Doheny	188	16	4	0	2.53
S. Leever	222	15	7	2	2.39

1904-05 NEW YORK GIANTS

Mathewson and McGraw. Seldom has a great team been defined by two such disparate personalities. On the bench was the short, fiery, hardscrabble manager John McGraw, raised on a baseball diet of rugged, rule-breaking play. On the mound was Christy Mathewson—tall, college educated, genteel, and honest—whose greatest vice may have been his ego when it came to his skill at checkers.

Mathewson had already been a 20-game winner in 1901 when McGraw arrived in mid-1902 to take over the Giants' reins. Previous managers had been uncertain whether Mathewson was best as a pitcher or a fielder. McGraw put a quick end to *that* nonsense. He gave Mathewson 42 starts in 1903; the 22-year-old finished 37 of them and won 30 games. Aided by Joe McGinnity's 31 victories, the Giants, who had been pretty much stumbling around the National League's second division for 10 years, shot to second, just 6½ games behind the powerful Pirates.

The next year, they were absolutely unstoppable. They put together 106 wins and finished 13 lengths ahead of the Cubs. McGraw, always looking for the extra winning edge, dealt for shortstop Bill Dahlen before the season started. In early July, he sent Moose McCormick to Cincinnati for Turkey Mike Donlin. The defense was solid. The offense led the league in runs scored without having a single .300 hitter in the lineup.

The key was the masterful pitching of Mathewson and McGinnity—the original "M&M boys." McGinnity started 44 games and finished 38 of them. The year before, Joe had set the modern National League record with 434 innings pitched; in '04, he settled for "only" 408. He collected 35 wins and lost just eight times. He also led the league with nine shutouts and a remarkable 1.61 ERA. Mathewson added 33 wins in 45 decisions with an ERA barely over 2.00. His 368 innings ranked third in the National League. Rounding out the pitching staff were deaf-mute Dummy Taylor, whose 21-15 record was his best season ever, and 23-year-old lefty Hooks Wiltse, who went 13-3. There was no postseason series between the American and National Leagues that year, largely because McGraw and Giants owner John T. Brush refused to dignify Ban Johnson's league with a "World's Championship." It would be the last autumn without a World Series until 1994.

Things were different in 1905, as the Giant offense perked up. Donlin hit .356, third in the league, and led the NL in runs scored. With Donlin on base, outfielder Sam Mertes was able to knock in 108 runs, second in the NL. Roger Bresnahan began to display the catching savvy that would eventually earn him a place in the Hall of Fame. And he batted .302 too.

The pitching may have been less spectacular than the 1904 staff, but it was no less effective. Mathewson completely dominated NL batters the way McGinnity had the year before. His 31 wins were eight more than the second-best finisher. He led the league in shutouts, strikeouts, and ERA with a sensational 1.28 figure. Although it would be surpassed later (once by Mathewson himself), at the time it was the lowest ERA for a full season in the 30-year history of the National League.

While McGinnity "fell off" to a 21-15 record and a 2.87 ERA, youngster Red Ames earned 31 starts and finished 22-8. Taylor won 16 and Wiltse 15. Not surprisingly, the Giants moved into first place on April 23, and they never left. With McGraw's and Brush's tempers having cooled, the two leagues worked out an agreement for a World Series. The Giants would play the AL-champion Philadelphia Athletics.

And there Mathewson put on a clinic, the greatest individual pitching show the World Series would ever see. He started against the A's in Games 1, 3, and 5, shutting them out three times, allowing just 14 hits, striking out 18, and surrendering only one base on balls. McGinnity tossed a five-hit shutout in Game 4. The Giants had won their first world championship.

The same Giant nucleus finished second and fourth the next two years before losing the 1908 pennant by one game, due largely to the play that

has become known as "Merkle's boner." It was the Giants' ability to win, and win hugely, when confronted with teams of equally monstrous talent—the Pirates and Cubs—that earns them their place among the top 10 teams of all time.

1904 GIANTS
105 Wins   48 Losses

Pos	Player	AB	BA	HR	RBI
1B	D. McGann	517	.286	6	71
2B	B. Gilbert	478	.253	1	54
SS	B. Dahlen	523	.268	2	80
3B	A. Devlin	474	.281	1	66
RF	G. Browne	596	.284	4	39
CF	R. Bresnahan	402	.284	5	33
LF	S. Mertes	532	.276	4	78
C	J. Warner	287	.199	1	15
C	F. Bowerman	289	.232	2	27
OF	M. McCormick	203	.266	1	26

Pitcher	IP	W	L	SV	ERA
J. McGinnity	408	35	8	5	1.61
C. Mathewson	368	33	12	1	2.03
D. Taylor	296	21	15	0	2.34
H. Wiltse	165	13	3	3	2.84
R. Ames	115	4	6	3	2.27

1906-08 CHICAGO CUBS

NO TEAM HAS EVER dominated a league the way the 1906-08 Cubs did. For those three years, they won *an average* of 107 games a season. The first of those three, they won 116 games—the most by any team ever—and took the pennant by 20 games. In 1907, they won by 17 lengths. Yet such was the intense competition with the other two splendid aggregations of the time, the Pirates and Giants, that when the Cubs took their third straight title, they had to do it by winning a game that had to be replayed because of a New Yorker's baserunning gaffe. The "gift" victory gave the Cubs a one-game edge over the tied Bucs and Giants. Maybe it was no fun to be a National League fan in Boston or St. Louis during that decade, but if you lived in Pittsburgh, Chicago, or New York, those were the best of times.

These Cubs were the team built by brainy manager Frank Selee, called by some the best pilot ever. Under Selee, the Cubs moved from sixth in 1901 to fifth, then to third, then to second. The tubercular Selee had to retire in mid-1905, and the reins of management were handed to first baseman Frank Chance. The husky 27-year-old soon earned the moniker "The Peerless Leader."

Between 1905 and '06, the Cubs obtained outfielder Jimmy Sheckard and third sacker Harry Steinfeldt, and their starting eight was set for the next three glorious seasons. Chance held down first, sour-tempered but baseball-keen Johnny Evers played second, and Joe Tinker was at short. The outfield was patrolled by Wildfire Schulte, Jimmy Slagle, and Sheckard, none a great hitter but all excellent fielders.

The Chicagoans were a unit. Other clubs featured league-leading individual stars, but the Cubs didn't find it necessary. On the 1906 team, three Cubs were league leaders in one or another offensive category; in 1907 and '08, none were.

The Chicago club was built on speed, defense, slashing if not powerful hitting, a sturdy pitching staff ably handled by catcher Johnny Kling, and brains. The Steinfeldt-Tinker-Evers-Chance infield was not just solid, it was smart. Of course, it must be noted that, despite the famous poem, the Tinker-Evers double-play combination was no record-breaker.

The pitching staff was superb. With the deep and reliable starting unit of Mordecai "Three Finger" Brown, Jack Pfiester, Ed Reulbach, Carl Lundgren, and Orvie Overall, no Cub hurler had to risk blowing out his arm. The Cubs didn't need a 30-game winner (although Brown won 29 in '08); they just had two 20-game winners each year, plus a few other guys sprinkled in the teens.

In 1906, the Cubs and Giants played even through April, but then the Cubs took off and never looked back. The next season, the two teams were actually close through mid-May, but it was functionally over soon after that.

The 1908 National League pennant race has gone down in baseball legend and lore. The Cubs, Pirates, and Giants maintained a furious pace. By late September, the three contenders were bunched at the top, 10 games above the next team. On September 22, the Cubs swept a doubleheader from the Giants in the Polo Grounds and the race tightened further. The next day, the Giants thought they had won the game 2-1 in the last of the ninth when Al Bridwell singled home Moose McCormick with two out and Fred Merkle on first. But 1) Merkle failed to touch second before he left the field, 2) eagle-eyed Evers spotted the fact, and 3) after a scuffle for the ball, Evers showed the umpire he had the ball on second. Merkle was forced out and the game was declared a tie, to be replayed the day after the last scheduled game. At season's end, the Giants and Cubs were tied for first. In the make-up game, the Cubs won 4-2 to win the title.

The 1906 World Series featured both Chicago teams: the indomitable Cubbies and the "Hitless Wonder" White Sox, whose team batting average was nearly 50 points below the league leader. The North Siders took the South Siders too lightly. Even though Reulbach pitched a one-hitter in Game 2, the Sox spanked Brown and Pfiester with two losses each. Ed Walsh won two for the Sox and the mighty Cubs were defeated in six games.

The story was quite different for the World Series contests of 1907 and '08. The Cubs dominated the Ty Cobb-led Tigers in both, winning eight of the 10 games played. One ended in a tie. With only one change in the starting eight, but the addition of a few new pitchers, the Cubs won 104 games in 1910 to take the pennant once more.

1906 CUBS
116 Wins   36 Losses

Pos	Player	AB	BA	HR	RBI
1B	F. Chance	474	.319	3	71
2B	J. Evers	533	.255	1	51
SS	J. Tinker	523	.233	1	64
3B	H. Steinfeldt	539	.327	3	83
RF	W. Schulte	563	.281	7	60
CF	J. Slagle	498	.239	0	33
LF	J. Sheckard	549	.262	1	45
C	J. Kling	343	.312	2	46
C	P. Moran	226	.252	0	35
UT	S. Hofman	195	.256	2	20

Pitcher	IP	W	L	SV	ERA
T. Brown	277	26	6	3	1.04
J. Pfiester	251	20	8	0	1.56
E. Reulbach	218	19	4	3	1.65
C. Lundgren	208	17	6	2	2.21
J. Taylor	147	12	3	0	1.83
O. Overall	144	12	3	1	1.88

1927 NEW YORK YANKEES

THEY CAME TO CALL IT "Five O'Clock Lightning." The Yankees of the 1920s and '30s were such a powerful group of hitters that almost no opposing pitcher could hold them back for a full game. After the pitcher had faced the Yank lineup once or twice and tired a bit (about five in the afternoon, since most games started at three), the slugging men from the Bronx had seen all they needed, and they were almost certain to break the game open. As their owner, Jacob Ruppert, said, "Close games make me nervous." His idea of a perfect day at the ballpark was "when the Yankees score eight runs in the first and slowly pull away."

Every list of the greatest teams of all time begins with the 1927 Yankees. Yankee manager Miller Huggins, in his 10th year as their skipper, was known for being irascible and moody, but all he had to do in 1927 was sit back and watch.

As an offensive powerhouse, the Yanks were simply awesome. Historically speaking, it should be remembered that the "big bomber" mentality had not yet taken over the game. As the 1927 season began, only three men in major-league history had swatted 40 or more homers in a season. That year, Babe Ruth belted 60 and Lou Gehrig 47. Ruth's record and the Ruth-Gehrig combo total stood until 1961, when Roger Maris and Mickey Mantle topped them in an expansion year. The

1927 Yankees weren't riding the wave of a livelier ball or other offensive fluke season; the league batting average was actually lower than it had been two of the previous three years. Twice in the previous three seasons, the American League as a whole had scored more runs.

The '27 Yankees had the top three run scorers in the American League; the top two in hits, RBI, and triples; the top three in home runs and total bases; the top two in walks; two of the top five in batting average; two of the top three in on-base percentage; and the top two in slugging percentage. As a team, they led the AL in hits, triples, homers (102 more than the runnerup), batting average, on-base percentage, and slugging average (no team has ever topped their .489 mark). Not surprisingly, they scored 130 more runs than the next highest-scoring team. Their 110 victories (in a 154-game season) is the second best by any American League team ever.

The Yankee starting eight was mostly blossoming young talent, with only third baseman Joe Dugan, outfielder Bob Meusel, and Ruth qualifying as veterans. Gehrig, in his third full year, set a record for slugging percentage by anyone not named Babe Ruth (which still holds today). In addition to his 47 circuit clouts, he led the AL in doubles with 52 and tied for second in triples with 18. His 175 RBI were the most in baseball history at that time and are still fourth best. Second baseman

Tony Lazzeri, just a rookie the season before, finished third in the league (and on the Yanks) with 18 homers and knocked in 102 runs. Switch-hitting shortstop Mark Koenig, in his third full season, swatted 11 triples and scored 99 times. Earl Combs, the speedy center fielder also in his third full season, had the best totals he would ever have in hits, triples, and batting average.

And then there was the Babe. His 60 home runs were 18 more than anyone else had ever hit. His 158 runs scored tied himself for second (he was also first) for runs in the 20th century, and he drove in 164 runs too. In a word, it was simply another "Ruthian" year.

Naturally, the Yankee pitching staff enjoyed having such a crop of sluggers around. They were basically a group of seasoned veterans. Staff ace Waite Hoyt led the team in wins with 22. Herb Pennock (age 33), Urban Shocker (36), and Dutch Ruether (33) each started more than 25 games. Pennock chalked up 19 wins, Shocker 18, and Ruether 13. Ace swingman Wilcy Moore (30) started a dozen games and relieved in 38 others. He was around when Five O'Clock Lightning hit often enough to earn 19 wins, and he's credited (retroactively) with 13 saves. He also led the league with a 2.28 earned-run average, although Hoyt and Shocker were right behind him.

With the exception of one inning, the 1927 Yankee power didn't show up for that year's World

Series. But it didn't matter. Aided by Pirate errors and two final-game, ninth-inning wild pitches by Pirate hurler John Miljus, the Yanks easily swept the Bucs in four games. It was the first of three consecutive sweeps by the Yanks: 1927, 1928, and 1932.

1927 YANKEES					
110 Wins 44 Losses					
Pos	Player	AB	BA	HR	RBI
1B	L. Gehrig	584	.373	47	175
2B	T. Lazzeri	570	.309	18	102
SS	M. Koenig	526	.285	3	62
3B	J. Dugan	387	.269	2	43
RF	B. Ruth	540	.356	60	164
CF	E. Combs	648	.356	6	64
LF	B. Meusel	516	.337	8	103
C	P. Collins	251	.275	7	36
2B	R. Morehart	195	.256	1	20
C	J. Grabowski	195	.277	0	25

Pitcher	IP	W	L	SV	ERA
W. Hoyt	256	22	7	1	2.63
W. Moore	213	19	7	13	2.28
H. Pennock	210	19	8	2	3.00
U. Shocker	200	18	6	0	2.84
D. Ruether	184	13	6	0	3.38
G. Pipgras	166	10	3	0	4.11

1929-31 PHILADELPHIA A'S

O F ALL THE TEAMS that merit ranking in baseball's top 10 of all time, the Athletics of 1929-31 were the most complete. They had sluggers who hit both for power and for average, their defense was first-rate, and their pitching was superior. Three of their starting eight those years are now in the Hall of Fame. Their ace pitcher, another Cooperstown resident, might be the greatest lefty of all time. They won 104, 102, and 107 games those three years. They dominated their National League opponents in two of the three World Series they played. And perhaps most impressively, they had to beat out the Yankees of Ruth and Gehrig every year just to get there.

The A's were managed and owned by Connie Mack, the angular patrician who wore a business suit in the dugout, not a baseball uniform. Mr. Mack managed 20 years longer than anyone else ever did, which is why he won nearly a thousand games more than the next most successful manager. Mack had sold off the stars of his early-teens pennant-winners, then it took him eight years to get out of last place and another four to reach the first division. But by 1925, his minions finished second, and they'd be there or in first or third the succeeding nine years.

After having caught and played third and first in previous years, Jimmie Foxx was given the first base job for the 1929 season. All he did was hit .354 with 33 homers and 118 RBI. He scored 123 times too. Outfielder Al Simmons swatted 34 circuit clouts himself, led the league with 157 RBI, and batted .365.

But the Athletics' run-scoring was no two-man tag team. Leadoff hitter and second baseman Max Bishop hit just .232, but he walked 128 times, most in the majors, which drove his on-base percentage up to nearly .400. He crossed the plate 102 times. Along with Simmons in the outfield were Bing Miller and Mule Haas. Miller belted the ball at a .335 clip and drove in 93. Haas hit .313 and knocked home 82 runners. Catcher Mickey Cochrane, such a potent batsman that Mack batted him third in the order (catchers had always been eighth-place hitters), hit for a .331 average and drove in 95 runs.

On the mound, George Earnshaw won 24 games to lead the league, losing just eight. But Lefty Grove had a better winning percentage, topping all other American League hurlers with a 20-6, .769 mark. Thirty-two-year-old Rube Walberg tossed in 18 more victories. Even 45-year-old Jack Quinn won 11. The staff ERA of 3.44 was the best in baseball by a half-run.

The A's toppled the Cubs in the World Series with dispatch. The Cubs thought they were in the thick of things when in Game 4, up 8-0 in the seventh inning of a game that would have tied the

Series, they were struck by Philadelphia lightning. The A's ran around the bases to score 10 times that inning. Two days later, the Cubs blew a 2-0 lead in the last of the ninth on a Bishop single, a Haas homer, and Simmons and Miller doubles, and the Series was over in five games. So devasting were the '29 Athletics that they appeared on the cover of *Sports Illustrated* in 1996. The subtitle read "The 1929 Philadelphia A's, not the Yankees, may have been the greatest baseball club ever assembled."

The 1930 season was an instant replay. Foxx batted .335 with 37 homers and 156 RBI. Simmons swatted the ball at a .381 clip to win his first of two consecutive batting titles; he hit one less homer than Foxx and drove in 165. Cochrane's .357 average included 42 doubles. Even defensive specialist Jimmy Dykes joined Miller to top the .300 mark. Grove went 28-5, 2.54 to lead the league in wins and ERA. Earnshaw won 22 and Quinn, now 46, was 9-7. In the World Series, the Cardinals found Earnshaw and Grove nearly unhittable as each won two games. (Grove allowed only five hits in his one loss.) Series to Philadelphia in six.

Then to prove it was no fluke, they did it again. Homers and batting averages fell off for most A's in 1931, as they did for the entire league, but the A's hurlers took up the slack in grand style. Grove had the greatest season of his great career, winning 31 (16 in a row) and losing just four. His .886 winning percentage was the major-league record for 47 years. He had 27 complete games in 30 starts and his league-leading ERA was 2.06. Earnshaw won 21 times; Walberg 20. Even the surprising World Series loss to the red-hot Pepper Martin and the Cardinals could not diminish the remarkable achievements of the A's of 1929-31.

1929 A's
104 Wins   46 Losses

Pos	Player	AB	BA	HR	RBI
1B	J. Foxx	517	.354	33	118
2B	M. Bishop	475	.232	3	36
SS	J. Boley	303	.251	2	47
3B	S. Hale	379	.277	1	40
RF	B. Miller	556	.335	8	93
CF	M. Haas	578	.313	16	82
LF	A. Simmons	581	.365	34	157
C	M. Cochrane	514	.331	7	95
UT	J. Dykes	401	.327	13	79

Pitcher	IP	W	L	SV	ERA
L. Grove	275	20	6	4	2.81
R. Walberg	268	18	11	4	3.60
G. Earnshaw	255	24	8	1	3.29
J. Quinn	161	11	9	2	3.97
B. Shores	153	11	6	7	3.60
E. Rommel	114	12	2	4	2.85

1936-39 NEW YORK YANKEES

WERE THE YANKEES of 1936-39 the greatest team of all time? It's not a difficult claim to make. Consider: During that span, they averaged 102 wins a season. They won the pennant each year by an average of nearly 15 games. In each of those seasons, they scored more runs than any team in baseball, averaging more than 80 runs per year more than the second-best AL team. They beat the other guys by seven or more runs one game out of every four. At least 10 times each year, their margin of victory was 10 runs or more.

In each of those seasons, the Yankees' pitching staff won the ERA title. And after dominating the American League each summer, they did the same to the National League in the World Series, with a 16-3 record in Series games and two four-game sweeps. While the Yankees of the Ruth-Gehrig era were potent, and their counterparts in the Mantle-Stengel era were winners, the 1936-39 Yanks were simply awesome.

These were the Yankees of Lou Gehrig and Joe DiMaggio. The 1936 season was DiMaggio's first; '39 was the year Gehrig's career ended. Piloted by brainy Joe McCarthy, who keenly used his pitching staff and acted quickly to fill anything resembling a gap, these Yanks had no competition.

The left side of their infield was the same for the four-year span. Red Rolfe held down third, hitting over .300 three times and leading the league in doubles one year and triples another. Not a great hitter, slick-fielding shortstop (and later long-time Yankee coach) Frankie Crosetti had some power and did lead the AL in stolen bases one year. The 1936 and '37 campaigns were second sacker Tony Lazzeri's final two as a Yank, and when he fell to a .244 average and just 14 homers, he was replaced by Joe Gordon, who banged 25 and 28 homers in 1938 and '39, respectively. First base belonged to Gehrig, of course, until his illness forced him out of the lineup forever after just eight games in '39. From 1936 through '38, Gehrig averaged .334 with 38 homers, 142 RBI, and 140 runs scored.

Bill Dickey was the catcher. In addition to being a superb defensive player and handler of pitchers, his lowest batting average during that span was .302; his highest, .362. The outfield is where McCarthy did his most tinkering. In June of 1937, Ben Chapman was hitting just .266, so McCarthy had him swapped to the Senators for Jake Powell, who batted .306 as a Yank that year. Tommy Henrich joined the team in 1938, Charlie Keller in '39. George Selkirk and Joe DiMaggio remained the other outfielders for all four years.

The 1936 campaign was DiMaggio's rookie season, and he showed why he was on his way to Cooperstown, batting .323 with 44 doubles, 15 triples (leading the league), and 29 homers. He also drove in 125 runs and scored 132. Joe suffered no "sophomore jinx." In 1937, he led the league with 46 home runs and 151 runs scored, and he drove in 167. In 1939, he won his first batting title with a .381 average.

McCarthy relied on two ace pitchers during the four years, Lefty Gomez and Red Ruffing. Ruffing won 20, 20, 21, and 21 in a remarkably consistent style. Gomez won 21 in 1937 and 18 in '38. Surrounding them was a less-than-superstar cast that McCarthy knew exactly how to use. Johnny Murphy was 13-4 and 8-2 in 1937 and '38 as the top reliever. Others who contributed a dozen wins or more in at least one of those seasons included Monte Pearson, Bump Hadley, Pat Malone, Johnny Broaca, Spud Chandler, and Atley Donald. Malone, at the end of his career, had pitched well for McCarthy as a Cub; Joe knew when to bring him back. Chandler would enjoy two 20-win seasons as a Yank in the '40s. The rest were journeymen at best but perfect matches for the McCarthy approach.

This Yankee team was capable of fireworks that made earlier teams look puny in comparison. On May 23, 1936, in Philadelphia's Shibe Park, the Yanks made mincemeat of Athletics hurlers, winning a doubleheader 12-6 and 15-1. The Yanks belted seven homers that day, had 30 hits and 61 total bases. The A's starter in Game 1 was rapped

out of the box in the second inning. Connie Mack brought him back in Game 2 and he gave up six more runs. The next day, the Yankees really went to town, hammering the A's 25-2. Lazzeri hit two grand slams that day (the first player ever to accomplish the feat) and added a third homer and a triple. DiMaggio homered and Crosetti slugged a pair out of the park.

1939 YANKEES
106 Wins   45 Losses

Pos	Player	AB	BA	HR	RBI
1B	B. Dahlgren	531	.235	15	89
2B	J. Gordon	567	.284	28	111
SS	F. Crosetti	656	.233	10	56
3B	R. Rolfe	648	.329	14	80
RF	C. Keller	398	.334	11	83
CF	J. DiMaggio	462	.381	30	126
LF	G. Selkirk	418	.306	21	101
C	B. Dickey	480	.302	24	105
OF	T. Henrich	347	.277	9	57
P	R. Ruffing	114	.307	1	20

Pitcher	IP	W	L	SV	ERA
R. Ruffing	233	21	7	0	2.93
L. Gomez	198	12	8	0	3.41
B. Hadley	154	12	6	2	2.98
A. Donald	153	13	3	1	3.71
M. Pearson	146	12	5	0	4.49
O. Hildebrand	127	10	4	2	3.06
S. Sundra	121	11	1	0	2.76
J. Murphy	61	3	6	19	4.40

1949-53 NEW YORK YANKEES

DESPITE FOUR PENNANTS in the 1940s, Yankee management by 1949 saw it was time for new blood. They called on former big-league clown (but successful minor-league manager) Casey Stengel to take charge. The final days of the legendary 1949 season saw the Yankees win the pennant in dramatic fashion, and the most successful Yankee dynasty was born.

The heavy-hitting Red Sox swept the Yanks in a three-game Fenway set on the next to last weekend of the season to move into first place. When the teams met for the last two games, the Sox were one game in front. Stengel's team, beset by injuries all year long, topped the Sox twice to take the flag in one of the greatest pennant races in history. The Yankees once again rolled over the Dodgers in the Series.

Then Casey began to build his dynasty, starting with a steady starting-pitcher crew of Vic Raschi, Eddie Lopat, and Allie Reynolds and improved by the midseason call-up of 21-year-old Whitey Ford. Joe DiMaggio had a brilliant comeback year after an injury-plagued '49, and Phil Rizzuto hit about 50 points higher than his lifetime average to win the league MVP Award. Yogi Berra, still rough-hewn as a catcher, was a born hitter. He batted .322

and belted 28 homers, driving in 124 runs. New York swept the "Whiz Kid" Phillies in the Series and Casey's men were world champs for the second year in a row.

The 1951 season marked the appearance of Mickey Mantle and the final year of DiMaggio. Both Boston and a promising young Cleveland team pushed the Yankees to a pennant race that wasn't decided until mid-September. Stengel was in full platoon form now: Bobby Brown/Gil McDougald and Hank Bauer/Gene Woodling were good players who became excellent combos sharing time. Johnny Mize and Joe Collins were spotted against certain pitchers. Peppery infielder Billy Martin, in his second year, quickly became one of Casey's all-time favorite players. In the World Series, Lopat pitched two complete-game wins and Reynolds one as the Yankees offed the "Miracle Giants" in six games.

The 1952 campaign looked to be the year the Yankee string would be broken. DiMaggio had retired and infielders Brown and Jerry Coleman joined Ford in the military. Stengel's team looked weaker than it had in years. But Martin stepped in to fill the second base slot with flash, and he and Rizzuto teamed up to be a superb keystone combo. Mantle replaced DiMaggio in center and hit .311 with 23 homers and 87 RBI. Berra's average fell to .273, but he still tagged 30 homers and drove home 98 to lead the team. Thirty-seven-year-old Allie Reynolds remained staff ace, winning 20 and topping the AL with a 2.06 ERA. Raschi added 16 wins. Though no one else had a dozen, 14 different hurlers won at least one each.

The 1952 World Series, New York vs. Brooklyn, was the toughest one for the Yanks in decades. Two games were decided by one run, four by a pair. The Yanks were up 4-2 in the bottom of the seventh of Game 7 when two Dodger walks and a single loaded the bases with one out. The fearsome Duke Snider and Jackie Robinson were coming up. Stengel called on his large lefty, Bob "Sarge" Kuzava, who calmly induced a Snider pop-up. Then Robinson also undercut a breaking pitch and lofted it behind the pitcher's mound. Sarge didn't see it; first sacker Collins didn't move. Two Dodger runners had already crossed the plate by the time Martin, charging in at full speed, snatched the ball from the air. Two innings later, the Yankees had tied the all-time record for consecutive world championships with four.

The next year, they broke it. There was no pennant chase in 1953, as the Yanks were securely in first place by May 1. For the first time in Casey's tenure, the Yankees outscored everyone else in the league. They also led in team ERA. Ford and Lopat were the aces and Reynolds, in a swing role, won 13 games and saved 13 more.

The 1953 World Series belonged to Martin. He set a record with a dozen hits, including two triples and two homers, and tallied eight RBI. And he added the only moment of real drama when he singled in the winning run in the last of the ninth in the final game against the Dodgers.

Unlike the Murderer's Row Yanks who simply pounded the ball, the Stengel teams of 1949-53 were carefully constructed and polished, season by season, game by game. Stengel was the genius who pushed his team to an unheard-of five consecutive world championships.

1953 YANKEES
99 Wins   52 Losses

Pos	Player	AB	BA	HR	RBI
1B	J. Collins	387	.269	17	44
2B	B. Martin	587	.257	15	75
SS	P. Rizzuto	413	.271	2	54
3B	G. McDougald	541	.285	10	83
RF	H. Bauer	437	.304	10	57
CF	M. Mantle	461	.295	21	92
LF	G. Woodling	395	.306	10	58
C	Y. Berra	503	.296	27	108
OF	I. Noren	345	.267	6	46
1B	D. Bollweg	155	.297	6	24

Pitcher	IP	W	L	SV	ERA
W. Ford	207	18	6	0	3.00
J. Sain	189	14	7	9	3.00
V. Raschi	181	13	6	1	3.33
E. Lopat	178	16	4	0	2.42
A. Reynolds	145	13	7	13	3.41
J. McDonald	130	9	7	0	3.82

1954 CLEVELAND INDIANS

ONLY FOUR MODERN major-league teams have won 110 or more games in one season. Two of those teams were from the first decade of this century. The third was the 1927 Yankees. The Cleveland Indians of 1954 were the fourth, and their 111 W's are the all-time American League record and the most by any major-league team over the last 90 years. Some might claim that this was a fluke year for the team from Cleveland. The facts indicate otherwise.

The Indians, who won the American League flag in 1948, were one of the quality teams in the AL in the '50s; unfortunately for them, the other was the Yankees. Cleveland finished second to the Yanks in 1951, '52, and '53. The frustration finally ended in 1954.

The Tribe manager was Al Lopez, a longtime catcher who took over the managerial reins from Lou Boudreau after the 1950 season and later won induction into baseball's Hall of Fame for both his catching and managing. Lopez had a great pitching staff to work with. Bob Feller, aging but still tough, won 22 games in 1951. Mike Garcia and Early Wynn each won 20 that year, and Bob Lemon chalked up 17. Those four were still the heart of the staff for the '54 champions.

The changes Lopez brought to the team took place elsewhere. Second sacker Bobby Avila

replaced former Yank Joe Gordon. George Strick-
land moved into Ray Boone's slot at short. Luke
Easter, already 34 when the breaking of the color
line allowed him a major-league shot in 1949, was
gone. Only Larry Doby remained from the 1951
outfield.

Before the season started, Lopez announced that
"the Yankees can be had." All they had done was
win five straight pennants *and* World Series, but
Lopez remained undaunted. Until the middle of
July, New York and the White Sox stayed in the
chase. But the Indians just wouldn't fold. The
notion that the Yankees collapsed is a falsehood, as
the boys from the Bronx won 103 games themselves that year. The Yanks were mighty good; the
Indians were just that much better. Some have
speculated that if the Yanks had truly had a bad
year, the Indians would not have felt pressured and
probably wouldn't have reached that record-setting
win total.

Jim Hegan was the sure-handed Indian catcher.
Considered as fine a handler of pitchers as had ever
been, he helped the staff stay on track throughout
the season. He had the highest fielding average of
any catcher in the AL that season. According to
Total Baseball's "fielding runs" stat, he was the best
defensive catcher in major-league history.

Offensively, the Tribe was solid too. Hegan hit 11
homers to join the Indians' league-leading effort in
that department. Doby hit 32 and drove in 126 to

lead the league in both categories. Al Rosen belted 24 with 102, and Avila slugged 15 homers and won the batting crown with a .341 average. Wally Westlake added 11 homers off the bench. Overall, the Indians finished second in the American League in scoring, trailing the Yankees.

The pitching staff was phenomenal. Garcia went 19-8, allowing his opponents a measly .284 on-base percentage, and his 2.64 ERA led the league. Of course, Lemon and Wynn finished second and third in ERA. Wynn and Lemon tied for the AL lead in wins with 23. Lemon's 21 complete games tied for league best. He also added a pair of his 37 lifetime homers (second ever for pitchers) that season. Garcia's five shutouts tied for the league lead. Art Houtteman sported a 15-7 record, and old warhorse Feller made 19 starts and finished 13-3. Another old pro, Hal Newhouser, joined youngsters Ray Narleski and Don Mossi to handle bullpen chores. They combined for 27 saves and 16 victories.

Sad to say, the Indians' terrific season-long performance didn't pay off in the World Series, as the New York Giants pulled a pair of heroes out of their caps. One was Dusty Rhodes, a part-timer who belted two key homers off the bench. The other was Willie Mays, whose full-speed, over-the-shoulder catch of Vic Wertz's monumental eighth-inning fly ball—and equally impressive peg to the infield—seemed to take the heart out of the Indians in Game 1. The Giants prevailed in just four games.

The Indians remained solid, finishing second in 1955, '56, and '59. They then entered their legendary dry spell, which lasted 35 years.

1954 INDIANS
111 Wins   43 Losses

Pos	Player	AB	BA	HR	RBI
1B	B. Glynn	171	.251	5	18
2B	B. Avila	555	.341	15	67
SS	G. Strickland	361	.213	6	37
3B	A. Rosen	466	.300	24	102
RF	D. Philley	452	.226	12	60
CF	L. Doby	577	.272	32	126
LF	A. Smith	481	.281	11	50
C	J. Hegan	423	.234	11	40
1B	V. Wertz	295	.275	14	48
OF	W. Westlake	240	.263	11	42

Pitcher	IP	W	L	SV	ERA
E. Wynn	271	23	11	2	2.73
M. Garcia	259	19	8	5	2.64
B. Lemon	258	23	7	0	2.72
A. Houtteman	188	15	7	0	3.35
B. Feller	140	13	3	0	3.09
D. Mossi	93	6	1	7	1.94
R. Narleski	89	3	3	13	2.22

1975-76 CINCINNATI REDS

THEY CALLED THEM the "Big Red Machine," because they rolled over their opponents like a bulldozer in knickers, taking National League West titles in 1970, '72, '73, '75, and '76 and four times advancing to the World Series.

But of all those great Reds teams, it was the back-to-back world champions of 1975 and '76 that stand the tallest. Manager Sparky Anderson and the boys won their division by 20 and then 10 games, swept through two League Championship Series undefeated, played heroically to win one of the greatest World Series ever, and then stopped the famous Yankees in four straight in the next fall classic.

These were absolutely complete teams. The Reds featured exceptional defense, in the infield, in the outfield, and behind the dish. Their pitching lacked star quality, but it was sturdy, workmanlike, and quietly effective. A lefty/righty bullpen duo could be counted on to snuff out most fires. They were a marvelous scoring machine, combining power, speed, and intelligent hitting. They could steal bases to change the complexion of a key inning. And they were driven by two of the most engaging personalities in major-league history.

The 1975 Reds didn't have a single starting pitcher win 16 games, but three won 15 and seven won 10 or more. In the bullpen, left-hander Will

McEnaney posted 15 saves and five wins, while right-hander Rawly Eastwick led the league with 22 saves. In 1976, only Gary Nolan could muster 15 victories, but six won 11 or more and Eastwick added 26 saves, again leading the NL.

The starting eight for the two seasons was identical: RBI machine Tony Perez at first, back-to-back MVP (and now Hall of Famer) Joe Morgan on second, slick fielder Dave Concepcion at short, all-time hit leader Pete Rose at third, and an outfield of slugging George Foster, ball hawk Cesar Geronimo, and speedster Ken Griffey. Behind the plate was arguably the best catcher in baseball history, Johnny Bench, both an offensive and defensive superstar who's now in the Hall of Fame. Anderson, who would favor the platoon system with later clubs, knew not to mess with this unit.

The 1975 team led the National League in runs scored and stolen bases. The 1976 team led the league in seemingly everything: runs, hits, doubles, triples, homers, walks received, batting average, slugging average, and on-base percentage. And stolen bases again.

The core of the team lay in the uniquely paired duo of Rose and Morgan. Both men were driven to excellence by a passion that makes the rest of the world look like edgy wimps. Yet off the field, the two were quite different. Rose was one of the boys, affable, happy, and always ready with a quick quip. Morgan's studied intensity never left him. Smiles didn't come easily to Joe Morgan the ballplayer. Unlike Rose, who had burst onto the baseball scene full of brashness and won Rookie of the Year honors, Morgan struggled his first years in the league. And until he joined the Reds, many felt "high potential, but..." would be his legacy.

In 1975, Morgan batted .327, hit 17 homers, drove in 94 runs, and led the league in on-base percentage. He was named Most Valuable Player. Then in 1976, he hit 27 home runs, drove in 111, and led the league in both on-base percentage and slugging average. Who else could they have given the MVP to? While Rose's batting-title days were behind him, he batted .317 and .323 those two years and led the league in doubles both times.

In the 1975 World Series, the Reds took on the Boston Red Sox. The two played the Series at a level of breathtaking excellence, overcoming deficits, making brilliant clutch plays, and providing one of the greatest Series ever. Game 6 was the all-time classic tied by Red Sox Bernie Carbo's three-run homer in the eighth and won by Carlton Fisk's 12th-inning dinger. The Reds came back to win Game 7.

The 1976 World Series was anticlimactic, as the Yankees scored just eight runs in the four games. After the sweep was complete, Reds president Bob Howsam was being interviewed in the ecstatic locker room by an effusive announcer, who congratulated him on having "a truly great team."

"Yes," Howsam answered, "and it's probably the last great team." The specter of free agency was on the doorstep, and building and keeping a team long enough to make it a dynasty was passing from baseball forever.

1975 REDS					
108 Wins 54 Losses					
Pos	**Player**	**AB**	**BA**	**HR**	**RBI**
1B	T. Perez	511	.282	20	109
2B	J. Morgan	498	.327	17	94
SS	D. Concepcion	507	.274	5	49
3B	P. Rose	662	.317	7	74
RF	K. Griffey	463	.305	4	46
CF	C. Geronimo	501	.257	6	53
LF	G. Foster	463	.300	23	78
C	J. Bench	530	.283	28	110
1B/OF	D. Driessen	210	.281	7	38
OF	M. Rettenmund	188	.239	2	19
Pitcher	**IP**	**W**	**L**	**SV**	**ERA**
G. Nolan	211	15	9	0	3.16
J. Billingham	208	15	10	0	4.11
F. Norman	188	12	4	0	3.73
D. Gullett	160	15	4	0	2.42
P. Darcy	131	11	5	1	3.57
P. Borbon	125	9	5	5	2.95
W. McEnaney	91	5	2	15	2.47
R. Eastwick	90	5	3	22	2.60

CHAPTER 4

10 BEST GAMES

LIKE A FOUR-STAR MOVIE, *a great
ballgame consists of heroic
characters, twists and turns, swings
of emotion, and, of course, a
dramatic climax. It helps too if the
stakes are high. Featured here are
the 10 most extraordinary major-
league baseball games in history.*

Carlton Fisk, Game 6, 1975 World Series

CUBS 1, GIANTS 1
SEPTEMBER 23, 1908

THE 1908 NATIONAL LEAGUE season was the culmination of a thrilling beginning to the 20th century. The Pirates (who had won the pennant in 1901, '02, and '03) were tangled in a bristling pennant race with the Giants (who had won in 1904 and '05) and the Cubs (winners in '06 and '07). And the entire season turned on one bizarre play in one game—a play that unfortunately labelled a rather smart ballplayer, Fred Merkle, a "bonehead" for the rest of his life.

The day before, the Cubs had helped knot the race even tighter by sweeping the Giants in a doubleheader. New York desperately wanted to avoid being swept at home. Legendary pitcher Christy Mathewson started for New York; Jack "The Giant Killer" Pfiester was the starting pitcher for Chicago.

Both pitchers were "on." Mathewson allowed only five hits for the contest. One was a fifth-inning line drive scorched by Cubs shortstop Joe Tinker into the outfield. Apparently, outfielder Mike Donlin tried to stop the ball with his shoe, but it rolled into the overflow crowd held back by ropes. Tinker circled the bases for an inside-the-park homer.

The Giants scored their lone tally in the sixth on a single, an error, a sacrifice, and a single. The sky was darkening when the Giants came to bat in the last of the ninth.

With one out, Giant third sacker Art Devlin singled off Pfiester. Next up, Moose McCormick figured if he pulled the ball to the right side, Devlin could advance to second. He was half right, because second baseman Johnny Evers flagged down McCormick's hard grounder and forced Devlin.

Batting next was Fred Merkle. Merkle was playing because regular first baseman Fred Tenney was out with a sore back. It was the only game Tenney failed to start at first that entire season for John McGraw's men. Merkle would not be 20 years old for three more months, but he responded to the occasion, rifling a single over first baseman Frank Chance's head down the right-field foul line. McCormick hustled into third. When Giants shortstop Al Bridwell followed with a liner into right-center, McCormick trotted across the plate, and the sellout mob at the Polo Grounds went roaring home. Some even carried Mathewson on their shoulders as they celebrated on the field.

The problem was, Merkle (apparently) never touched second. A little more than two weeks earlier, the Cubs had been involved in a similar situation in Pittsburgh. A Pirate single drove in the apparent winning run in the last of the 10th, and the Pirate runner on first failed to step on second. Keen-eyed Johnny Evers appeared with the ball, stepped on the base, and announced the third out, which meant the run couldn't count. Umpire Hank

O'Day (the only ump) muttered something to the effect that no one ever bothered to enforce that rule, which was true, even though the books stated it clearly. The Cubs protested; it was disallowed.

But when the same thing happened in New York, O'Day was the umpire again. Even though the fans were pouring onto the field and the place was bedlam, O'Day headed toward second to see if Merkle touched the sack. After a scrap to get the ball away from at least one Giant and several fans (some maintain to this day that the real ball never reached second), Evers once again appeared on second with a ball and announced the runner was out.

This time O'Day was on the spot, and he ruled in favor of Evers, although not until after he left the field. He chose the wisdom of avoiding a riot. After meeting with National League president Harry Pulliam that night, he stated that the runner was out, and because of the thousands of fans on the field and impending darkness, the game was to be declared a 1-1 tie.

The papers of the day were full of charges and countercharges. Mathewson assured everyone that he had grabbed Merkle by the arm and made certain the youngster had touched second. In fact, Matty claimed that if the league officials ruled against the Giants in this matter, he would never play professional baseball again, period. The league did uphold O'Day's tardy decision, and the game entered the record books as a tie. And ever since then, the rule that you must touch the next base has been dutifully enforced.

Because of that tie, the Cubs and Giants finished the pennant race in a dead heat. The game was replayed when all the other games had been played, and the Giants and Mathewson lost to the Cubs and Pfiester 4-2. Poor Fred Merkle never lived down his "Bonehead" nickname.

CUBS 1, GIANTS 1

Chicago	AB	R	H	RBI	New York	AB	R	H	RBI
Hayden rf	4	0	0	0	Herzog 2b	3	1	1	0
Evers 2b	4	0	1	0	Bresnahan c	3	0	0	0
Schulte lf	4	0	0	0	Donlin rf	4	0	1	1
Chance 1b	3	0	1	0	Seymour cf	4	0	1	0
Steinfeldt 3b	2	0	0	0	Devlin 3b	4	0	2	0
Hofman cf	3	0	1	0	McCormick lf	3	0	0	0
Tinker ss	3	1	1	1	Merkle 1b	3	0	1	0
Kling c	3	0	1	0	Bridwell ss	4	0	0	0
Pfiester p	3	0	0	0	Mathewson p	3	0	0	0
Totals	29	1	5	1	Totals	31	1	6	1

Chicago	0	0	0		0	1	0		0	0	0
New York	0	0	0		0	0	1		0	0	0

DP: Chicago 3, New York 1. LOB: Chicago 4, New York 7. HR: Evers.
SH: Chance, Steinfeldt, Bresnahan.

Chicago	IP	H	R	ER	BB	SO
Pfiester	9	6	1	0	2	0
New York						
Mathewson	9	5	1	1	0	9

HBP: McCormick (by Pfiester). T: 1:03

RED SOX 3, GIANTS 2
1912 WORLD SERIES, GAME 8

THE 1912 WORLD SERIES between the Giants and Red Sox was an almost nightmarish drama of emotional swings for fans of both teams. Close plays, backbreaking errors, great pitching, and clutch hitting were the order of the day. And, appropriately enough, the final game was the most sensational of them all.

These were two powerful teams. Both had scored around 800 runs to lead their respective leagues and had out-homered all of their competition. The Red Sox had led the American League in slugging average; the Giants had topped the NL in batting average. Sox center fielder Tris Speaker had just set the modern major-league record for doubles in a season.

But the pitching matchups promised the most excitement. The Giants featured a lefty/righty duo of Rube Marquard and Christy Mathewson; the Sox countered with Smokey Joe Wood (of whom Walter Johnson said, "No man alive threw harder") and Hugh Bedient. Wood won Games 1 and 4 but was roughed up in Game 7. Mathewson threw 11 innings in Game 2 (declared a tie because of darkness) and lost Game 5 to Bedient, although he allowed only five hits and no earned runs.

Mathewson and Bedient squared off again in Game 8, the final game. The Giants took the lead when outfielder Red Murray doubled in Josh Devore in the third. In the top of the fifth, Larry Doyle hit a screaming drive deep to right field. Boston right fielder Harry Hooper leaped into the air, snagged the fly, then had it pop out of his mitt (remember how small these gloves were). But miraculously, Hooper was able to reach out with his bare hand and grab it before he tumbled into the stands. Some called it the greatest catch they had ever seen.

The Sox tied it in the bottom of the seventh when a pinch-hitter batting for Bedient rapped a double to drive in a run. Sox manager Jake Stahl brought in Wood, who had lasted just one inning the day before. Now the two staff aces were opposing each other. The heat was on.

Neither team could muster offense through the eighth and ninth innings. In the top of the 10th, Murray doubled for the Giants. Next up was "Bonehead" Fred Merkle, who singled past second base. Center fielder Speaker bobbled the ball momentarily and Murray hustled home. Speaker's miscue was amazing in itself; just the day before, the remarkable Speaker had performed an unassisted double play—the only time an outfielder has ever done that in a Series.

The last of the 10th was one that put every fan of both teams through an emotional wringer of preposterous dimensions. Wood, normally a good hitter, had injured his hand making the final play of the top of the inning and couldn't bat. So Stahl looked down his bench and found Clyde Engle, a .234 hitter for the season. Mathewson needed just three outs to put the world-championship flag in New York's pocket.

Engle lifted a lazy fly ball to center, where reliable Fred Snodgrass camped under it. But when the ball hit his glove, it kept going. Snodgrass instantly landed a place in baseball's pantheon of postseason bumblers, as his error became known as the "$30,000 muff." Engle reached second. Snodgrass's mother, "watching" the game via an electronic scoreboard in a Los Angeles movie theater, acted appropriately. She fainted.

Next up was Hooper, who slugged a shot deep into center. Snodgrass, taking no time to brood over his error, outran the ball to make a spectacular catch of a sure triple, then fired the ball back to the infield—and just barely missed doubling up Engle on his way back to second. Then, most atypically, Mathewson issued a walk to Steve Yerkes. (Christy had walked just 34 men in 310 innings that year.) At the plate was the dangerous Speaker.

One of Mathewson's famous fadeaways fooled Speaker, and Tris could only loft a short foul pop between home and first. But first baseman Merkle stopped as if frozen in his tracks and catcher Chief Meyers had to exert a furious dive to try and catch the foul. He came up short, and Speaker had life. Allegedly, someone was shouting "Chief!" for the catcher to make the play. If that person was Mathewson, he made the wrong call. If it was the tricky Speaker, he made the right one.

The now-furious Mathewson heaved one that Speaker was able to line into right. Engle scored to tie the game and the runners moved up on the throw home. After an intentional walk, Larry Gardner poked a fly to right deep enough to score Yerkes with the winning run. It was a most dramatic conclusion to a most dramatic Series.

RED SOX 3, GIANTS 2

New York	AB	R	H	RBI	Boston	AB	R	H	RBI
Devore rf	3	1	1	0	Hooper rf	5	0	0	0
Doyle 2b	5	0	0	0	Yerkes 2b	4	1	1	0
Snodgrass cf	4	0	1	0	Speaker cf	4	0	2	1
Murray lf	5	1	2	1	Lewis lf	4	0	0	0
Merkle 1b	5	0	1	1	Gardner 3b	3	0	1	1
Herzog 3b	5	0	2	0	Stahl 1b	4	1	2	0
Meyers c	3	0	0	0	Wagner ss	3	0	1	0
Fletcher ss	3	0	1	0	Cady c	4	0	0	0
McCormick	1	0	0	0	Bedient p	2	0	0	0
Shafer ss	0	0	0	0	Henriksen	1	0	1	1
Mathewson p	4	0	1	0	Wood p	0	0	0	0
					Engel	1	1	0	0
Totals	38	2	9	2	Totals	35	3	8	3

New York	0	0	1	0	0	0	0	0	0		1
Boston	0	0	0	0	0	0	1	0	0		2

E: Doyle, Snodgrass, Speaker, Gardner 2, Stahl, Wagner. LOB: New York 11, Boston 9. 2B: Gardner, Henriksen, Herzog, Murray 2, Stahl. SB: Devore. SH: Gardner, Meyers.

New York	IP	H	R	ER	BB	SO
Mathewson (L)	9.2	8	3	2	5	4
Boston						
Bedient	7	6	1	1	3	2
Wood (W)	3	3	1	1	1	2

T: 2:37 Att: 17, 034

SENATORS 4, GIANTS 3
1924 WORLD SERIES, GAME 7

WALTER JOHNSON was one of the greatest pitchers in baseball history. Unfortunately, he played for a rotten team. The Washington Senators of Johnson's era were routinely second-division fodder. Walter could win, but few others could. It had gotten so bad by 1924 that the 36-year-old Johnson, winner of 354 big-league games, announced he would retire after the season.

His team rallied behind him and knocked over the three-consecutive American League champs, the Yankees, by two games to give Washington its first pennant ever, in 38 seasons of professional D.C. baseball. Led by their spunky second baseman/manager, Bucky Harris, the Senators faced off in the Series against NL powerhouse New York. John McGraw's Giants, four straight NL winners and twice world champions, were the opposite of the new-kid winners in Washington.

But matters started poorly for the Washingtonians. In Game 1, Johnson was rapped around for 14 hits and four runs as he took the loss in a 12-inning thriller. The two teams took turns winning in Games 2, 3, and 4, but Johnson was mistreated by Giant bats in Game 5, allowing 13 hits and six runs in another Senator defeat. The Nats took Game 6, though, setting up the wonderful machinations and weird events of Game 7.

The first chess move belonged to Harris. In an attempt to get red-hot lefty hitter Bill Terry out of the Giant lineup, he started seldom-used right-hander Curly Ogden, then switched to lefty George Mogridge after just one out in the first inning. McGraw didn't take the bait; Terry started and stayed in the game. For a while.

Giant starter Virgil Barnes held the first 10 Nats hitless, but then Harris got his team rolling with a solo homer. In the sixth, his pitching ploy worked. With two on and none out, McGraw sent in a pinch-hitter for Terry. And Harris promptly inserted relief specialist Firpo Marberry. Terry's left-handed power was gone from the game, but it didn't hurt—yet. A fly ball, a single, and two consecutive infield errors pushed three Giants across.

The score stayed 3-1 till the bottom of the eighth. The exceptionally durable Muddy Ruel, who had caught all but seven of the Nats' games that year and every inning of the World Series, picked the perfect time for his first Series hit, as he advanced a runner to third. Then, with the bases loaded and two men out, Harris grounded sharply to third, where 18-year-old Freddy Lindstrom (the youngest player ever in a World Series) could only watch in dismay as the ball hit a pebble and bounced over his head into short left field. Two runners scored. The game was tied. And coming in to pitch for the Senators was none other than Walter Johnson.

He faced some tough situations, including a one-out triple by Frank Frisch in the ninth (Terry would have batted that inning), and two men on in the 11th. All in all, six batters reached against him. But when things were tough, Walter was tougher. Relying on grit and smarts, he kept the Giants off the scoreboard, fanning five of them in four innings. When it came to the last of the 12th, the score was still knotted at 3.

With one out, Ruel came to bat and lifted a foul pop-up around home plate. Giant catcher Hank Gowdy tossed his mask aside and waited for the ball to drop. But as Hank circled under it, he stepped into his mask. "It stuck on my foot like a bear trap," he recalled later. Trying to shake the mask off his foot and simultaneously chase the pop, Hank failed at both. The ball fell for an error, and Ruel responded by rapping a double past third.

Next up, Walter Johnson. Harris had no intention of removing his superstar now, especially since Johnson was an excellent hitter. He slapped a grounder to short, where Travis Jackson fumbled the ball. Johnson was safe at first, and Ruel held at second.

Then lightning struck twice. As historian Fred Lieb said, "All the gremlins and other little imps were working for Washington." Earl McNeely grounded to third, but the ball bounded over Lindstrom's head—again! Was it the same pebble? Ruel romped home, and the Senators had become world champs in highly improbable fashion. As for Johnson, he decided not to retire. He stuck around and took the Nats to the Series again in 1925.

SENATORS 4, GIANTS 3

New York	AB	R	H	RBI	Washington	AB	R	H	RBI
Lindstrom 3b	5	0	1	0	McNeely cf	6	0	1	1
Frisch 2b	5	0	2	0	Harris 2b	5	1	3	3
Youngs rf-lf	2	1	0	0	Rice rf	5	0	0	0
Kelly cf-1b	6	1	1	0	Goslin lf	5	0	2	0
Terry 1b	2	0	0	0	Judge 1b	4	0	1	0
Meusel lf-rf	3	0	1	1	Bluege ss	5	0	0	0
Wilson lf-cf	5	1	1	0	Taylor 3b	2	0	0	0
Jackson ss	6	0	0	0	Leibold	1	1	1	0
Gowdy c	6	0	1	0	Miller 3b	2	0	0	0
Barnes p	4	0	0	0	Ruel c	5	2	2	0
Nehf p	0	0	0	0	Ogden p	0	0	0	0
McQuillan p	0	0	0	0	Mogridge p	1	0	0	0
Groh	1	0	1	0	Marberry p	1	0	0	0
Southworth	0	0	0	0	Tate	0	0	0	0
Bentley p	0	0	0	0	Shirley	0	0	0	0
					Johnson p	2	0	0	0
Totals	45	3	8	1	Totals	44	4	10	4

New York	0	0	0		0	0	3		0	0	0		0	0	0
Washington	0	0	0		1	0	0		0	2	0		0	0	1

DP: New York 2, Washington 1. E: Jackson 2, Gowdy, Judge, Bluege 2, Taylor. LOB: New York 10, Washington 8. 2B: Goslin, Leibold, Lindstrom, McNeely, Ruel. 3B: Frisch. HR: Harris. SB: Youngs. SH: Lindstrom, Meusel.

New York	IP	H	R	ER	BB	SO
Barnes	7.2	6	3	3	1	6
Nehf	.2	1	0	0	0	0
McQuillan	1.2	0	0	0	0	1
Bentley (L)	1.2	3	1	1	1	0
Washington						
Ogden	.1	0	0	0	1	1
Mogridge	4.2	4	2	1	1	3
Marberry	3	1	1	0	1	3
Johnson (W)	4	3	0	0	3	5

T: 3:00 Att: 31,667

ATHLETICS 10, CUBS 8
1929 WORLD SERIES, GAME 4

BABE RUTH INTRODUCED the era of the "Big Bang" to baseball in 1920, but it wasn't until the late '20s that the game truly began to be dominated by big, brawny sluggers who scowled, flexed their muscles, and hit the ball a mile. In 1929, four teams scored more than 900 runs and three others totalled more than 896. That year, each league topped 6,100 runs scored. Only 10 years earlier, *both leagues combined* for just 8,657 runs.

The 1929 World Series matched two teams of bruisers. The Philadelphia Athletics featured muscle-on-muscle Jimmie Foxx, banger of 33 homers that season, plus Al Simmons, who cracked 34 and drove in 157 runs to lead the league. And these weren't one-dimensional hitters: Foxx batted .354 and Simmons .365, and Al hit 41 doubles too. Bing Miller and Mickey Cochrane hit over .330.

The Chicago Cubs countered with some meat of their own. Hack Wilson cleared the NL fences 39 times. His 159 RBI led the league. Rogers Hornsby, called by many the greatest right-handed hitter ever, matched Wilson in homers and chipped in 47 doubles, a .380 batting average, and a league-leading .679 slugging percentage. Joining Wilson in the outfield were two more pretty fair hitters. Kiki Cuyler pounded the ball at a .360 clip and homered 15 times. Riggs Stephenson homered twice more than Kiki and batted two points higher. The three drove in 371 runs and scored 337. It was probably the most potent outfield ever to swing a stick.

Thus, it was no surprise when the turning point of the 1929 World Series was an offensive explosion. It just turned out to be one of the most dramatic such detonations in baseball history.

The Series opened in Chicago's Wrigley Field, always a hitter's favorite. But A's manager Connie Mack threw Chicago a curveball before the first game even started. Instead of opening with his ace, Lefty Grove, Connie put Howard Ehmke, a 35-year-old part-timer, in the box. All old Howard did was set a World Series record for strikeouts that would stand for 24 years, and the A's won 3-1. They took Game 2 9-3. When the Series moved to Philadelphia for Game 3, a three-run inning was all the Cubs needed, as Guy Bush held the A's to just one run.

In Game 4, Charlie Grimm's fourth-inning two-run homer brightened the day for the visiting Cubs. They then exploded with five straight singles in the sixth on their way to five more runs. When they tacked on their eighth run in the seventh, the Cubs looked certain to tie the Series at two games each.

Cubs starter Charlie Root had allowed just three hits as the last of the seventh began. So when Simmons led off with a homer, the Cubs weren't frightened, even though the hit landed on the roof atop the left-field stands. Foxx followed with a sharp single. Miller's short fly to center dropped in front of Wilson, who lost the ball in the sun. Then Jimmy Dykes smacked a single to left and the A's had another run. At this point, Mack offered his men some sage advice: Since Root is losing it, he'll be trying to groove every pitch. Swing at everything.

Joe Boley responded by rapping a single, and the score was 8-3. A pop to short by the next batter didn't slow things down, because Max Bishop swatted in another run with a liner over Root's head. Cubs manager Joe McCarthy had seen enough, and he brought in veteran Art Nehf to face Mule Haas. Wilson lost Haas's fly ball in the sun, but this time it went over his head. By the time he chased it down, Haas had a three-run, inside-the-park homer. The A's were just one run down.

And they weren't through. Cochrane was walked, a new pitcher was called in, and Simmons came to bat again. Al grounded to third, but a weird hop sent the ball over the third baseman's head. Foxx then swatted his second hit of the inning and Cochrane scored the tying run. McCarthy called in his fourth pitcher of the inning, who promptly hit Miller with a pitch and then gave up a two-run double to Dykes, which was nearly flagged down by a diving Stephenson.

The A's had scored 10 runs. Wilson, normally a good fielder, bore the brunt of the criticism for his

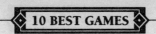

two bad plays on a terribly sunny day. As for the Series, the A's won it in Game 5 with three runs in the bottom of the ninth.

ATHLETICS 10, CUBS 8

Chicago	AB	R	H	RBI	Philadelphia	AB	R	H	RBI
McMillan 3b	4	0	0	0	Bishop 2b	5	1	2	1
English ss	4	0	0	0	Haas cf	4	1	1	3
Hornsby 2b	5	2	2	0	Cochrane c	4	1	2	0
Wilson cf	3	1	2	0	Simmons lf	5	2	2	1
Cuyler rf	4	2	3	2	Foxx 1b	4	2	2	1
Stephenson lf	4	1	1	1	Miller rf	3	1	2	0
Grimm 1b	4	2	2	2	Dykes 3b	4	1	3	3
Taylor c	3	0	0	1	Boley ss	3	1	1	1
Root p	3	0	0	0	Quinn p	2	0	0	0
Nehf p	0	0	0	0	Walberg p	0	0	0	0
Blake p	0	0	0	0	Rommel p	0	0	0	0
Malone p	0	0	0	0	Burns	2	0	0	0
Hartnett	1	0	0	0	Grove p	0	0	0	0
Carlson p	0	0	0	0					
Totals	35	8	10	6	Totals	36	10	15	10

Chicago	0	0	0	2	0	5	1	0	0
Philadelphia	0	0	0	0	0	0	10	0	x

DP: Philadelphia 1. E: Wilson, Cuyler, Miller, Walberg. LOB: Chicago 4, Philadelphia 6. 2B: Cochrane, Dykes. 3B: Hornsby. HR: Grimm, Haas, Simmons. SH: Boley, Haas, Taylor.

Chicago	IP	H	R	ER	BB	SO
Root	6.1	9	6	6	0	3
Nehf	0	1	2	2	1	0
Blake (L)	0	2	2	2	0	0
Malone	.2	1	0	0	0	2
Carlson	1	2	0	0	0	1
Philadelphia						
Quinn	5	7	6	5	2	2
Walberg	1	1	1	0	0	2
Rommel (W)	1	2	1	1	1	0
Grove (SV)	2	0	0	0	0	4

HBP: Miller (by Malone).

T: 2:12 Att: 29,921

Phillies 4, Dodgers 1
OCTOBER 1, 1950

THE BROOKLYN DODGERS of the late 1940s and early '50s were a true powerhouse. In fact, if they hadn't lost two games (this one and Game 3 of the '51 playoffs), they would have been National League pennant-winners *five times in a row,* and seven out of eight. Interestingly, those two games are both listed here among the 10 best contests of all time.

The Dodgers were sluggers: Gil Hodges, Duke Snider, and Roy Campanella all hit more than 30 home runs in 1950; Jackie Robinson, Carl Furillo, and Snider all topped the .300 mark. They led all National League teams in runs, hits, homers, stolen bases, batting, and slugging. The Dodgers had two 19-game winners on their staff: Don Newcombe and Preacher Roe.

The Phillies were the opposite of a dynasty. They hadn't won a pennant since 1915 and had been dubbed the "Phutile Phils" for their routine second-division finishes. But the 1950 squad had some talented young players, as well as a fierce desire to win. Only one Phillie regular in 1950 was 30 years old. Even their starting pitching was young, with 23-year-old Robin Roberts and 21-year-old Curt Simmons the mainstays. Quickly dubbed the "Whiz Kids," they moved into first in late July. By September 18, they had a 7½-game lead over Boston, with Brooklyn 8½ back. It looked as though the Kids would coast.

But before long, weird things began to happen. Two of their starting pitchers got hurt and were out for the season. Simmons, sporting a 17-8 record, was called into the military in mid-September. Ace hurler Roberts slumped, failing at six chances to win his 20th game. And the Dodgers were coming on. The Phillies lost seven of nine games; Brooklyn won 12 of 15. The Phils were two in front, with the season's final two games scheduled in Brooklyn. The Dodgers took the first game 7-3 to close the gap to one.

Not surprisingly, the final game was attended by the largest crowd of the season at Ebbets Field—35,073. Some reports said 30,000 other fans were turned away. Newcombe, looking for his 20th win, was to square off against Roberts, still stuck on 19. Roberts was pitching for the third time in five days; manager Eddie Sawyer saw little use in saving his star for the future.

Roberts had the Dodgers eating out of his hand, allowing just one hit through the first four innings. The Phils were hitting singles against Newcombe, but they could get no farther, managing just one run through six innings.

The Dodgers evened the score in the bottom half of the sixth, and in a most Dodger-like way. Shortstop Pee Wee Reese hit a fly ball that got stuck between the screen and the right-center-field wall.

When no one could reach it, the umps ruled it a home run. The Dodger faithful could see their prayers coming true.

The Phils put men on base in the seventh, eighth, and ninth, but Newcombe held firm. In the last of the ninth, Dodgers outfielder Cal Abrams led off with a walk. Reese singled him to second. Snider could have bunted the runners over, but instead he lined a single to center. Phils center fielder Richie Ashburn charged the ball, snatched it on one hop, and threw a perfect strike home to catcher Stan Lopata. Abrams, unwisely sent in by the third base coach, was a dead duck. The Dodgers hadn't won—yet. But now they had men on second and third, still with one out.

Robinson was walked intentionally. Furillo then popped out foul on the first pitch from Roberts. Dodger slugger Hodges skied a long fly to right-center, but Del Ennis snagged it. The Phils and Dodgers were going to extra innings to determine the NL pennant-winner.

Roberts led off for the Phils, as manager Sawyer knew he had his best in the game and saw no reason to change that. The pitcher smashed a single off Newk. A single by Eddie Waitkus followed, but Newcombe pounced on an Ashburn bunt and courageously threw out Roberts at third. (On his headfirst slide, Robin got an eyeful of lime.) Next up was Dick Sisler, 29 years old but playing in only his fourth full season. On a 1-2 pitch, Sisler popped a fly to left that just barely cleared the fence, 348 feet away. A three-run homer.

Roberts's lime-impaired vision and the darkening skies weren't enough to derail the Philadelphia express. A fly ball, strikeout, and pop-up were all the three Dodger batters could muster. Robin Roberts finally had his 20th victory, and the upstart Phils had won the pennant against the potent Dodgers.

PHILLIES 4, DODGERS 1

Philadelphia	AB	R	H	RBI	Brooklyn	AB	R	H	RBI
Waitkus 1b	5	1	1	0	Abrams lf	2	0	0	0
Ashburn cf	5	1	0	0	Reese ss	4	1	3	1
Sisler lf	5	2	4	3	Snider cf	4	0	1	0
Mayo lf	0	0	0	0	Robinson 2b	3	0	0	0
Ennis rf	5	0	2	0	Furillo rf	4	0	0	0
Jones 3b	5	0	1	1	Hodges 1b	4	0	0	0
Hamner ss	4	0	0	0	Campanella c	4	0	1	0
Seminick c	3	0	1	0	Cox 3b	3	0	0	0
Caballero	0	0	0	0	Russell	1	0	0	0
Lopata c	0	0	0	0	Newcombe p	3	0	0	0
Goliat 2b	4	0	1	0	Brown	1	0	0	0
Roberts p	2	0	1	0					
Totals	38	4	11	4		33	1	5	1

Philadelphia	0	0	0	0	0	1	0	0	0	3
New York	0	0	0	0	0	1	0	0	0	0

DP: Philadelphia 1, Brooklyn 1. LOB: Philadelphia 7, Brooklyn 5. 2B: Reese. HR: Reese, Sisler. SH: Roberts.

Philadelphia	IP	H	R	ER	BB	SO
Roberts (W)	10	5	1	1	3	2

Brooklyn	IP	H	R	ER	BB	SO
Newcombe (L)	10	11	4	4	2	3

T: 2:35   Att: 35,073

GIANTS 5, DODGERS 4
1951 NL PLAYOFFS, GAME 3

No RIVALRY has ever surpassed the one between the New York Giants and Brooklyn Dodgers. These cross-borough, intraleague battles were amazing even when the two teams weren't very good. When both teams were solid, and fighting fiercely for the league championship, their confrontations were unlike anything else in the world.

And no game typified this brash, brilliant rivalry more than the third game of the 1951 playoffs. It was the culmination of a merely sensational pennant race featuring the greatest come-from-behind charge to the top ever, which ended the season in a flat-footed tie. Yet the winner would not be crowned until another comeback in the final half of the final inning of the final playoff game, with the outcome ultimately sealed by the most dramatic home run in baseball history—the "Shot Heard 'Round the World."

The Dodgers, who had won the pennant in 1947 and '49 and narrowly missed in '50, were expected to win the National League once again. By the middle of May, they established themselves in first; the Giants were in the second division.

But then two important things happened. The Giants brought up Willie Mays from Minneapolis, where he was batting a mere .477, and manager Leo Durocher (whose "defection" from Brooklyn to the hated Giants in '48 had made him anathema among the Flatbush faithful) installed the youngster in center field. Mays wasn't ready to hit .350 or 50 homers just yet, but it was clear to anyone with eyes that he would soon. Even despite a poor start, Durocher made it clear to Willie that the kid would be in center field "as long as I'm the manager." With Mays in center, a place had to be found for Bobby Thomson. He obligingly took over the third base spot, and the team began to click.

By early July, the Giants had moved into second place, but the Dodgers were still comfortably in front. On August 11, in fact, Brooklyn had a 13½-game lead, and Dodger manager Charlie Dressen (a Durocher protégé) offered this opinion to a writer: "The Giants is dead."

Durocher's boys didn't take to that. They went on an incredible tear, winning 39 of 47 games, including the last seven of the regular season. It took a 14th-inning home run by Jackie Robinson on the final day of the season to keep the Dodgers from winding up in second. The two teams finished with identical 96-58 records, and the National League prepared for its second-ever playoff, a best-of-three confrontation.

Monte Irvin and Thomson homered off Ralph Branca to give the Giants a 3-1 victory in Game 1 in Brooklyn, but Clem Labine shut them out 10-0 in the Polo Grounds in Game 2. The amazing season was down to one game again.

For Game 3, the teams started their aces: Don Newcombe for Brooklyn, Sal Maglie (nicknamed "The Barber" for his willingness to throw close to batters) for New York. Maglie stumbled in the first, allowing two walks and a single to give the Dodgers a run. After that, he was untouchable for six innings. Newcombe was unscored on till the seventh, when the Giants tallied on a double, bunt, and sacrifice fly.

In the eighth, the Dodgers punched out four singles around a wild pitch and intentional walk for three runs and a lead that looked insurmountable. From his station in the third base coaching box, Durocher had been heckling Newcombe. But Newk wasn't being affected. He put the Giants down in order in the last of the eighth.

But in the bottom of the ninth, Newcombe tired. Al Dark beat out an infield single. Don Mueller pushed a single to right past Gil Hodges's outreaching glove. One out later, lefty hitter Whitey Lockman went with a Newcombe outside pitch and comfortably slapped it into the left-field corner. One run scored to make it 4-2, and runners were on second and third.

Dressen called for a new pitcher. Two Dodgers were warming: Carl Erskine and Branca. Coach Clyde Sukeforth answered the manager's question with, "Branca's got more stuff," and Ralph replaced Newcombe, even though Branca had been victimized by a Thomson homer in Game 1.

The second pitch was a high inside fastball, which Thomson muscled down the left-field line. It cleared the fence 315 feet away. The fans went bonkers. Giants broadcaster Russ Hodges screamed "The Giants win the pennant!" into his mike nine times. The Giants had come back again. No one had ever seen anything like it.

GIANTS 5, DODGERS 4

Brooklyn	AB	R	H	RBI	New York	AB	R	H	RBI
Furillo rf	5	0	0	0	Stanky 2b	4	0	0	0
Reese ss	4	2	1	0	Dark ss	4	1	1	0
Snider cf	3	1	2	0	Mueller rf	4	0	1	0
Robinson 2b	2	1	1	1	Hartung	0	1	0	0
Pafko lf	4	0	1	1	Irvin lf	4	1	1	0
Hodges 1b	4	0	0	0	Lockman 1b	3	1	2	1
Cox 3b	4	0	2	1	Thomson 3b	4	1	3	4
Walker c	4	0	1	0	Mays cf	3	0	0	0
Newcombe p	4	0	0	0	Westrum c	0	0	0	0
Branca p	0	0	0	0	Rigney	1	0	0	0
					Noble c	0	0	0	0
					Maglie p	2	0	0	0
					Thompson	1	0	0	0
					Jansen p	0	0	0	0
Totals	34	4	8	3		30	5	8	5

Brooklyn	1	0	0	0	0	0	0	3	0
New York	0	0	0	0	0	0	1	0	4

DP: Brooklyn 2. LOB: Brooklyn 7, New York 3. 2B: Irvin, Lockman, Thomson. HR: Thomson. SH: Lockman.

Brooklyn	IP	H	R	ER	BB	SO
Newcombe	8.1	7	4	4	2	2
Branca (L)	0	1	1	1	0	0
New York						
Maglie	8	8	4	4	4	6
Jansen (W)	1	0	0	0	0	0

WP: Maglie.
T: 2:28 Att: 34,320

PIRATES 10, YANKEES 9
1960 WORLD SERIES, GAME 7

IN THE FIRST 90 YEARS of World Series play, the Series went to the ultimate game just 32 times. Most of those final games were not terrifically close, nor very exciting. Only 11 were decided by one run. But of those 11 one-run seventh games, one stands out for having the least likely script of all: Game 7 of the 1960 Series between the Yankees and Pittsburgh.

When Rocky Nelson homered for the Pirates with Bob Skinner on first in the last of the first inning, Pirate fans may have seemed relieved, but they knew they couldn't get too cocky. They knew this Yankee club could score. (In their three Series victories, they had pulverized the Pirates 16-3, 10-0, and 12-0.) The Pirates tacked on two more in the second for a 4-0 lead, but the hair-raising roller-coaster ride was just getting started.

Through the first four innings, Pirates starter and Cy Young winner Vern Law allowed only two small singles. A fifth-inning homer by Bill Skowron put the Yanks on the board. Yankee power exploded in the sixth. After a single and a walk, Law was replaced by Roy Face. After one out, Mickey Mantle singled and Yogi Berra crushed a three-run homer. The Yankees had regained the lead, 5-4.

Face disposed of the first two Yankees in the top of the eighth, then walked Berra. Two singles and a double later, the New Yorkers had quickly extended their lead to 7-4. The Pirates were three runs down with just six outs to go. However, the Pirates had built a deserved reputation as masters of the comeback. Of their 95 wins that season, 28 were come-from-behind efforts in games they were losing in the sixth inning or later. A leadoff single by pinch-hitter Gino Cimoli got the amazing eighth off and rolling for Pittsburgh. The next batter, Bill Virdon, chopped down on a pitch and grounded it toward short, a likely double-play ball. But Yank shortstop Tony Kubek, uncertain how to play the wicked hops of the notorious Forbes Field infield, hesitated, moved back, then in, and the ball hit him in the throat. Both baserunners were safe with nobody out.

Dick Groat, National League bat champ and MVP, rapped a single to left, scoring Cimoli. Yanks hurler Bobby Shantz was replaced by Jim Coates. A sacrifice bunt moved runners to second and third, and then Nelson hit a short fly-out. The Bucs' last chance was Roberto Clemente, hitless in this game. Clemente chopped one to first, where Skowron gloved it and waited to toss to Coates for the third out. But Clemente was in full flight, and he outhustled the pitcher to the bag. Another run in, 7-6 Yanks.

Hal Smith, a former Yankee farmhand, got around on a pitch from Coates and powered it over the left-field wall, making himself one of the most unlikely heroes in World Series history (he would be one-upped in that regard minutes later). Three Pirates scored, and the Bucs had turned the tide once again. Now they took a 9-7 lead into the top of the ninth.

But the Yankees weren't done, either. To try and end the Series, Bucs manager Danny Murtaugh brought in Bob Friend, the burly right-hander who had won 18 games in the regular season but who had been no puzzle for Yank batters; they had swatted him around for 11 hits and eight runs in just six innings of work. Bobby Richardson and former Pirates slugger Dale Long quickly rapped singles, and Harvey Haddix entered the game in relief.

With one out, Mantle singled in Richardson and the score was 9-8 Bucs. Then Mantle provided one of the most electrifying moments in World Series history. Berra lined a one-hopper down the first base line that Nelson speared. He stepped on first and then raised his arm to throw to second for the tag on Mantle that would end the Series.

But Mantle had not gone to second. His remarkable baseball instincts sent him back to first, where his diving dance-step kept him away from Nelson's attempted tag. This allowed the runner on third to score, and the Yankees had impossibly retied the score at nine runs each.

Then Bill Mazeroski, one of the greatest *defensive* players of all time, opened the last of the ninth with a home run over the left-field fence. The Pirates had won a World Series in highly improba-

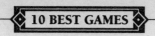

ble fashion, in a game marked by twists and turns and freaks and flukes—and brilliance. Shortly afterward, the Yankees fired manager Casey Stengel.

PIRATES 10, YANKEES 9

New York	AB	R	H	RBI	Pittsburgh	AB	R	H	RBI
Richardson 2b	5	2	2	0	Virdon cf	4	1	2	2
Kubek ss	3	1	0	0	Groat ss	4	1	1	1
DeMaestri ss	0	0	0	0	Skinner lf	2	1	0	0
Long	1	0	1	0	Nelson 1b	3	1	1	2
McDougald 3b	0	1	0	0	Clemente rf	4	1	1	1
Maris rf	5	0	0	0	Burgess c	3	0	2	0
Mantle cf	5	1	3	2	Christopher	0	0	0	0
Berra lf	4	2	1	4	Smith c	1	1	1	3
Skowron 1b	5	2	2	1	Hoak 3b	3	1	0	0
Blanchard c	4	0	1	1	Mazeroski 2b	4	2	2	1
Boyer 3b-ss	4	0	1	1	Law p	2	0	0	0
Turley p	0	0	0	0	Face p	0	0	0	0
Stafford p	0	0	0	0	Cimoli	1	1	1	0
Lopez	1	0	1	0	Friend p	0	0	0	0
Shantz p	3	0	1	0	Haddix p	0	0	0	0
Coates p	0	0	0	0					
Terry p	0	0	0	0					
Totals	40	9	13	9		31	10	11	10

New York	0	0	0	0	1	4	0	2	2
Pittsburgh	2	2	0	0	0	0	0	5	1

DP: New York 3. E: Maris. LOB: New York 6, Pittsburgh 1. 2B: Boyer. HR: Berra, Mazeroski, Nelson, Skowron, Smith. SH: Skinner.

New York	IP	H	R	ER	BB	SO
Turley	1	2	3	3	1	0
Stafford	1	2	1	1	1	0
Shantz	5	4	3	3	1	0
Coates	.2	2	2	2	0	0
Terry (L)	.1	1	1	1	0	0
Pittsburgh						
Law	5	4	3	3	1	0
Face	3	6	4	4	0	0
Friend	0	2	2	2	0	0
Haddix (W)	1	1	0	0	0	0

T: 2:36 Att: 36,683

RED SOX 7, REDS 6
1975 WORLD SERIES, GAME 6

WHEN IT COMES TO EXCITING COMEBACKS and thrilling plays, there have been more great *sixth* games in World Series history than *seventh* games. But this one in 1975 earned itself the honorific title, now and forever, as "Game 6."

The Reds and Red Sox seemed almost destined to meet there, as neither had much trouble disposing of their divisional or LCS foes. They played themselves into a taut, emotional World Series. And even though no one knew it at the time, these two teams would change baseball forever.

Cincinnati was the "Big Red Machine," a high-scoring attack supported by a brilliant defense, excellent team speed, and a manager willing to deal for a pitching advantage on a moment's notice—Sparky "Captain Hook" Anderson. Two of its starters, Joe Morgan and Johnny Bench, are in the Hall of Fame. A third starter, Pete Rose, is considered by many to deserve a spot there too.

The Red Sox, on the other hand, seemed stitched together. Their great rookie tandem of Fred Lynn and Jim Rice was only half-there for the Series; Rice was out hurt. Elder statesman Carl Yastrzemski was now a first baseman, but the whole team played Yaz-style, making heady plays when they had to.

Game 6 was delayed three days by a steady Boston rain. It was as if the gods were mercifully forestalling the inevitable; Boston had reached the Series only twice since 1918 and had lost each time. They trailed in this Series three games to two.

But soon after the game began on October 21, Lynn pounded a two-out Gary Nolan pitch into Fenway's center-field bleachers, and the Sox had a delightful 3-0 lead. Pitching magician Luis Tiant lost the lead to the Reds in the fifth, with the key hit being a two-run triple by Ken Griffey on which Lynn banged hard against the wall in pursuit. As Lynn lay crumpled against the fence, some people feared he was dead.

In the seventh, a two-out double by George Foster sent Griffey and Morgan home, and the Reds' lead was 5-3. Cesar Geronimo's homer added the sixth run in the top of the eighth. The spirits of Bostonians were flagging.

Lynn opened up the last of the eighth with a single off the leg of relief pitcher Pedro Borbon, and Rico Petrocelli worked the pitcher for a walk. Anderson immediately called for his bullpen ace, Rawley Eastwick. Two outs later, Bernie Carbo was sent to hit for pitcher Roger Moret. Carbo had belted a pinch homer in Game 3, but Eastwick seemed to have his number. Carbo barely stayed alive by getting wood on a 2-2 pitch to send it foul.

But then Eastwick made a mistake, and Carbo crushed it into the center-field stands, a hit one sports writer described as "a giant electric jolt." Fenway Park was rocking. The Red Sox had miraculously tied the game. The Sox seemed seconds away from winning it when they loaded the bases with none out in the last of the ninth. But a fly ball down the left-field line by Lynn was grabbed by Foster, and George made a perfect throw home to double up Denny Doyle on a risky dash home.

By the top of the 11th, everyone—players, fans, TV audience—had this game firmly stuck in their gut. The ever-boyish Rose understood. He spoke for everyone when he came to bat and said to catcher Carlton Fisk, "This is a great game, isn't it? Isn't this fun?" Rose was hit by a pitch and forced at second. Morgan then smacked a ball into right field that looked like a sure home run. But Sox outfielder Dwight Evans went dashing back, made a sensational twisting, turning catch, and doubled off the runner who had left first and not returned.

All America was breathless when Fisk led off the bottom of the 12th. "Pudge" got under Pat Darcy's sinker and lifted it down the foul line, over the "Green Monster." The Red Sox had won one of the most thrilling games in history.

Perhaps even more important was the impact this game had on baseball. Experts of the time who had written off baseball as too slow and dull were proven wrong, as Game 6 was watched by 62 million people; 75 million tuned in to Game 7, won by Cincinnati. Baseball had recaptured the hearts of America, and the sport went on to unprecedented growth in the 1980s.

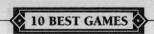

RED SOX 7, REDS 6

Cincinnati	AB	R	H	RBI	Boston	AB	R	H	RBI
Rose 3b	5	1	2	0	Cooper 1b	5	0	0	0
Griffey rf	5	2	2	2	Drago p	0	0	0	0
Morgan 2b	6	1	1	0	Miller	1	0	0	0
Bench c	6	0	1	1	Wise p	0	0	0	0
Perez 1b	6	0	2	0	Doyle 2b	5	0	1	0
Foster lf	6	0	2	2	Yastrzemski lf-1b	6	1	3	0
Concepcion ss	6	0	1	0	Fisk c	4	2	2	1
Geronimo cf	6	1	2	1	Lynn cf	4	2	2	3
Nolan p	0	0	0	0	Petrocelli 3b	4	1	0	0
Chaney	1	0	0	0	Evans rf	5	0	1	0
Norman p	0	0	0	0	Burleson ss	3	0	0	0
Billingham p	0	0	0	0	Tiant p	2	0	0	0
Armbrister	0	1	0	0	Moret p	0	0	0	0
Carroll p	0	0	0	0	Carbo lf	2	1	1	3
Crowley	1	0	1	0					
Borbon p	1	0	0	0					
Eastwick p	0	0	0	0					
McEnaney p	0	0	0	0					
Driessen	1	0	0	0					
Darcy p	0	0	0	0					
Totals	50	6	14	6		41	7	10	7

Cincinnati	0	0	0		0	3	0		2	1	0	0 0 0
Boston	3	0	0		0	0	0		3	0	0 1

DP: Boston 1, Cincinnati 1. E: Burleson. LOB: Cincinnati 11, Boston 9. 2B: Doyle, Evans, Foster. 3B: Griffey. HR: Carbo, Fisk, Geronimo, Lynn. SB: Concepcion. SH: Tiant.

Cincinnati	IP	H	R	ER	BB	SO
Nolan	2	3	3	3	0	2
Norman	.2	1	0	0	2	0
Billingham	1.1	1	0	0	1	1
Carroll	1	1	0	0	0	0
Borbon	2	1	2	2	2	1
Eastwick	1.1	2	1	1	1	2
McEnaney	.2	0	0	0	1	0
Darcy (L)	2	1	1	1	0	1
Boston						
Tiant	7	11	6	6	2	5
Moret	1	0	0	0	0	0
Drago	3	1	0	0	0	1
Wise (W)	1	2	0	0	0	1

HBP: Rose (by Drago). T: 4:01 Att: 35,205

METS 7, ASTROS 6
1986 NLCS, GAME 6

A T LEAST ONE BOOK has been written calling this the greatest game ever played. That statement may be true considering the game's length (4:42 to play 16 innings) and its importance. Had the Mets lost, they would have been forced to face Astros hurler Mike Scott again. Scott had already held them to one run in two complete-game victories in the Series. This was a super contest, and one that certainly made a difference.

These were the first two National League expansion teams, both starting out in 1962. The Mets had twice before tasted postseason play—in their "Miracle" year of 1969 and again in 1973, winning both LCS. The Astros' only postseason appearance had happened in 1980, when they lost an intense five-game series to Philadelphia.

The Mets lost Game 1 of this series to Scott, as Glenn Davis's homer was the game's only run. Bob Ojeda pitched a complete game in Game 2 to get the Mets even. After the Mets scored four times in the sixth inning of Game 3 to tie the score, the Astros took a one-run lead into the bottom of the ninth. But Wally Backman bunted himself on and Lenny Dykstra slugged a homer to win it for New York. Game 4 was another Scott masterpiece.

Game 5 went 12 innings, as Nolan Ryan faced Dwight Gooden, and the two were knotted at one run each after nine innings. Backman singled in the 12th, took second on a wild pickoff throw, and scored the winning run on a Gary Carter single.

With the prospect of a Game 7 against Scott staring them in the face, the Mets hoped to get out to a good start in Game 6 against Bob Knepper. But it was the Astros who jumped ahead. They scored three times off Ojeda—and would have had more if a suicide squeeze attempt hadn't been bungled. Another baserunning blunder cost Houston a scoring chance in the fifth.

But it didn't matter to Knepper, who held the Mets to two hits through eight innings. After eight, Houston was up 3-0. Dykstra led off for the Mets in the ninth, pinch-hitting for Rick Aguilera, and whistled a triple into center field. Mookie Wilson followed with a hard single that the Astros' second sacker couldn't glove, and one batter later Keith Hernandez belted a double that brought home Wilson. The Mets were within one run.

Dave Smith was brought in to replace Knepper, but his control left him. Two consecutive walks to Carter and Darryl Strawberry loaded the bases. Ray Knight hit a long fly to right that brought Hernandez in. The Mets had fought their way back to a tie, and the game soon entered extra innings. Neither team could push across any runs through the 13th inning. Roger McDowell held the Astros in check; Smith and Larry Andersen teamed up to stifle the Mets. The tension mounted.

In the top of the 14th, Carter singled and Strawberry walked. A too-hard bunt by Knight forced Carter at third, but Backman came through again, singling in the lead run. The Mets turned to their relief ace, Jesse Orosco, to close the door. Orosco got out the first hitter in the bottom of the 14th, but then always-clutch Billy Hatcher knocked an Orosco pitch into the foul-pole screen in left. The Astros had dramatically retied the game.

The Mets came rolling back again, scoring three times in the top of the 16th. Hatcher misplayed a Strawberry pop-fly into a double, then Knight singled Strawberry home. A walk to Backman and two wild pitches by Jeff Calhoun, followed by another Dykstra base hit, sent the Mets into the last of the 16th up by three runs.

But the cantankerous Astros were not to be dismissed so easily. They came back with a roar. With one man out, former Dodgers star Davey Lopes appeared as a pinch-hitter and reached base on a walk. Both Bill Doran and Hatcher singled to bring one run home. After a force-out at second, Davis—the hero of Game 1—also responded with a single. New York's lead was down to 7-6, with two out and two men on.

Orosco and Kevin Bass battled it out to a 3-2 count before Bass chased an Orosco slider and missed. The Mets stormed to the mound and mobbed Orosco. New York had prevailed in the longest postseason game ever played.

METS 7, ASTROS 6

New York	AB	R	H	RBI	Houston	AB	R	H	RBI
Wilson cf-lf	7	1	1	1	Doran 2b	7	1	2	0
Mitchell lf	4	0	0	0	Hatcher cf	7	2	3	2
Elster ss	3	0	0	0	Garner 3b	3	1	1	1
Hernandez 1b	7	1	1	1	Walling 3b	4	0	0	0
Carter c	5	0	2	0	Davis 1b	7	1	3	2
Strawberry rf	5	2	1	0	Bass rf	6	0	1	0
Knight 3b	6	1	1	2	Cruz lf	6	0	1	1
Teufel 2b	3	0	1	0	Ashby c	6	0	0	0
Backman 2b	2	1	1	1	Thon ss	3	0	0	0
Santana ss	3	0	1	0	Reynolds ss	3	0	0	0
Heep	1	0	0	0	Knepper p	2	0	0	0
McDowell p	1	0	0	0	Smith p	0	0	0	0
Johnson	1	0	0	0	Puhl	1	0	0	0
Orosco p	0	0	0	0	Andersen p	0	0	0	0
Ojeda p	1	0	0	0	Pankovits	1	0	0	0
Mazzilli	1	0	0	0	Lopez p	0	0	0	0
Aguilera p	0	0	0	0	Calhoun p	0	0	0	0
Dykstra cf	4	1	2	1	Lopes	0	1	0	0
Totals	54	7	11	6		56	6	11	1

New York	0	0	0	0	0	0	0	0	3	0	0	0	0	1	0	3
Houston	3	0	0	0	0	0	0	0	0	0	0	0	0	1	0	2

DP: Houston 2. E: Bass. LOB: New York 9, Houston 5. 2B: Garner, Davis, Hernandez, Strawberry. 3B: Dykstra. HR: Hatcher 1. SB: Doran 2. SH: Orosco. SF: Knight.

New York	IP	H	R	ER	BB	SO
Ojeda	5	5	3	3	2	1
Aguilera	3	1	0	0	0	1
McDowell	5	1	0	0	0	2
Orosco (W)	3	4	3	3	1	5
Houston						
Knepper	8.1	5	3	3	1	6
Smith	1.2	0	0	0	3	2
Andersen	3	0	0	0	1	1
Lopez (L)	2	5	3	3	2	2
Calhoun	1	1	1	1	1	0

WP: Calhoun 2.

T: 4:42 Att: 45,718

METS 6, RED SOX 5
1986 WORLD SERIES, GAME 6

FOR A GAME ENDING that moves past improbability and somehow begins to tickle the realm of science fiction, Game 6 of the 1986 World Series is unsurpassed. Both the Mets and the Red Sox had been through debilitating League Championship Series. Both had fought back from near-certain defeat with near-miraculous effort. The Sox, in fact, were down three games to one and losing by three runs in the ninth inning of ALCS Game 5. They came back to win that game (on a Dave Henderson homer), and the next two as well.

With all that emotion spent on the part of these two teams, no one would have been astonished if one or the other had rolled over to a quick, painless World Series loss. But what nobody could have predicted was how much fight was still left in these two teams. The Sox won the first two games; the Mets the next two. The Red Sox took a tough 4-2 decision in Game 5.

Leading three games to two, the Red Sox had their chance to avenge both the "Curse of Babe Ruth" (for selling Ruth to the Yankees, the story goes, the Red Sox were supernaturally forbidden to win a World Series) as well as ugly comments about their character and guts. They were glad to have their ace, Roger Clemens, starting. The Mets countered with Bob Ojeda.

The Sox scored in the first, on a single by American League batting champion Wade Boggs and a Dwight Evans double. Then they scored again in the second inning, on singles by Spike Owen, Boggs, and Marty Barrett. Clemens set down six of the first nine Mets he faced on strikes. Darryl Strawberry walked to open the fifth, however, and after a stolen base, a single, and an error, the Mets were able to plate the tying run when Danny Heep grounded into a double play.

Boston reclaimed the lead in the top of the seventh. Barrett walked to lead off and moved to second on Bill Buckner's ground-out. Ray Knight gloved a smash by Jim Rice but threw poorly to first. Rice was safe; Barrett went to third. Then the Mets botched an Evans double-play grounder and Barrett scored. Rich Gedman singled to left but Mookie Wilson made a huge throw, nailing Rice trying to score.

The Mets came right back in the eighth to tie. Lee Mazzilli hit a pinch single, and Dykstra was safe when Sox hurler Calvin Schiraldi (who had replaced blister-fingered Clemens) tried to turn his bunt into a force at second but made a bad throw. When next hitter Wally Backman bunted too, Schiraldi made the wise play. Both runners advanced. After an intentional walk, Gary Carter's fly to left was deep enough for Mazzilli to tag and score. The first two Mets reached in the last of the ninth, but Schiraldi hung tough.

The 10th inning was almost too much to believe. First, Henderson yanked a Rick Aguilera pitch over the left-field wall. Two outs later, the Boggs/Barrett tandem struck again: a double, a single, and Boston had a two-run lead heading into the bottom of the 10th inning.

Schiraldi got both Backman and Keith Hernandez to fly out, and some of the Mets faithful began to leave the ballpark. Red Sox fans, meanwhile, began the process of uncorking the champagne that would celebrate 68 years of waiting. What happened next was "Twilight Zone" material. Gary Carter lofted a soft single to left field. Kevin Mitchell rapped a pinch single up the middle. Knight's bloop to center barely fell in for a single, scoring Carter and moving Mitchell to third.

Schiraldi was replaced by Bob Stanley to pitch to Wilson. The result was one of the greatest at-bats in Series history. With the count 2-2, Mookie fouled off consecutive Stanley offerings. The seventh pitch was wild inside; Mookie bent himself in half to avoid the pitch, and Mitchell roared home, with Knight heading to second. The game was tied.

After two more foul balls, Wilson topped the 10th pitch down the first base line. There stood Bill Buckner, long a solid defensive first sacker but now, at age 36, past his prime. The ball rolled under his glove, between his legs, and into short right. The Mets had pushed home three runs to stave off World Series defeat in spectacular—and bizarre—

fashion. The Mets took the title two days later, winning the seventh game 8-5.

METS 6, RED SOX 5

Boston	AB	R	H	RBI	New York	AB	R	H	RBI
Boggs 3b	5	2	3	0	Dykstra cf	4	0	0	0
Barrett 2b	4	1	3	2	Backman 2b	4	0	1	0
Buckner 1b	5	0	0	0	Hernandez 1b	4	0	1	0
Rice lf	5	0	0	0	Carter c	4	1	1	1
Evans rf	4	0	1	2	Strawberry rf	2	1	0	0
Gedman c	5	0	1	0	Aguilera p	0	0	0	0
Henderson cf	5	1	2	1	Mitchell	1	1	1	0
Owen ss	4	1	3	0	Knight 3b	4	2	2	2
Clemens p	3	0	0	0	Wilson lf	5	0	1	0
Greenwell	1	0	0	0	Santana ss	1	0	0	0
Schiraldi p	1	0	0	0	Heep	1	0	0	0
Stanley p	0	0	0	0	Elster ss	1	0	0	0
					Johnson ss	1	0	0	0
					Ojeda p	2	0	0	0
					McDowell p	0	0	0	0
					Orosco p	0	0	0	0
					Mazzilli rf	2	1	1	0
Totals	42	5	13	5		36	6	8	3

Boston	1	1	0	0	0	0	1	0	0 — 2
New York	0	0	0	0	2	0	0	1	0 — 3

DB: Boston 1, New York 1. E: Buckner, Evans, Gedman, Knight, Elster. LOB: Boston 14, New York 8. 2B: Evans, Boggs. HR: Henderson. SB: Strawberry 2. SH: Owen, Dykstra, Backman. SF: Carter.

Boston	IP	H	R	ER	BB	SO
Clemens	7	4	2	1	2	8
Schiraldi (L)	2.2	4	4	3	2	1
Stanley	0	0	0	0	0	0
New York						
Ojeda	6	8	2	2	2	3
McDowell	1.2	2	1	0	3	1
Orosco	.1	0	0	0	0	0
Aguilera (W)	2	3	2	2	0	3

HBP: Buckner (by Aguilera) WP: Stanley

T: 4:02 Att: 55,078

CHAPTER 5

10 BEST STADIUMS

PHYSICALLY, they're little more than steel, concrete, and sod, but to baseball fans these 10 classic ballparks each have delightful personalities: Some are quirky, some are festive, and some embrace the spirits of legends past. Overall, they are the best places to sit back, kick up your feet, and watch a ballgame.

Ebbets Field

DODGER STADIUM

IN CINCINNATI, around the turn of the century, they had a ballpark with the affectionate but grandiose name of "Palace of the Fans." The only park in major-league baseball today with a legitimate claim to that title is Dodger Stadium in Los Angeles.

Everything about Dodger Stadium is pretty: the grass, the palm trees beyond the fence, even the special combination of crushed red brick and calcium chlorate that makes up the infield dirt and outfield warning track. With rose bushes and other flowers, it takes a full-time staff of gardeners to keep things in bloom. Dodger Stadium has been the only ballpark completely repainted every off-season. It is more than 30 years old, but it looks and feels absolutely new.

Opened in 1962, the stadium was originally called Chavez Ravine after its site (they didn't want the Angels, who also played there, to feel like second-class citizens). Its seating capacity was 56,000, huge for its time; and with foresight, the architect designed ways to expand it to 85,000. However, that hasn't been necessary. This was the first park to be built using cantilevers instead of poles, so the seats are not as close to the field as they might be. Yet despite that and the large number of seats, sight lines are uniformly excellent. There are no obstructed-view seats.

The scoreboard is first-rate, with the lineup for both teams showing at all times. The scoreboard crew is so good, it is said, that they've been borrowed for some Super Bowls. The ushers are friendly and the restrooms are cleaner than yours at home.

It's no surprise that Dodger Stadium has been called "baseball's Taj Mahal," or that the Dodgers were the first team to break the three-million mark in single-season attendance. Perhaps the rarest thing about Dodger Stadium is that it is the last ballpark since Yankee Stadium in 1923 (and most likely the last ever) to be built totally with private funds. Of course, there was some public incentive: Walter O'Malley agreed to give L.A. the old Wrigley Field park (truly *primo* real estate by that point in time), and in return the Los Angeles city fathers politely condemned the land so it could be razed for the park. Thus, he was given the site almost for free.

The only real drawback (according to some fans) is that *grilled* Dodger Dogs are now available only on the blue level, upstairs. Dodger Dogs sold elsewhere are now boiled, as they are in most parks. Most people agree that the authentic Dodger Dog runs a close second to the Fenway Frank as the best authentic hot dog sold in a major-league park today.

In a world where the films with the biggest and loudest explosions seem to rate highest at the box office, and where fans love the 16-14 game, another aspect of special charm about Dodger Stadium is that it is unashamedly and unequivocally a pitcher's park. The expanse of foul territory is obviously detrimental to the hitter. Some batters claim that the pitching mound in Dodger Stadium is still higher than it is anywhere else. Don't go to Dodger Stadium in search of a seven-run inning.

Sandy Koufax, rated by many experts as the best left-hander in NL history, pitched most of his career here. Koufax was a supreme craftsman on the mound, never satisfied with anything less than brilliance. His perfect game on September 9, 1965, in Dodger Stadium was an absolute masterpiece. It almost had to be. Cubs opponent Bob Hendley allowed just one hit and one walk.

The scowl of Don Drysdale signified another style of superb Dodger pitching. Drysdale threw his fifth consecutive shutout in Dodger Stadium in 1968 on his way to the record for consecutive scoreless innings, which stood until another stellar Dodger righty, Orel Hershiser, broke it 20 years later. Dodger Stadium was the home of Mike Marshall, whose 106 appearances in 1974 was 14 more games than his own record, set in 1973. No one has come closer than a dozen since. Fernando Valenzuela enchanted fans with his mysterious motion and baffled hitters with his elusive screwball from the Dodger Stadium mound, and Japanese sensation Hideo Nomo sparked new magic in 1995.

When you look at the Dodger Stadium infield, it's easy to blink your eyes and see the infield tandem of Steve Garvey, Davey Lopes, Bill Russell, and Ron Cey still stationed there. From 1974 through 1981, that was the Dodger infield—the longest stint of unity in baseball history.

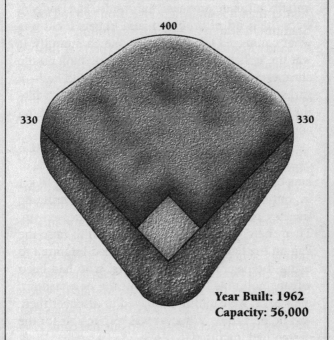

400

330

330

Year Built: 1962
Capacity: 56,000

EBBETS FIELD

THE NEW YORK BOROUGH OF BROOKLYN was always known for being baseball-mad. Part of the reason was Ebbets Field. Ebbets was the field that today's new parks pay homage to, if not actually imitate: intimate, unusual, enjoyable. The Dodgers were the heart of Brooklyn, and Ebbets Field was what connected the Dodgers to the community. It was the archetypal neighborhood park, built on the cheapest land owner Charles Ebbets could find—a garbage dump known as "Pigtown." And just like the slightly off-kilter nature of Brooklyn, anything could happen at Ebbets Field. And often did.

The first day Ebbets Field opened, April 9, 1913, offered a clue to what was to come. Thousands of fans bought bleacher seats and were waiting to get in, but couldn't. Whoever had the job of bringing the key to the bleacher section had messed up. Then there was the ceremonial march to raise the flag on the flagpole. But someone had forgotten to bring the flag. The sports writers, who had been writing columns of praise about the new stadium for weeks, were a little dismayed to discover there was no press box. Whoever was responsible for the design had forgotten it.

Ebbets Field was the home of great fans, like Hilda Chester, the loud woman in the bleachers with the clanging cowbell. It was the home of the "Dodger Sym-Phony," a noisy bunch of musicians who loved to play "Three Blind Mice" when the umps appeared (at the time, only three umpires worked each game). Of course, the Sym-Phony had to compete with legendary organist Gladys Gooding. Ebbets was the home of the first legendary piece of ballpark advertising. Clothier Abe Stark made this promise to batters: "Hit Sign, Win Suit." Abe's sign got him so much attention that he was actually elected the borough of Brooklyn's president.

The fans in Ebbets were close to the players, physically and otherwise. Cal Abrams talks about having conversations with the fans as he knelt in the on-deck circle. Nowhere before or since has a town and a team been so closely intertwined. This helps explain the many Brooklyn Dodger fans whose love for their team did not move to California in 1958. These fans reflexively curse at the mere hint of the name Walter O'Malley, the owner who moved the team.

Ebbets Field's upper deck hung out over the field, meaning a routine fly ball could nick the upper deck on the way down and the outfielder could catch a home run. The right-field wall and scoreboard were not a masterpiece of functional design, either. The scoreboard jutted out from the wall at a 45-degree angle for five feet; as a result, there were dozens of weird angles. Anything could happen on a ball hit down there. Once Dodger George Cutshaw hit a "ground-ball homer." His hit bounced crazily off the right-field concrete wall and over the fence.

In the 1920s and '30s, the ballclub became known as the "Daffiness Boys," as they incorporated the spirit of the park in their play. Ebbets Field is where Babe Herman did not triple into a triple play (as legend goes), but he was one of three Dodgers to wind up on third at the same time, so he doubled into a double play. This led to one of the great Dodger lines of all time. For years afterward, when one Dodger fan relayed the information to another that the Dodgers had three men on base, the response was, "Yeah? Which base?"

Casey Stengel had been a beloved member of the Daffiness bunch, and when he returned as a Pirate, the fans in Ebbets greeted him loudly. Casey responded by politely doffing his cap to the crowd. A bird flew out.

But in its 45 years of existence, a great deal of serious baseball history was made there too. Ebbets Field was where Jackie Robinson and Branch Rickey tore down the color line that had stood in baseball for more than 60 years. Ebbets Field's first night game, in 1938, was doubly historical; Redleg Johnny Vander Meer pitched a no-hitter that night, his second consecutive one. No one mentioned that the lights might not have been very good.

In the 1940s, the Dodgers changed from Bums to Champs, leading to some dramatic events. Dodger Mickey Owen cost the team Game 4 when he failed to hold on to a third strike in the 1941 World Series. Yankee Bill Bevens took a no-hitter two outs into the ninth inning of Game 4 of the '47 World Series, only to lose the no-hitter *and* the game on one swing of Cookie Lavagetto's bat. But in the glorious World Series of 1955, the Dodgers won all three games played at Ebbets. Johnny Podres beat the Yankees twice, and the world championship flag flew over Brooklyn for the only time.

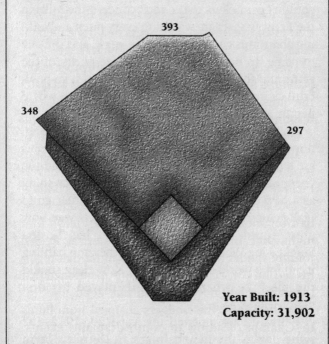

393

348

297

Year Built: 1913
Capacity: 31,902

FENWAY PARK

WHEN YOU GO TO A GAME IN FENWAY PARK, you can feel the history oozing out between the seats. It's now in its ninth decade of hosting major-league baseball, and no other park carries with it a greater sense of how baseball is forever linked to its past. The fans who go to games there know it. Even on a hot summer Friday night when other parks are filled with people who are there because they couldn't get tickets to the rock concert, the folks in the Fenway seats are watching every pitch and talking about this game, the one last week, and the one to come. In no place on Earth is the purity of the game and the fan's honest experience of it so powerful as in Fenway Park. It's not just a place where people go to watch baseball; it *is* baseball.

It's true that Fenway Park is not sweet-smelling, nor is it brand-spanking clean. But these attributes are overrated. Shopping malls smell great, and the "new wave" stadiums of the 1970s can be as shiny as a new dime. But where would you rather go to really enjoy a ballgame? To put it another way, how great could something smell that has hosted Smokey Joe Wood and Christy Mathewson battling it out for a world championship? How clean should the place be where Babe Ruth played his first major-league game?

Fenway Park opened on April 20, 1912, the same day as the new ballpark in Detroit, Navin

Field (later to become Tiger Stadium), opened. Both openings were delayed several days by bad weather. That year, the Red Sox won the pennant and took the World Series in Fenway. It was one of the most memorable Series ever—the Series of "Snodgrass's Muff" and Tris Speaker's title-winning single. The Red Sox also won pennants there in 1915 and '16, although they played the Series in larger Braves Field. When the Sox won the World Series in Fenway in 1918, the stars were an old unknown named George Whiteman and a kid pitcher named Ruth.

From the beginning, the Fenway field had some quirks that made playing there special. The grade of the field resulted in a slope up to the base of the left-field wall that rose 10 feet. Before long, it was known as "Duffy's Cliff" because Sox fielder Duffy Lewis played it like he owned it. Duffy's opposite was Smead Jolley. When he was traded to Boston in 1932, Jolley got a full day's special tutoring in dealing with the terrain. The next day, a batter lifted a long fly to left with the bases loaded and Jolley gracefully climbed the embankment. But when he realized he had overrun the ball and tried to come back to it, he fell head over heels. Jolley explained, "You spent all day teaching me how to run up that hill, but you never taught me how to get back down!"

In fact, there is more great baseball history in left field alone in Fenway Park than in many other places. This is where Ted Williams was stationed, where his fierce desire to win and his pride at being a great hitter shackled him during the 1946 World Series, the only one he ever appeared in. This is where Carl Yastrzemski patrolled, playing the wall like a violin and, in that star-crossed season of 1967, contributing one of the hottest bats ever to drive the Sox to a pennant.

In 1947, the ads that had covered the left-field wall were removed forever, and thus was created the "Green Monster"—that looming beast that to this day terrifies certain pitchers. The officially stated distance down the left-field line is 315 feet. Several measurements indicate this is an exaggeration by as much as seven feet, but the Red Sox refuse to let anyone perform an accurate measurement. It's part of the mystique.

This is the wall over which Carlton Fisk hit *the* home run in Game 6 of the 1975 World Series, the home run he somehow pushed into fair territory by the frantic waving of his arms. It's also the wall over which Bucky Dent homered to end what could have been another storybook season (1978). (Only twice has the American League been forced to go to a playoff to determine a league or division champion. Both times the games were played in Fenway. Both times the Red Sox lost.) In 1976, the steel panels that had covered the wall were removed and sold in pieces to benefit the Jimmy Fund, a favorite charity of Boston baseball stars.

Other notes: In 1940, the Sox felt that the 332-foot right-field fence was damping the homer stroke of up-and-coming superstar Ted Williams, so it was brought in 28 feet. And on May 17, 1947, a seagull decided it wasn't hungry anymore and dropped a three-pound smelt on the mound, landing in front of St. Louis Brown pitcher Ellis Kinder.

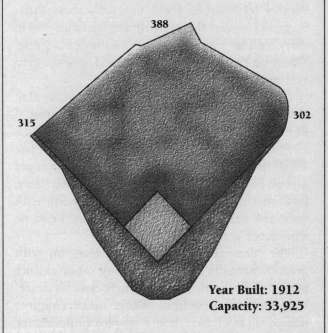

Year Built: 1912
Capacity: 33,925

FORBES FIELD

WHEN FORBES FIELD OPENED IN 1909, the reviews were raves. "For its architectural beauty, imposing size, solid construction, and public comfort and convenience, it has not its superior in the world," said the *1910 Reach Guide*. By the time the Pirates left Forbes Field in 1970, most Pittsburghers agreed the old ballpark was run-down, dirty, and an unpleasant place to watch a game. "Bring on the new stadium!" seemed to be the general consensus.

It's hard to believe how quaint that sounds today. Nowadays, architects are being paid large sums of money to try to re-create the magic that places such as Forbes Field had. Somehow, the fans of the late 1960s had forgotten how memories stay alive in old places, how ghosts call you back to previous times, how sharing a bleacher seat one afternoon with your son can connect you to sharing the same experience with your father.

The memory of Forbes Field lives on with greater intensity than that of any other extinct park. Ask the local chapter of the Society for American Baseball Research. While other chapters named themselves to honor *people* of importance to their baseball history, the Pittsburgh SABR members call themselves the "Forbes Field Chapter." Every October 13, a cadre of fans stands by the remaining left-field wall and listens to the radio broadcast of Game 7 of the 1960 World Series, ended by a homer at that very spot.

Forbes Field was built on top of a hill in an area of the city that was considered remote by most experts. But before long, the city began to grow up around the park, its bustling neighbors, and two universities—the University of Pittsburgh and what is now Carnegie-Mellon University. By the 1950s, the neighborhood was one of the city's most congested, noisy, and exciting. Forbes Field was built with a capacity of 23,000. By 1925, the seating was increased by 18,000.

Forbes Field truly had a park setting. And inside, the vast expanse of immaculately tailored grass was positively magical in its message. The deepest part of the park was 457 feet from home, just left of center field. Out there sat the batting cage, rolled out after batting practice. It was in play. Left field was an imposing 365 feet away down the line and 406 to left-center. The right-field line was just 300 feet away, but it was 375 feet in right-center, and the screen that ran from there to the line was 24 feet high. There were no cheap homers hit in Forbes Field.

But there were some monumental ones. Babe Ruth hit his last three on one afternoon there in 1935, and the final shot cleared the right-field roof—something no one had ever done before and something that would be done only 15 more times in the next 35 years. Bill Mazeroski hit a homer over the left-field wall that won the '60 Series over the dominating Yankees. It was the first Series win for the city in 35 years, an event that turned Pittsburgh inside-out with joy.

Ralph Kiner had the benefit of having left field moved in 30 feet to create "Greenberg Gardens" (later "Kiner's Korner"). Dale Long began and ended his streak of homering in eight consecutive games in Forbes Field. And Negro League great Josh Gibson of the Homestead Grays and Pittsburgh Crawfords rapped many a long one out of sight while playing in Forbes.

Forbes Field was noted for great defensive play. Honus Wagner, Roberto Clemente, and Mazeroski are all members of the all-time great glove team. In a 1909 game, the skies were threatening when the Giants' Red Murray made a spectacular bare-handed catch to end the game as a flash of lightning simultaneously lit up the yard. Yet no pitcher ever pitched a no-hitter in Forbes Field. Owen Wilson *did* hit 36 triples as a Pirate in 1912—a record much less likely to be broken than Roger Maris's 61 homers.

The grass may have been green, but for many years the infield was legendarily rock-hard. Pirate infielders loved the crisp bounces they got and often led the league in double plays. But when a newcomer was faced with "the rock pile," problems often ensued, such as the misplayed hopping ball that struck Yankee Tony Kubek in the throat and kept alive the Bucs' chances in the eighth inning of Game 7 of the '60 World Series.

For the ballpark's last 15 years, a statue stood outside the left-field wall of Forbes Field. It was a huge homage to a hugely talented and loveable ballplayer, the Pirates' Wagner, still the greatest shortstop of all time.

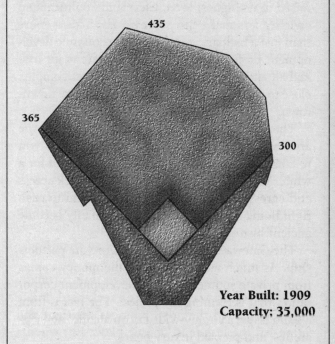

435

365

300

**Year Built: 1909
Capacity: 35,000**

JACOBS FIELD

IF ORIOLE PARK AT CAMDEN YARDS was the first attempt to build a ballpark in the heart of a city in order to bring economic revitalization to the area, then Jacobs Field—part of the vast Gateway Project in downtown Cleveland—is that concept raised to its highest level. Cleveland's political and civic leaders make the point clearly: This is more than just a ballpark; it is part of an economic development project that includes a new arena for basketball and hockey and an entertainment complex close to public transit, all meant to revitalize downtown.

There are new restaurants and sports bars in the area, and the thrust is clear: Cleveland wants you to come to an Indians game and stick around for a while. The 1970 belief that "fans want quick access and egress, so let's make it easy for them to rush right home after the game" has essentially become ancient history.

The Gateway Project is a public/private partnership. As much as two-thirds of the money comes from private sources, says the development corporation that is running the project. The rest is from a bond issue, a county-wide tax on alcohol and cigarettes, and prepaid luxury boxes.

The success of the overall effort at economic development is hard to measure in total (economists haggle over such things), but it is clear that

Indian attendance is higher than ever. After approaching a record attendance year (even with the strike) in 1994, the Tribe announced in early June of '95 that they had already sold more tickets than they had in their previous best year, 1948. In 1994, nearly 30,000 people took the tour of the new park, which helped raise over $40,000 for local charity.

Interestingly, the old parks built around the turn of the century were *not* usually in the center of town. They were frequently off at the end of the trolley line. Some parks were actually called "trolley parks," and the teams were often owned by the same people who owned the trolleys. It was a way to increase business in the outskirts of town. However, as cities grew, they often grew up around the bustle of the park, which became a part of the city's core.

The way the Cleveland ballpark melds into the city skyline is part of its exceptional charm, which led Paul Goldberger, architecture critic for *The New York Times,* to ponder the connection between city and country: "[It is] a place in which the idea of baseball and the idea of civic architecture come together, and in this sense...is part of the long tradition of ballparks.... [It] is in the meeting of...the soft perfection of the field with the hard lines of the city that the special quality of ball parks lies. The infield, finite and measured and in a sense urban itself, giving onto the outfield, vast and stretching and of no particular dimension—from the juxtaposition of these two things...comes the truth of the ball park, now rediscovered in our time."

In many ways, Jacobs Field surpasses Camden Yards as a fan's haven. In Camden, once you leave the seating area, you are blocked from a view of the game. But Cleveland's park has plenty of open areas and, in general, feels less confining than Camden. As you wait in line for your hot dog, you can turn around and watch the game. Then you can munch on your dog as you walk completely around the park and hardly ever miss a pitch.

Jacobs Field has the largest freestanding scoreboard in the United States, and it's a great one, providing the fans with tons of data on the game they're watching. It also offers the scores of every other big-league game, references to history, and, of course, baseball trivia. The main scoreboard actually has three sections: the Sony Jumbotron full-color instant replay board (26′ x 37′); the game-in-progress board (34′ x 64′), where you'll find the lineups and stats; and the Starburst color board (26′ x 37′), where you'll find everything else. The scoreboard makes the field asymmetrical.

With the exception of those in the uppermost seats, the 42,865 fans who can fit into Jacobs Field feel close to the action. In fact, the ground-level luxury box seats behind home plate put the fans 10 feet closer to the catcher than the pitcher is. Many feel that this cozy, delightful ballpark has ignited the players themselves. In the previous 34 years in the cavernous, dreary Municipal Stadium, the Indians didn't contend once for the pennant—despite several teams that had the talent to do so. In the first three years at Jacobs Field, the Tribe posted sensational records of 66-47, 100-44, and 99-62. Coincidence?

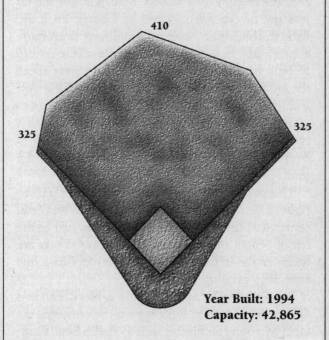

410

325   325

Year Built: 1994
Capacity: 42,865

ORIOLE PARK AT CAMDEN YARDS

WHEN THEY WERE EXCAVATING to build Oriole Park at Camden Yards, archaeologists uncovered the remains of a saloon. Research indicated it was the tavern once owned by George Ruth Sr., Babe Ruth's father. Nothing could have been more appropriate, because Camden Yards was meant to be built on the past—to take what was great about the old parks and combine it with the spiffiest new technologies and amenities. The objective was to make the ballgame experience as pleasurable as it could be. Camden Yards revolutionized the art of ballpark design forever. No one will ever build a multi-purpose, cookie-cutter oval again.

The park is delightfully asymmetrical: 318 to right, 333 to left, and 400 to dead center. But dead center isn't the deepest part of the park. Just to the left of center, the fence is 410 feet away. There are funny angles in the outfield to make extra-base hits especially exciting.

But Camden Yards' innovation is more than just design; it's location. Building on the concepts set forth by young architects such as Philip Bess, Camden Yards is part of the urban landscape. It fits in, in a friendly way, and in doing so becomes a hub for revitalization of the area. This makes it much more valuable to the city. The park then offers the community vastly increased revenue over and above what a suburban, all-alone stadium could do.

And Camden Yards has succeeded. Hugely. When it opened on April 6, 1992, it was called a "jewel" and a "miracle," and it still is one of the toughest tickets to get for any baseball game anywhere, regardless of whether the Orioles are playing terrifically or miserably. The Baltimore Inner Harbor development, already a hit before Camden Yards, is now even more popular. The first year there, the Orioles increased their attendance by more than a million fans (at higher ticket prices) over Memorial Stadium.

The park feels like it already has a history because of the historic elements in and around it. The warehouse beyond the right-field fence has become the park's signature element—like the ivy on the walls at Wrigley or the Green Monster at Fenway. Armrests on the aisle seats incorporate a hundred-year-old Oriole logo, echoing a similar design touch in the Polo Grounds. The architects and Oriole planning team had no qualms about borrowing from the past inside the park, because their design also respected the architecture of historic buildings outside the park. And Janet Marie Smith, Oriole planning coordinator, said, "It didn't cost any more than had we built a concrete round stadium."

The objective was fan intimacy. The front row of seats was 20 feet closer to the baselines than comparable seats in Memorial Stadium. Rex Barney, a former Dodger and a long-time Oriole P.A. announcer, paid it the highest compliment: "As close to Ebbets Field as any place I've ever seen."

The story of how Camden Yards came to be the marvelous creation that it is, and not just another Three Rivers or Veterans Stadium, makes marvelous reading in Peter Richmond's *Ballpark: Camden Yards and the Building of An American Dream*. The architectural firm had to be poked, prodded, cajoled, and scolded into making Camden Yards a place with historic evocations; it was what the Orioles wanted. The book's inside-front cover shows what the architect originally proposed. The inside-back displays what finally happened. For one thing, they planned to tear down that dumb old warehouse building. For another, they wanted to make the park symmetrical. Luckily, Orioles owner Eli Jacobs and team liaison Smith decided otherwise.

Of course, there were problems when the park opened. It was discovered that many of the seats didn't face home plate at all. Instead, they were aimed at someplace out behind second base. (Since then, many of them have been realigned.) Long-time Oriole fans complained about the higher prices for everything. Naturally.

Nevertheless, Camden Yards has earned a special reputation among those who have wondered for years why it was so hard to get a decent meal in a baseball park. Camden Yards' food is superb, from five kinds of hot dogs to authentic Maryland crab cakes to Boog Powell's marvelous barbecue (the street between the right-field stands and the warehouse is a kind of food court).

Camden Yards ushered in the new age of baseball parks, and did it in grand style. It was a change baseball desperately needed.

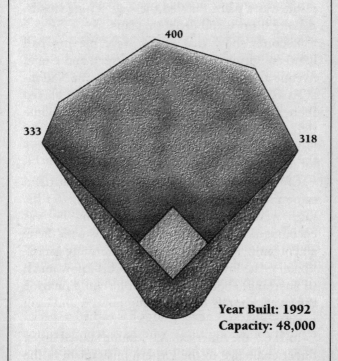

400

333

318

Year Built: 1992
Capacity: 48,000

Sportsman's Park
(Original)

The original Sportsman's Park had a long tradition of baseball history at the site. But it also had the greatest team in the innovative and important American Association, as well as the most ebullient, noisy, and cantankerous owner ever. The result was a place that led the way, setting trends, making history, and delighting fans.

Records show that teams were playing ball between Spring Avenue, Dodier Street, and Grand Avenue as early as 1866. In the 1870s, the National Association St. Louis Brown Stockings played there and the park was known as Grand Avenue Grounds. When the NA folded, replaced by the National League in 1876, St. Louis had a team there for just two seasons.

Chris Von der Ahe, a German immigrant and saloon keeper, had noticed how much better his sales were when a game was on, and he was encouraged to buy the land, build a new park there, and organize a team to play in barnstorming games. Von der Ahe loved the plan. He didn't know much (if anything) about baseball, but he could imagine the sweet sounds of beer being poured and cash registers ringing.

In 1882, the American Association started up, in direct challenge to the Eastern puritanism of the

National League. The Midwestern AA owners were savvy. They knew that baseball's future lay with the workingman, and that the workingman wanted to be able to have a refreshing alcoholic beverage while he watched the game, something the NL owners forbade. The American Association also offered its games for just 25 cents, half of the lowest ticket for an NL game. So the Eastern bigwigs gave the AA a nickname: "The Two-Bit Beer and Whiskey League." And Von der Ahe, of course, owned the St. Louis franchise.

The snooty comments of the NL owners got them nowhere. Within a few years, the AA was winning head-to-head battles in competing cities from the NL. And no team was more successful than Von der Ahe's Browns.

Von der Ahe was baseball's first brilliant huckster. If the Browns were at home, he'd raise a flag of a giant gold ball with the words "Game Today," which could be seen all over town. He ran newspaper ads touting the quality of his players and the excitement they offered (even if he sometimes seemed to miss the subtleties of the game). He had a phone line strung from the park to downtown so the team could keep fans not at the park informed about scores via large bulletin boards.

And it worked. In 1886, he had to double the capacity of Sportsman's Park from 6,000 to 12,000 to handle the abundant crowds. His beer garden in right field remained in play; a fielder could chase a ball among the patrons sitting at their tables (ducking their beer mugs if he was an opponent) and throw the ball in.

The pinnacle of American Association excitement happened in Sportsman's Park in 1886. In 1884, the two leagues had their champions play each other in the first example of a "World Series." Most people, though, didn't take it seriously; it was just another postseason exhibition series. In 1885, when they did it again, the Browns beat the Chicago White Stockings, and the National League team was miffed. They had "underrated" the St. Louis nine, and even though this "championship" stuff was no big deal, they were embarrassed. So in 1886, when the champion Browns met Chicago again, the stakes (at least in terms of pride) were high.

St. Louis won the best-of-seven Series in six games when Curt Welch came steaming home on a wild pitch in the last inning of the final game. It went down in history as "Curt Welch's $15,000 slide."

After winning the AA championship four straight seasons, the penurious Von der Ahe began selling off his superstars, and the team stopped winning. When the AA folded, Von der Ahe bought into the National League for the 1892 season and looked for new ways to encourage people to come to Sportsman's. He instituted nightly horse races, installed shoot-the-chutes rides, and put in a honky-tonk, announcing he intended to make his park "the

Coney Island of the West." For history and excitement, Sportsman's Park was the first great ballpark in baseball history.

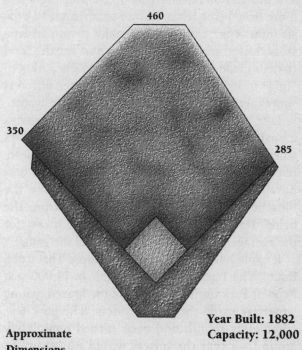

460

350

285

**Approximate
Dimensions**

**Year Built: 1882
Capacity: 12,000**

TIGER STADIUM

NO BALLPARK HAS EVER HAD ITS FANS FIGHT for it the way Detroit fans have battled to keep Tiger Stadium from being replaced by a suburban mall-type stadium. They have written books, instituted lawsuits, raised money for studies and repairs, and (twice) made a human chain around the park—to "hug" it. And with good reason. Tiger Stadium is simply one of the best places to watch a ballgame.

Like Wrigley, like Fenway (with which it shares a birthday), Tiger Stadium was built in the days when the average fan mattered. Ballparks then were not built with tax dollars and kept afloat with corporate luxury boxes (which always move the bleacher/grandstand fan farther away from the field). Tiger Stadium was built to make it easy for the average fan to have a great view of the game.

It could have been called "The House That Cobb Built." The Tigers were comfortable in 14,000-seat Bennett Park until the arrival of the brazen, young superstar made them contenders. The park was completely rebuilt and even turned completely around, so that the hitters would no longer be blinded by late afternoon sunlight. In addition, a dark hitter's background was installed—the first of its kind—so that batters would not have to look into white shirts. (Within two years, Major League Baseball decreed that all parks must have a hitter's background.) The result was a hitter's paradise.

The new park was renamed Navin Field in honor of the team's owner. By 1923, further expansion was necessary and a second deck was added from first to third. From 1935 through 1938, owner Walter Briggs expanded the seating to 58,000 by adding an outfield upper deck. He changed the name to honor himself—Briggs Stadium. In 1961, new owner John Fetzer asked the fans what name they wanted to give the place, and "Tiger Stadium" was the answer. It cost $20,000 to change the name. It could have cost more except that it was necessary to buy only two new letters ("T" and "E") to turn "Briggs" into "Tiger."

With a short right-field fence (325 feet) and reachable fences in left-center and right-center, the ballpark has been cozy for both fans and hitters. Some of the game's greatest batters ever were regulars at Tiger Stadium—Cobb, Harry Heilmann, Hank Greenberg, Mickey Cochrane, Al Kaline, and Cecil Fielder. The park's 440-foot center field (deepest in the majors) has led to some exciting three-base hits.

In its early days, the ballpark was tailored for its most outstanding player. The groundskeeper kept the dirt in front of home plate soaked down, so that Cobb's bunts wouldn't reach the infielders too quickly. Maybe they kept it a little too wet; the spot became known as "Cobb's Lake."

Tiger Stadium hosted consecutive World Series in 1934 and '35. When Tiger Goose Goslin singled in player/manager Cochrane in the last of the ninth in Game 6, 1935, with the winning run, Detroiters went bonkers. In four previous tries, they had never won a World Series.

But the fan proximity caused a real problem in the 1934 Series, providing baseball with one of its most embarrassing moments. The "Gashouse Gang" Cards and Tigers were similar in style—hard-nosed battlers. The Tigers had a 3-2 lead in games when the teams returned to Tiger Stadium for Game 6. But the Cards, behind Paul Dean, toppled them 4-3 to knot the Series. The Tigers and their fans were ready for another tough contest in Game 7, but they didn't get one. The Cards pummeled them with seven runs in the third, and when Joe Medwick tripled in another in the top of the sixth, he slid hard into Tiger Marv Owen. The two grappled for a while.

But the Tiger fans had something waiting for Medwick when he took his left-field position in the last of the seventh. Garbage. They threw fruit, sandwiches, pop bottles—anything they could find. Medwick had to leave the field. When they seemed to have quieted down, he came out again, but he once again was chased away by flying food. The game was delayed (Pepper Martin and Ernie Orsatti stayed loose by tossing a grapefruit back and forth) and commissioner Kenesaw Mountain Landis was ultimately forced to remove Medwick from the game for his own safety.

When Tiger Stadium added lights for night baseball in 1948, it was the last ballpark to do so—except for Wrigley Field, which held out for another 40 years. The right-field "Homer Deck" was copied and used by the Texas Rangers in their new home, The Ballpark in Arlington.

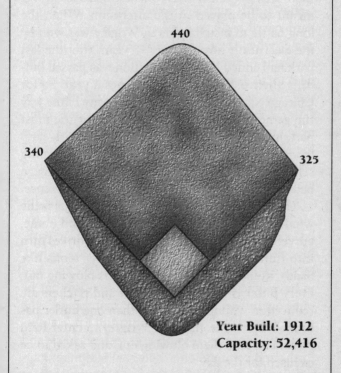

440

340

325

Year Built: 1912
Capacity: 52,416

WRIGLEY FIELD

THE EXPERIENCE OF WATCHING a baseball game in Wrigley Field is absolutely unique for several very important reasons. Not only is Wrigley a lovely place in a lovely setting, but most of the games there are day games. Everyone knows baseball was meant to be played in the afternoon. When the long battle to install lights in Wrigley was won by the electrically advantaged (40 years after the last park had added lights), legislation was passed limiting their use to 18 season games a year. So for Chicago National League fans, the purity of the way the game was meant to be remains, for the most part, intact. The idea of ducking out of work early to catch a game (the adult version of skipping school) is still sinfully, deliciously alive in Chicago because of Wrigley Field, and it makes a difference.

The other reason why Wrigley is so special is the wind. When the wind is blowing in toward home, curveballs break nastily, screaming line drives turn into fluttering outs, and every pitcher looks like Sandy Koufax. But when the wind is blowing out, every hitter is Harmon Killebrew and pitchers are reduced to whimpering. More than one hurler has looked up at the flags on Wrigley's center-field bleachers, seen them blowing out, and asked to be excused for the day.

Those two elements—daytime pleasure and the wind-dominated sense that anything can happen—

are two of the most cherished joys of the sport of baseball. And only Wrigley Field has them so completely.

Only in Wrigley could a team have a 25-6 lead after four innings and have to struggle to hold on for a 26-23 win, getting the final out in the ninth inning with the bases loaded. It happened there on August 25, 1922. But in 1917, the Cubs and Redlegs played a 10-inning game there in which both teams combined for a total of only one hit.

It was here that Babe Ruth "called his shot." Or did he? We do know that the Babe loved hitting in Wrigley. During batting practice during that 1932 World Series, he announced in brazen Ruthian fashion to anyone who would listen, "I'd play for half my salary to hit in this dump every day." The Bambino belted two homers in the fabled Game 3.

The way Wrigley looks is potent, both for aesthetics and for baseball sense. The huge scoreboard, 60 years old, carries the inning-by-inning scores of every game in the majors (and is the model for the scoreboards being built in today's new retro-parks). The flags of each team fly in order of that day's standings. The beautiful ivy vines on the outfield walls have led to craziness on the field: lost balls, a throw home of a paper cup.

Wrigley was designed from the start to be a fan's paradise. Originally constructed to be a Federal League park in 1914, the owner, Charles Weeghman, took it with him to the National League when the Feds folded after the 1915 season. Weeghman installed the first permanent concession stand in his park. He was also one of the first owners to let fans keep the balls that were fouled into the stands. (Before Weeghman's innovation became standard practice, it was common for rough-and-ready guards to snatch balls away from children.) When the Wrigley family took over the team, they maintained the excellent treatment of the fans.

The Sporting News, 1944: "There is overwhelming evidence that Mr. Wrigley's foresight in demanding neatness, comfort and beauty as an essential (and profitable) adjunct of baseball entertainment has proven a grand success." Paul Goldberger, architecture critic, *The New York Times:* "[Wrigley is] a baseball park that radiates joy."

When you don't have a team that always wins, making the ballpark a wonderful place to be anyway is the key to success. With the exception of the 1930s and two divisional titles in the '80s, the Wrigley-based Cubs have seldom been a very good team. The Wrigley Field experience makes that hurt a lot less. Just hearing Harry Caray wind up ("And a-one, and a-two...") before leading the fans in the Seventh Inning Stretch rendition of "Take Me Out to the Ballgame" is worth the price of admission.

And Wrigley was home to one of baseball's finest, Hall of Famer Ernie Banks, a gentleman and class act all the way. He was the man who loved baseball so much he could chirp "let's play two!" even when surrounded by a dismal bunch of fellow Cubbies, and a man who said of Wrigley Field, "I couldn't wait to get to the ballpark."

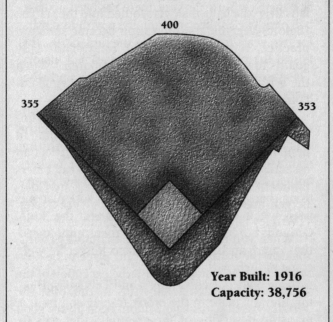

400

355

353

Year Built: 1916
Capacity: 38,756

YANKEE STADIUM

BECAUSE THERE HAS BEEN no team in history like the New York Yankees, there has been no base-ball park like Yankee Stadium. Even with its closing for two years for renovation in the mid-1970s, this is still the place to go to bask in baseball history. The ghosts are alive in Yankee Stadium, and what great ghosts they are.

A sports writer called it "The House That Ruth Built" when it opened on April 18, 1923. And he was right. After being the third-most interesting team in New York for nearly 20 years, the Yankees bought Babe Ruth from Boston in 1920 and every-thing changed. Ruth had been in New York just one year when the Giants, who owned the Polo Grounds but let the Yankees play there, announced the American Leaguers would no longer be wel-come in their park.

Team owners Jacob Ruppert and Tillinghast Hus-ton found a place in the Bronx to play and built a mansion deserving of the greatness that was to come. And who hit the first home run in the brand new ballpark? Who do you think? In appropriate Yankee fashion, general manager Ed Barrow announced the crowd at 74,217, which turned out to be at least 12,000 more fans than the place could hold. By 1927, they had expanded it to 82,000 by adding second and third decks to left-center, and 85,265 folks were there for a September 9, 1928, game against the hard-charging, young Athletics of Connie Mack. Second and third decks were added to right in 1937.

The facade at the top of the stadium is instantly identifiable. It's a stately, simple, repeated arch motif that evokes the grandeur of the Yankee image. In the outfield, there were three monuments in deep center field—one honoring Miller Huggins in the middle, ones for Ruth and Lou Gehrig on either side. The story is told that manager Casey Stengel, waiting too long for his center fielder to track down a ball, shouted, "Ruth! Huggins! Gehrig! Somebody throw that thing in here!" When the stadium was renovated in 1976, these monuments were moved behind the fence.

Thirty-one World Series and a remarkable 83 Series games have been played in Yankee Stadium. The Yanks, by the way, have won 52 of them. The stadium's great Series moments would fill a book by themselves: Casey Stengel's two home runs to win games in the 1923 Series, the first one being an inside-the-park job most notable for his unusual gait in the process; Babe Ruth trying to steal second in the ninth inning of Game 7 of the '26 Series and being thrown out to send the Yanks down to defeat; the Ruth/Gehrig slugfests of 1927, '28, and '32; the seven-run inning in Game 1 of the '37 Series; back-to-back sweeps in 1938 and '39; Allie Reynolds's two-hitter to open the '49 Series; Don Larsen's perfect game in '56; Whitey Ford's breaking of Babe Ruth's consecutive-scoreless-inning string in '61; Mickey Mantle's ninth-inning homer to win Game 3 against St. Louis in '64; Reggie Jackson's three home runs—all on the first pitch—in consecutive at-bats in 1977's Game 6; Graig Nettles's astonishing defense to turn around Game 3 in 1978.

Two of the most famous home runs ever were hit here: Ruth's 60th in 1927, off Tom Zachary, to break his own single-season home run record of 59; and Roger Maris's 61st in 1961, off Tracy Stallard, to break Ruth's record. In 1963, Mantle smashed a pitch from Bill Fischer off the third deck's facade. Estimates said it would have travelled 620 feet if the concrete hadn't gotten in the way. However, the only person said to ever hit a ball completely out of the park was the Negro League's Josh Gibson.

Beyond that, you can just list the names and listen to the magic: Ruth, Gehrig, Lazzeri, Combs, Meusel, Hoyt, Pennock. Leo Durocher, Bill Dickey, Red Ruffing, "Goofy" Gomez, "King Kong" Keller. Tommy Henrich, Phil Rizzuto, Snuffy Stirnweiss, Joe DiMaggio. Billy, Whitey, Yogi, and the Mick.

Not surprisingly, Yankee Stadium has been the site of some of baseball's most emotional farewells. On July 4, 1939, Lou Gehrig, his body tortured by a disease that would come to be named after him, told 61,808 fans gathered in his honor that he considered himself "the luckiest man on the face of the earth." Nine years later, Babe Ruth, no longer the

gallant, proud Yankee slugger but now an enfee-
bled, cancer-stricken old man unable to stand by
himself, bade farewell to New York on June 13. Two
months later, the Babe was dead.

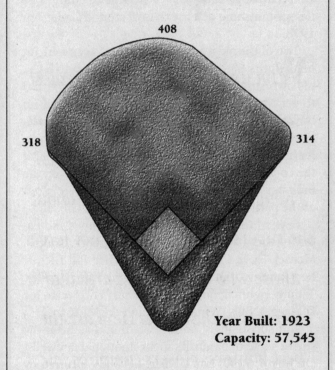

408

318

314

Year Built: 1923
Capacity: 57,545

CHAPTER 6

BEST OF THE REST

WHICH PITCHERS *had the speediest heaters? Who could really pick it at third? Who were the nuttiest fans? Though we love to reminisce about the superstars of yore, let's not forget those who excelled in particular aspects of the game. Here are the best bunters, closers, umpires, etc. in baseball history.*

Sandy Koufax

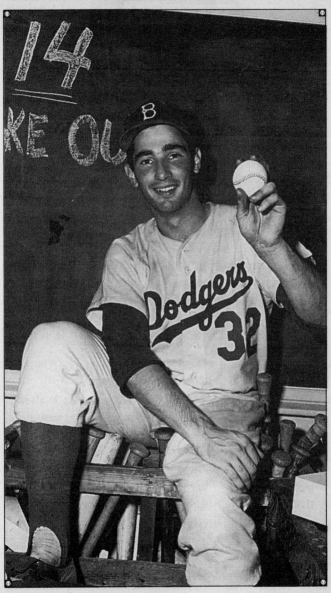

10 Best World Series

1912: Red Sox 4, Giants 3

THE WORLD SERIES was only just beginning to take hold on the psyche of America by the time 1912 rolled around. But this classic clinched the deal forever. Two powerhouse teams, led by ace pitchers Christy Mathewson (Giants) and Smokey Joe Wood, banged heads together for eight games; one game was called a 6-6 tie after 11 innings because of darkness. It couldn't have been wilder.

The Series was full of clutch plays and intrigue, spectacular pitching and snappy hitting. Even the Boston fans got into the act, costing their team a win. The final game had great catches, excruciating bobbles, and sensational craftiness. Boston, capitalizing on Fred Snodgrass's dropped fly ball in the 10th inning, took Game 8 3-2.

1924: Senators 4, Giants 3

THIS WAS THE YEAR that legendary hurler Walter Johnson was supposed to triumph because he had spent so many seasons without winning a pennant. But he lost his first two starts and Washington, under rookie manager Bucky Harris, was fighting to hold on. Three of the first six games were decided by one run, one in extra innings.

Managers maneuvered, but the seventh game was beyond belief. Giant catcher Hank Gowdy got his foot stuck in his face mask, and two hits bounced over Giant third baseman's Fred Lindstrom's head—including the winner in the 12th inning. The winning pitcher? Walter Johnson. Afterward, commissioner Kenesaw Mountain Landis said, "Are we seeing the high point of this thing we love? Are we looking at the crest of the institution we know as professional American baseball?"

1931: CARDINALS 4, A's 3

THEY WEREN'T CALLED THE "GASHOUSE GANG" just yet, but this Cardinal team was definitely smoking against the proud and potent A's of Connie Mack. This A's club could have been the finest ever; they were making their third consecutive World Series appearance, averaging more than 104 wins.

But the pesky Cards didn't care, even though the same A's had whipped them in six games in the '30 Series. The key was the amazing performance of Pepper Martin for St. Louis. He undressed the mighty A's with his boisterous batting (12-for-24) and bravado baserunning (five steals). And with two runs in and the winning run at the plate in the ninth inning of Game 7, the man who grabbed the fly ball to end it all was...Pepper Martin.

1947: YANKEES 4, DODGERS 3

THIS SERIES MATCHED TWO TEAMS that were each beginning a string of greatness. The Yanks of Ruth and Gehrig were gone; in their place were Joe DiMaggio, Yogi Berra, and Phil Rizzuto. The

Dodgers were about to become one of the greatest bunches in National League history. It was Jackie Robinson's first season; Pete Reiser and Pee Wee Reese were blossoming stars. It was hard to avoid the feeling that these two teams would be back to face each other again.

The most sensational game was the fourth, won by Brooklyn. With two out in the last of the ninth, pinch-hitter Cookie Lavagetto cracked the only hit the Dodgers had all game. But it was enough to score two men who had walked and gave Brooklyn a 3-2 win.

1955: Dodgers 4, Yankees 3

THE YANKS topped the Dodgers again in 1949, and the Dodgers narrowly missed reaching the Series in 1950 and '51. When the two teams met in 1952 and '53, the story was the same: Yanks win.

But the 1955 Dodgers had a new manager, Walter Alston, and a new set of heroes. Duke Snider clubbed four homers, which only Babe Ruth, Lou Gehrig, and Snider himself had done before. Roger Craig, a 25-year-old hurler, stifled the Yanks in Game 5. Johnny Podres won Games 3 and 7. In the last game, the Dodgers were hanging on to a 2-0 lead when Sandy Amoros—brought into the game for defensive purposes—made an impossible grab of a tailing Yogi Berra liner and turned a potentially game-tying double into a double play. "Next year" had arrived in Brooklyn.

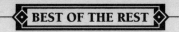

1960: Pirates 4, Yankees 3

I**T WAS HARD TO BELIEVE:** The New York Yankees had outscored the upstart Pittsburgh Pirates 55-27 and still lost the Series. When the Yankees won, they won big. But when the games were close, Pirate pluck and luck made the difference.

The Pirates, who had been a remarkable come-from-behind team all year, won Game 1 but were crushed in Games 2 and 3 (16-3 and 10-0). They weren't intimidated, however, winning Game 4 3-2 and Game 5 5-2. The 12-0 Yank win in Game 6 was more of the expected. But Game 7 turned on bad hops, bad pitching moves, poor defense, aggressive baserunning, and big-time homers—including the climactic blast by Bill Mazeroski in the bottom of the ninth to win it 10-9. The Pirates had startled the Yankees. Casey Stengel was fired; Mickey Mantle cried.

1962: Yankees 4, Giants 3

R**ALPH TERRY,** who had allowed the Bill Mazeroski homer that ended the '60 Series in such dramatic fashion, redeemed himself in the taut 1962 fall classic. For six games, the two teams jabbed at each other like testy prizefighters, neither able to establish any dominance. Nobody on either team had homered more than once or scored more than a handful of runs.

By the time Game 7 rolled around, each team's ace starter (Jack Sanford for the Giants, Terry for the Yanks) had won one and lost one game. They faced off against each other, and it wasn't over until Giant monster Willie McCovey rapped a line drive up the middle with two on and two out in the last of the ninth with the Yanks up 1-0—a line drive that second baseman Bobby Richardson snared to end the game.

1972: A's 4, Reds 3

IT WAS THE NEW WAVE vs. the old guard. The wild-haired, mustachioed A's against the clean-cropped, all-American Reds. Dick Williams managed Charlie Finley's wild brigade; Cincy manager Sparky Anderson headed up the Big Red Machine.

Before they were finished, every game but one had been decided by one run; superstar Johnny Bench, in the midst of an intentional walk on a 2-2 pitch, watched strike three zip past him; and Oakland's Gene Tenace, with four homers, had established himself as one of the Series' unexpected heroes. Rollie Fingers preserved a 3-2 win in Game 7 and the fuzzy misfits of Oakland won their first of three consecutive world championships.

1975: Reds 4, Red Sox 3

IT WOULD BE HARD to make a case that any Series was ever more exciting than this one. Neither of these two teams seemed to have the slightest willingness to accept defeat. They both kept banging at each other over and over again.

In six of the seven games, the team that won came from behind to do it. In one game, it came from behind twice. Five times the winning margin was only one run. Two games weren't decided until the ninth inning; two others went into extra innings. Carlton Fisk's 12th-inning dinger won the thrill-packed Game 6 for Boston, while the Reds took Game 7 4-3 with a run in the ninth. Whew!

1991: TWINS 4, BRAVES 3

THESE TWO TEAMS were not even supposed to be in the Series, as both had finished last in their respective divisions just the season before. In contrast to the 1975 Series, this fall classic was not noted for dramatic turnarounds or big comebacks. The two clubs just played each other about as deadly even as you possibly can, and they did it for seven games.

There were weird plays, marathon games, unexpected heroes, creative baserunning, home-plate collisions, and clutch homers. Kirby Puckett's stellar catch and 11th-inning, game-winning homer in Game 6 to stave off Series defeat was one of the classic gutsy performances of all time. In Game 7, Jack Morris—in another heroic performance—pitched a 10-inning shutout and Minnesota won in the bottom of the 10th on a Gene Larkin bases-loaded single. Taut, and tense, it was a Series that will long be remembered.

10 BEST SINGLE-GAME PERFORMANCES

JOE ADCOCK

JULY 31, 1954. It was hot and humid this day in Brooklyn, so the Braves' Adcock wasn't wasting time taking pitches from Dodger hurlers. He came out swinging and rapped four homers and a double on seven pitches (off four different pitchers). In doing so, he established the ML mark for total bases in a game.

JIM BUNNING

JUNE 21, 1964. Bunning had seven children, which may be why he pitched his best game on Father's Day. The Phillie hurler faced just 27 Mets that day, striking out 10 of them. He also doubled in a pair of runs to add to his 6-0 perfecto win. Manager Gene Mauch said, "We knew when he was warming up that this was something special."

TY COBB

MAY 5, 1925. Thirty-eight-year-old Cobb, tired of hearing how super Babe Ruth was, announced he was going for the home run that day. And did he ever! He swatted three out of the park, tacked on two singles and a double, and set a still-standing American League record for total bases in a game.

ED DELAHANTY

JULY 13, 1896. Some historians will tell you that Delahanty was the greatest right-handed hitter ever. On this day at Chicago, the Phillies slugger singled his first time up and crushed four inside-the-park homers. After the last one, the opposing pitcher was there at home to shake his hand.

HARVEY HADDIX

MAY 26, 1959. Pirate Haddix retired the first 36 Braves to face him on this cool night in May, yet he didn't throw a true no-hitter. For one and one-third games on this night, Haddix retired every Brave he saw. But he lost the game on an error and a hit in the unlucky 13th.

CATFISH HUNTER

MAY 8, 1968. The 1960s were definitely the decade of the pitcher. Hunter's perfect game against Minnesota on this date was the third perfecto in the decade. He fanned 11 Twins in the game. Hunter's A's won 4-0, and Catfish joined in the batting fun too, driving in three of the runs himself and hitting a homer.

ADDIE JOSS

OCTOBER 2, 1908. Both the National and American League pennant races were exceptionally tight in '08. Cleveland, Detroit, and Chicago were within percentage points of each other when

Joss faced off against rugged 40-game White Sox winner Ed Walsh. Walsh was excellent, pitching a four-hitter, fanning 15. Joss was sensational. He faced 27 batters and not one reached first.

DON LARSEN

OCTOBER 8, 1956. Only three men had ever pitched a one-hitter in a World Series game when Larsen took the mound for the Yankees in Game 5 of the '56 affair with the Series tied 2-2. Larsen achieved the ultimate: a World Series perfect game. He threw only 97 pitches. Only one Dodger saw "ball three" all day.

MARK WHITEN

SEPTEMBER 7, 1993. Twelve major-leaguers have hit four home runs in a game, and two have tallied 12 RBI in a contest. Whiten became the only player in both exclusive clubs when he teed off on the Reds in the second game of a doubleheader. One of his homers was, of course, a grand slam.

RICK WISE

JUNE 23, 1971. The story is told that in 1971, Wise was complaining about his teammate Phillies' bats and said, "To win around here, you have to pitch a shutout and hit a homer." He did even better than that on this day: He pitched a no-hitter against the Reds (only one batter reached base, on a walk) and slugged two homers.

10 Best Big-Game Performers

GROVER CLEVELAND ALEXANDER

THE BASES WERE LOADED in the last of the seventh inning of Game 7 of the 1926 World Series. In came aged hurler Alexander, who had won a complete game (and some say then celebrated heavily) the day before. But Pete fanned Tony Lazzeri and then nailed down the championship through the eighth and ninth as well. Alexander had his problems, but he was always ready in the clutch.

HOME RUN BAKER

IT WAS THE 1911 WORLD SERIES that he earned his one-of-a-kind moniker. In Game 2, he homered off Rube Marquard to untie the score for good. In Game 3, Baker homered off Christy Mathewson to tie the game in the top of the ninth, and the A's went on to win that game and the Series. Baker batted .363 in six World Series.

GEORGE BRETT

THREE TIMES THE KANSAS CITY ROYALS faced the New York Yankees in the ALCS (1976, '77, and '78), and despite heroic efforts by Brett, the Royals lost all three times. Things were different in 1980, as Brett's majestic three-run homer in Game 3 turned the tide. Brett holds LCS career records with nine homers and a .728 slugging percentage.

LOU BROCK

FOR ST. LOUIS IN 1964, Brock turned in a .348 average down the stretch, then batted .300 in the World Series. Three years later, he hit .414 with seven steals in the fall classic, and in 1968 he hit .464 in a losing cause against Detroit. For players who have played in more than 20 Series games, his .391 average is the highest ever.

ROBERTO CLEMENTE

CLEMENTE LOVED THE PRESSURE and the exposure of the big games, which is why he played so well in two World Series for the Pirates (1960 and 1971). He hit safely in every one of the 14 games played and compiled a .362 average. He dazzled the Orioles in the '71 Series not only with his .414 batting average but with his fielding excellence.

LENNY DYKSTRA

DYKSTRA HAS BEEN AN IGNITER. For example, he hit a two-run homer to snatch victory from defeat in Game 3 of the 1986 NLCS. He motivated the Mets in that series' Game 6 with only the fourth hit off Astro Bob Knepper—a triple. He batted .429 in the 1988 NLCS, and he batted .348 with nine runs and four homers in the 1993 World Series.

LOU GEHRIG

GEHRIG WAS THE ORIGINAL "MR. OCTOBER." His 1.727 slugging average in the 1928 World

Series may never be topped. The next Series he played in he slugged a phenomenal 1.118. Gehrig is in the top 10 lifetime in every major World Series offensive category.

REGGIE JACKSON

HE DESERVED THE NICKNAME "MR. OCTOBER" because Reggie adored the glitter and the glory of World Series time. In fact, in 30 World Series games, his slugging average (.755) is the highest of all time. And no one will ever forget Reggie's three 1977 Series homers in Game 6—all on the first pitch.

SANDY KOUFAX

KOUFAX WAS THE MAN the Dodgers counted on to win the big games. And he usually did, like when he threw a perfect game in September of the 1965 pennant race. He started Game 1 of the 1963 World Series against the Yankees and fanned the first five Yanks who came up to the plate. In 57 World Series innings, he compiled a 0.95 ERA.

CARL YASTRZEMSKI

THE RED SOX would not have been in several pennant races without the superb clutch efforts of Yastrzemski. He carried the team with a sensational Triple Crown season in 1967, burning it up down the stretch and hitting .400 in the World Series. In 1975, he hit .310 in the Series.

10 Best Team Leaders

Cap Anson

CAP WAS CHICAGO'S first player/manager in the National League, and his teams won five pennants. When he was canned in 1897, the team became known as the Orphans. Anson was tough on his men. Spring training, where the men could sweat off some winter weight and practice their skills, was his idea.

Don Baylor

HOW MANY MEN CAN YOU NAME who teams acquired explicitly for their leadership ability? The answer is one: Don Baylor, a proven winner who established a workmanlike sanity in every clubhouse he entered in the 1980s. He played on seven first-place teams. He was in the World Series each of his last three years—with three different teams.

Lou Boudreau

BOUDREAU BECAME THE YOUNGEST playing manager in American League history (24). He led by quiet example. And stellar performance. With his Indians in a furious flag race in 1948, Boudreau had his crowning season at the plate. Pinch-hitting after an injury had sidelined him, his key hit helped the Tribe sweep the Yanks. In the playoff game that season, he had four hits including two homers.

FRANK CHANCE

AS PLAYER/MANAGER, "the Peerless Leader" led the Cubs to four pennants and two world championships (1907 and '08). Chance was a large man who was forthright and honest. If a player stepped out of line, "Husk" wasn't afraid to push him back onto the right path. With his fists.

FRED CLARKE

CLARKE HAD SPENT JUST THREE YEARS in the majors when he was named player/manager of Louisville in 1897. Clarke was a tough, country-boy competitor with an inventive twist to his mind. (He patented several inventions.) He sparkled when he joined the Pirates and led them to three consecutive National League flags.

MICKEY COCHRANE

COCHRANE LEARNED HOW TO MANAGE as Connie Mack's catcher on the powerful A's teams of the late '20s and early '30s. Named player/manager for Detroit in 1934, he won pennants in '34 and '35. A beaning fractured his skull before he turned 35 years old, and he found managing without playing wasn't his style.

JOE CRONIN

CRONIN WAS ONLY 26 when he added the job of manager to his shortstop duties in Washington in 1933. His Senators won the pennant that year.

Called by Ted Williams "the greatest manager I ever played for," Cronin moved up to the Red Sox front office, and he later became president of the American League.

NAPOLEON LAJOIE

WITH HIS TALENT, grace, and pleasantly confident manner, Lajoie was the player the others looked up to. He preferred to lead by example, but the fans and owners wanted their beloved star as their manager too. Lajoie's Cleveland team took "Naps" as their name, and they finished second to the Tigers in 1908 by just a half-game.

PEE WEE REESE

REESE'S STYLE OF LEADERSHIP happened on the field and in the clubhouse as the unofficial manager's representative. Kentuckian Reese helped silence the revolt by racist players against Jackie Robinson's entry into the bigs when he put his arm around his teammate in full view of everyone.

WILLIE STARGELL

WHEN STARGELL CAME TO PITTSBURGH, he was a frightened kid. But when he watched Roberto Clemente, he saw how a proud and powerful leader behaved. Stargell's grandest year was 1979, when Pops handed out "Stargell Stars" to worthy Pirate teammates and led them to the world title.

10 Classiest Players

Ernie Banks

Ernie was a Hall of Fame talent in the 1950s and '60s whose sunny disposition made him the most beloved player in Chicago Cub history. How could you not love a man heard to say, "What a great day for a ballgame! Let's play two!"? He was the first Cub to have his number retired. He definitely earned the sobriquet "Mr. Cub."

Roberto Clemente

Clemente came to a racially backward town in 1955 and barely spoke the language. The Pittsburgh press ridiculed his poor English and called him a malingerer, but the fans weren't swayed. They could see his pride and class. One of the great humanitarians in the game's history, Clemente lost his life trying to make sure that Nicaraguan earthquake victims would get needed supplies.

Joe DiMaggio

DiMaggio didn't say much, which made some people feel he was aloof. In truth, it was more a matter of shyness. He always carried himself royally and looked great at whatever he did. Perhaps no one ever combined such complete talent with such serious study of the game. No player ever reeked class, professionalism, and winning the way Joe D. did.

CHARLIE GEHRINGER

GEHRINGER WAS A PLAYER devoid of showmanship. He was always quiet but always an exceptional performer, both as a fielder and a batter. As his manager Mickey Cochrane put it, "Charlie says hello on Opening Day, goodbye on Closing Day, and in between hits .350."

WALTER JOHNSON

ONLY ONE PITCHER IN BASEBALL HISTORY won more games than Johnson, yet Walter played for a team that was almost always worse than mediocre. But he was never heard to complain. He just went out and did better than anyone could ever expect. His nicknames included "Sir Walter" and the "White Knight."

AL KALINE

AS ERNIE BANKS WAS "MR. CUB," Kaline was "Mr. Tiger." In every inning he played from 1953-74, he demonstrated nothing but exceptional skill backed up with sensational class. He played spectacularly through pain. He is one of a handful of players who reached the Hall of Fame without ever playing in the minors.

STAN MUSIAL

HERE'S WHAT STAN MUSIAL'S fellow players had to say about him on a plaque they gave him: "An outstanding artist in his profession...a gentleman in every sense of the word." From a Polish-American family in a rugged steel town, Musial's quiet excellence on the field and humanitarian generosity off it earned him deep affection throughout the game.

ORATOR O'ROURKE

THIS 1800S STAR EARNED his nickname because he was never at a loss for words, and when he argued with an umpire, he was eloquent. The fans loved him. When he decided he shouldn't have to pay for his own uniform, the fans pitched in to raise the necessary $20. He became both an umpire and an executive after his playing career.

BROOKS ROBINSON

AT THIRD BASE, Robinson made the spectacular look simple. And when a Robinson play looked difficult, it was verging on impossible. Brooks was always kind, gentle, and generous. When he had difficulties, he never complained. He later served as president of the Major League Baseball Players Alumni Association.

JACKIE ROBINSON

NO PLAYER EVER HAD TO FACE the challenge Jackie Robinson did, as ordered by Branch Rickey: No matter what they do or say to you, you cannot fight back. It wasn't easy, but he did it. And his unbreakable spirit made it possible for the color line in baseball to be broken forever. In a 1947 popularity poll, only Bing Crosby was ahead of him.

10 Grittiest Players

Ty Cobb

COBB MAY HAVE BEEN THE FIERCEST competitor ever to put on a baseball uniform. He never gave an inch. He was driven to excel, to be the best. Maybe the least-liked player of all time, he knew baseball wasn't a popularity contest. Maybe he didn't sharpen his spikes, but he pretended he did and that scared the dickens out of his opponents.

Bob Gibson

THE INTIMIDATION FACTOR when a batter faced Gibson was immense. Burning with a furious pride not just to win but to dominate, Gibson was head and shoulders above all other pitchers in his era. And in three World Series, he dominated like few others have.

Don Hoak

THEY CALLED HIM "THE TIGER," but the story that best indicates the character and drive of Hoak is that he lied about his age to enter the U.S. Marine Corps. He was also a pro boxer as a teenager in the '40s. A brawler, battler, and throwback, Hoak died of a heart attack while chasing a burglar.

Billy Martin

MARTIN WAS A LONG-TIME FAVORITE of Casey Stengel for his aggressive play that maximized his minimal talent. Martin was scrappy, hard-working, and driven to succeed. His heads-up play on a pop-up in no-man's-land saved the 1952 World Series. He said about his youth, "I awoke every morning knowing there was a good chance I was going to have to get in a fight with somebody."

PEPPER MARTIN

MARTIN WAS A WILD MAN on the basepaths, with sensational head-first slides. His nickname of "Pepper" was high praise in his day: It meant he had the guts and the energy to win no matter what. His most glorious moment was taking charge of the 1931 World Series (12-for-24) like few have done before or since.

JOHN MCGRAW

MCGRAW KNEW HOW TO GET THE MOST out of his skills on the field. He did so by fighting for every edge possible, often using his fists. On the 1890s Baltimore Orioles, a team known for nasty "inside" baseball, McGraw was the nastiest and maybe the toughest. As a manager, he battled with umpires, team owners, and even league presidents.

FRANK ROBINSON

ROBINSON CROWDED THE PLATE, and if a pitcher tried to back him off, Frank dug in that much harder. His brutal slide into Eddie Mathews in 1959 precipitated one of the first true brawls between black and white stars—a sad but necessary footnote to the integration of the game.

JACKIE ROBINSON

WHEN BRANCH RICKEY signed Robinson, the Dodger GM made it clear to Jackie that he had to take it all without fighting back for three years. So Robinson retaliated against the racial slurs and spike wounds with hard line drives, assertive baserunning, and the most intimidating response of all: the steal of home. When the three years were up, Robinson used his fists too.

PETE ROSE

I'D WALK THROUGH HELL in a gasoline suit to keep playing baseball," Rose said. Pete retired as the all-time games-played king as well as the hit king. He was a winner, leading six teams to pennants. Rose's defining moment came when he bulldozed catcher Ray Fosse in the 1970 All-Star Game.

ENOS SLAUGHTER

WHEN SLAUGHTER WAS in the minor leagues, his manager hollered at him for not hustling on and off the field. Slaughter learned his lesson; he epitomized the word "hustle" from then on. He was widely criticized for viciously spiking Jackie Robinson, an action that verified his racism as well as his hyper-aggressiveness. His "mad dash" home sealed the 1946 World Series for his Cards.

10 PUREST HITTERS

WADE BOGGS

THE THOUGHT OF A MODERN HITTER taking up residence among the hallowed names of Sisler, Lajoie, and Waner is almost incomprehensible. Everyone knows how much harder it is to hit for average nowadays, with night games, relief specialists, plane travel, and the rest. Yet there is Boggs, perched among them, the five-time bat champ with the perfect swing and the incredible batting eye.

DAN BROUTHERS

POSSESSOR OF THE SHARPEST BATTING EYE in the 19th century, Brouthers was the first person (some say) to counsel, "Keep your eye on the ball." His lifetime batting average (.342) is eighth best all time. Yet he won seven slugging titles too, and he did it for nine different National League teams.

PETE BROWNING

WHEN BROWNING BROKE A FAVORITE BAT, a local Louisville carpenter offered to make a new one—this time to his specifications. Browning thereby became the original "Louisville Slugger," the first player to have a custom-made bat. Also called "The Gladiator," Browning won four batting titles and holds the fourth-highest right-handed lifetime batting average (.341). He was the greatest hitter in American Association history.

ROD CAREW

WHILE OTHER BATTERS OF HIS TIME swung for the fences, Rod poked the ball where they weren't. As a result, he won seven batting titles, hit over .330 10 times, and sported a lifetime average of .328. In 1977, he hit .388—the highest mark in the ML since 1941. For 15 consecutive seasons, Carew batted over .300.

TY COBB

COBB WON 10, 11, OR 12 BATTING TITLES, depending on your reading of history. He was the very first player elected to the Hall of Fame. He was the most dominant hitter in history until Babe Ruth. His lifetime average (.366) is 30 points higher than almost anyone who has played in the past 50 years.

TONY GWYNN

GWYNN IS THE GREATEST singles hitter alive today. He has already won seven batting titles and his lifetime average is .337. His .394 average in 1994 was the best in the National League in 64 years. He owns a superb batting eye; the most he's ever fanned in a season has been 40 times.

ROGERS HORNSBY

UNIVERSALLY CONCEDED to be the greatest right-handed batter ever, Hornsby owned a lifetime average (.358) that was just eight points less than Ty Cobb's, and Rogers had considerably more power. For the five years from 1921-25, he averaged .400. No one else has ever done that. His .424 in '24 is the highest NL average this century.

JOE JACKSON

THEY SAY BABE RUTH modeled his hitting style after Jackson's. "Shoeless Joe" may have been the most "natural" hitter of all time. He never won a batting title (Ty Cobb had to be first, remember), but from 1911-20 he finished second, third, or fourth seven times. His lifetime average of .356 sits him right behind Cobb and Rogers Hornsby.

NAP LAJOIE

AFTER FIVE YEARS IN THE NATIONAL LEAGUE, Lajoie heeded the call to jump to Ban Johnson's new American League in 1901. He was a large factor in the new circuit's success. He batted .426 that season—.149 above the league average and the highest mark this century. He won four slugging titles along with his four (some say three) batting titles.

TED WILLIAMS

WILLIAMS SAID HE WANTED to be known as the greatest hitter of all time. Many say he achieved his goal. He was as pure a line-drive, eagle-eye artisan as any, the last .400 hitter, yet he was also a fearsome slugger who belted 521 homers. Amazingly, Williams lost nearly five years of his career flying jets in the U.S. military.

10 STRONGEST SLUGGERS

JIMMIE FOXX

FOXX EARNED HIS NICKNAME "The Beast." His rippling muscles terrified American League pitchers for years. When he slugged 58 homers in 1932, he became only the third player ever to top 50. Foxx was second in lifetime homers until Willie Mays surpassed him. Jimmie's pokes were oftentimes the longest balls ever hit in (or out of) the ballpark.

JOSH GIBSON

CALLED THE "BLACK BABE RUTH," Gibson is alleged to have done something Ruth (and no one else) never did: hit a homer completely out of Yankee Stadium. The color line kept Josh from the majors, but he set slugging-distance records that have become legendary. In his Negro League career (1930-46), he was the home run king nine times.

HARMON KILLEBREW

WHEN KILLEBREW SLUGGED LONG HOME RUNS, they didn't just go far; they sometimes caused damage. A long ball he clouted in 1967 in Minneapolis' Metropolitan Stadium went more than 530 feet and actually shattered two seats in the process. Eight times he hit more than 40 home runs on his way to a lifetime total of 573, fifth best of all time.

RALPH KINER

KINER'S CAREER was a short one (1946-55), as a bad back hampered him. But no one except Babe Ruth ever belted homers with a greater frequency than Ralph. And Kiner played his peak years in the caverns of Forbes Field. Twice he swatted more than 50 in a season.

DAVE KINGMAN

KING KONG" was not a good hitter, but boy, could he slug the ball. At 6'6", he wound up and sent balls high into the stratosphere. In 1976, he hit one out of Wrigley Field, *over* Waveland Avenue, and off Naomi Martinez's house on Kenmore Avenue.

MICKEY MANTLE

NO ONE EVER WALLOPED home runs from both sides of the plate like Mantle. Mantle is given credit for the longest ball ever hit in Yankee Stadium; the wall kept it from going 620 feet. A famous photo shows him smiling at the tattered ball he belted 565 feet in Washington.

WILLIE MCCOVEY

MCCOVEY DIDN'T HAVE RIPPLING MUSCLES like Jimmie Foxx or Harmon Killebrew, but when he connected the ball could almost be heard to whimper in pain. Only four men ever hit more homers in the National League than his 521. He hit full stride from 1963 through 1970, when he hit (in order) 44, 18, 39, 36, 31, 36, 45 and 39 home runs.

BABE RUTH

RUTH'S PROWESS AS A HITTER for distance so far surpassed anyone ever seen before that they had to invent a new word for it: "Ruthian." In his first game in the minor leagues, he hit a ball called the longest fans of that town (Fayetteville, North Carolina) had ever seen. The last homer he ever hit was the longest ball ever hit out of Forbes Field; it cleared the double-deck right-field grandstands.

WILLIE STARGELL

IT WAS A FRIGHTENING IMAGE: Willie Stargell, poised at the plate, motionless except for his bat as he wristed it in fat circles. The way he flipped it around, it seemed to weigh less than an ounce. Stargell hit homers completely out of Dodger Stadium; he's the only person to do it—and he did it twice, in 1969 and '73. Stargell also smashed more out of Forbes and Three Rivers than anybody else.

FRANK THOMAS

IN THE HOME RUN HITTING CONTEST before the 1994 All-Star Game, Thomas hit a ball farther than any other in the history of Three Rivers Stadium. Considering it came against a batting practice pitcher, the feat is even more remarkable. Thomas combines brute strength with a hawk's eye, so when he goes after a pitch, it is usually in his zone.

10 BEST BUNTERS

RICHIE ASHBURN

A THROWBACK IN PLAYING STYLE to the earlier part of the century, Ashburn was a superb fielder, marvelous singles hitter, and excellent bunter in an era (1950s) when big home runs were the offense of preference. He hit over .300 nine times, won two batting titles, and finished second two other years. He was one of the hardest players in baseball history to double up.

BRETT BUTLER

T HE DRAG-BUNTING EXPERTISE of Butler has made him one of the most successful leadoff hitters of all time. Another "throwback," he hits triples, walks frequently, hardly ever hits into a double play, and covers center field like a tarpaulin. From 1988-94, he ranked among the National League's top five performers in on-base percentage almost every year.

ROD CAREW

C AREW'S EXCEPTIONAL BUNTING ABILITY forced the defense to play him in tight, which made it easier for him to slap hits through the left side of the infield—which is a large reason why he was able to lead the American League in batting average seven times. In 1972, he was helped to the title by successfully bunting for a hit 15 times.

RAY CHAPMAN

ANOTHER MASTER OF "LITTLE BALL" in a big way, Chapman was probably on his way to the Hall of Fame until he was killed by a pitched ball. Chapman bunted like an artist, swiped bases, took walks, and scored runs. He set the American League record in 1917 with 67 sacrifice hits.

TY COBB

COBB LIKED TO BUNT DOWN THE FIRST BASE LINE in order to spike (or threaten to spike—same effect) the first baseman and pitcher. Cobb came to bat in an old-timer's game and cautioned catcher Benny Bengough: "Move back; I haven't swung one of these things in 20 years." Bengough moved back; Cobb laid down a perfect bunt.

EDDIE COLLINS

THE COLLEGE-EDUCATED (a rarity in his day) Collins was known for his braininess and impressive ability. The bunt was just one of the things he did very well. He's the majors' all-time leader with 511 sacrifice hits.

KID GLEASON

GLEASON MANAGED the 1919 Chicago "Black Sox," which will forever have him associated with the wrong crowd. But as a player, Gleason was a star, both as a pitcher and as a second baseman, where his defensive skills were noteworthy. As the man who suggested the first intentional walk, it's not surprising he was a superb bunter.

WILLIE KEELER

THIS TURN-OF-THE-CENTURY STAR was one of the game's greatest "scientific" hitters, using his smarts to overcome his small size, to wring every hit out of the dead ball he could. His bunting was a precision act, as he advised hitters simply to "hit 'em where they ain't." He was also a founding father of the "Baltimore chop," swatting the ball directly downward on the hard Oriole infield in order to beat it out for a hit.

MICKEY MANTLE

WITH HIS EXCEPTIONAL BASEBALL INTELLIGENCE and sensational natural speed, Mantle was a deadly bunter. Many "how to play baseball" books of the 1950s had Mantle as their bunt instructor. Mickey's forte was the drag bunt from the left side; while the pitcher and first baseman watched the ball, Mantle sped past them.

PHIL RIZZUTO

THE SCOOTER" wasn't a great hitter. But as a bunter, he was a marvel. Using the bunt either as a sacrifice to keep an inning alive or a hit to get things started, Rizzuto's offensive contributions were important to the slugging Yanks of the 1940s and '50s. Even from the broadcast booth, Phil kept calling for the bunt.

10 FASTEST BASERUNNERS

HARRY BAY

BAY WAS A SPEED MERCHANT in a brief career at the beginning of the 20th century. He played just four full years, but he stole 45 bases in 1903 to lead the American League and 38 bases in '04 to tie for the lead. Because of his speed, Bay was one of the first players to be featured in moving pictures.

COOL PAPA BELL

SATCHEL PAIGE SAID BELL was so fast he could turn off the light switch and be in bed before the room got dark. Starring in the 1920s and '30s, Bell routinely scored from second on fly-ball outs or infield groundouts, and he claimed he once stole 175 bases in a 200-game season.

GEORGE CASE

CASE WAS A SPEEDSTER in an era of sluggers, so he seldom got his due. But he led all major-leaguers in stolen sacks five consecutive years (1939-43). His 61 steals were an ML high from 1920-61. Case's speed was so highly thought of that he earned a race with Jesse Owens; Case lost.

VINCE COLEMAN

IT TOOK COLEMAN several years to learn how to be a baseball player, but it was impossible to keep his immense speed out of the bigs. His 145 stolen bases in 113 Sally League games established an all-time pro-baseball mark, and he was the first big-league rookie to steal over 100 bases (110 in 1985). Coleman topped the National League in steals his first six years, and he had a special fondness for swiping third.

BILLY HAMILTON

"Sliding Billy" didn't look like your archetypal basestealer. He was thick-legged and had a chunky build. But his 912 career steals were the record for nearly 80 years. Steals were different in Billy's day. Official scorers could award a "stolen base" if the runner advanced farther than he "should have" on a hit.

KENNY LOFTON

A former point guard at the University of Arizona, Lofton combines many baseball skills with his breathtaking speed. He has a good batting eye with power and he is a sensational center fielder. He led the American League in stolen bases in his first three seasons. In 1994, he led the AL in both hits and steals.

MICKEY MANTLE

Considering Mantle's injuries to his legs, it's remarkable that he is considered one of the fastest ever. He often played while bandaged from the hips to the feet. Early in his career, when the switch-hitting "Commerce Comet" batted from the left side, he would drag bunt for hits, using his 3.1-second speed from home to first.

DEION SANDERS

THE EPITOME OF THE MODERN-DAY ATHLETE—glitzy, self-glorifying—Sanders could nonetheless fly. He used his incredible amount of sheer physical talent to carve out a career in both big-league baseball and football. A big-time cornerback and punt returner in the NFL, Sanders batted .304 and led the NL with 14 triples in 1992.

EVAR SWANSON

FAST ENOUGH TO PLAY end in pro football for three years, Swanson left the bruising sport to become one of the fastest baseball players ever. He once circled the bases in 13.3 seconds, which is still considered the "record." Unfortunately he played from 1929-34, when teams concentrated on the long ball instead of the steal.

WILLIE WILSON

BASEBALL'S FASTEST MAN in the late 1970s, Wilson was a highly efficient basestealer. Yet he didn't use that weapon as often as he might, leading his league only once (although he did steal 83 bases that year, 1979, and was caught only 12 times). Wilson put his speed to work on the art of the triple. Five times he topped his league in the three-base hit.

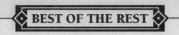

10 Hardest Throwers

Steve Dalkowski

A LEGENDARY FIGURE from the 1950s, Dalkowski was both faster and wilder than anyone ever before. They said he once blew a hole in a wooden fence 60 feet behind his catcher. They hooked up a device to measure how fast he threw, but he could not get the ball anywhere near the target. His wildness kept him out of the big leagues for too long, and before he got there his arm suddenly died.

Bob Feller

R APID ROBERT" was signed from an Iowa farm for $1 and an autographed ball. In his first major-league start, 15 St. Louis Browns went down on strikes. A few games later, he fanned 17 Athletics. When he struck out 348 men in 1946, it was the most anyone had fanned since 1904.

Walter Johnson

J OHNSON'S MOTION, a sidearm whip, was almost effortless, but the ball got to the plate so fast it was scary. It's why they called him "The Big Train." In 1908, his first full season, he was fifth in the American League in strikeouts. In 1909, he was second. For 12 of the next 15 years, no one in the AL struck out more batters than Walter Johnson. His lifetime mark (3,509) stood for more than 50 years.

SANDY KOUFAX

BEFORE KOUFAX, no National League pitcher had struck out 300 batters in the 20th century. Koufax did it three times in four years. From 1959 through 1966, he either led the league in K's or was in the top four. Despite arm trouble that ended his career early, many call him the greatest ever.

SAM McDOWELL

McDOWELL'S LEGEND has spoiled history's interpretation of him. He had major heat but also had a drinking problem, and he stayed wild enough to keep batters terrified. Yet "Sudden Sam" is one of a handful of pitchers in the 20th century to fan 300 batters in a season more than once.

AMOS RUSIE

CAN YOU IMAGINE A PITCHER who threw so fast that the baseball powers decided they had to move the pitching mound back 10 feet? That's what happened with Rusie. In 1893, home plate and the mound were separated from 50 feet to 60 feet six inches, largely because of "The Hoosier Thunderbolt." Rusie was a five-time strikeout leader.

NOLAN RYAN

RYAN WAS AN UNBELIEVABLE physical phenomenon—a man who pitched better (and some say faster) than he ever did when he was way past 40. Ryan's 100-mph fastball was matched by his incredible discipline and devotion. Six times he fanned more than 300 batters in one season. Ryan pitched seven no-hitters. He struck out 1,500 more batters than the next best pitcher.

HERB SCORE

IN HIS FIRST TWO SEASONS (1955-56), Score's amazing fastball had American Leaguers quaking in their cleats. He struck out more batters both those years than any other AL hurler. In 1956, the league batted just .186 against him as he won 20 games. But a Gil McDougald line drive hit Score in the eye, and he never really came back.

SMOKEY JOE WILLIAMS

TALL AND SKINNY, Smokey Joe's nicknames of "Cyclone" and "Strikeout" don't indicate how much control accompanied his blazing speed. As a Negro League star in the early part of the 20th century, he shut out major-leaguers in exhibition games a dozen times. In one 12-inning game, he threw a one-hitter and struck out 27 men.

SMOKEY JOE WOOD

AN INJURY SHORTENED the pitching career of Wood, but he returned to play good enough outfield to be a regular for several years. Joe was the star of the 1912 Boston Red Sox champions, with a 34-5 record. He was right behind Walter Johnson in K's in 1911 and 1912. Johnson said of him: "No man alive can throw harder than Joe Wood."

10 CRAFTIEST PITCHERS

GROVER CLEVELAND ALEXANDER

EVEN WITH ALCOHOLISM and epilepsy tearing his mind and body apart, Alexander was able to stick around by throwing strikes and outsmarting hitters. He is tied with Christy Mathewson for lifetime NL victories (373) and holds the league's career marks for complete games (437) and shutouts (90).

LEW BURDETTE

THE TEAM THAT SIGNED HIM was the Yankees, but when they couldn't wait for pitching help, they swapped him to the Braves. In 1957 (six years later), he made them pay, throwing two World Series shutouts against the Bronxmen. Burdette made people think he was always throwing a spitter, which worked just as well as if he really was.

WHITEY FORD

FORD KEPT HITTERS OFF BALANCE with an assortment of stuff (some artificially altered) and a preponderance of control, which is why he hardly ever lost. The lifelong Yankee holds many World Series records, including most consecutive scoreless innings (33, breaking Babe Ruth's of 29⅔). Ford's winning percentage of .690 is the highest of any modern 200-game winner.

BURLEIGH GRIMES

WHEN THEY BANNED the spitball in 1920, "Old Stubblebeard" was one of the few they let throw it until his career was over. His was a nasty pitch but, rugged competitor that he was, he preferred *not* to use it—just to suggest that he was.

EDDIE LOPAT

HE WAS THE MASTER of "junk," with an edgy and nervous disposition to match his mound behavior. Lopat was a keen student of the art of pitching who threw many different pitches from many different angles, which made him especially tough on free-swingers.

JUAN MARICHAL

PROBABLY THE GREATEST modern pitcher never to win a Cy Young Award, Marichal kept NL hitters dazzled with his high leg kick, baffling assortment of pitches, and sensational control. He walked only 709 batters in 3,509 innings. In his first major-league start in 1960, the Giant hurler held the Phils hitless until the eighth inning.

SATCHEL PAIGE

WHEN SATCH BEGAN HIS PITCHING CAREER, his fastball was radio-style (heard but not seen). But to make money outside of white baseball, he had to play a lot. In 1934, Paige claimed his barnstorming team played 105 games with Satchel pitching most of those. As his arm wore out, he replaced speed with savvy: a baffling windmill windup and a killer "hesitation pitch."

EDDIE PLANK

PLANK'S DELIVERY WAS DELIBERATE, to say the least. He'd fidget, mess with his belt, adjust his cap, check the dirt for pebbles, and irritate the snot out of hitters. Then he'd wing his wicked "crossfire" sidearm curve over the corner. Pitching the first 17 years of the 20th century, he had one season with a losing record—his last.

WARREN SPAHN

DECEPTION was at the heart of Spahn's pitching: a high leg kick, a sneaky fastball, a sharp curve, a dangerous slider, and flawless motion. No left-handed pitcher won more games than Spahn (363 from 1946-65). Someone once said, "If you had no idea what baseball was and you saw Spahn, you wouldn't know what he was doing, but you could tell he was the best there was at doing it."

LUIS TIANT

USING A HERKY-JERKY MOTION with arms and legs going every which way, Tiant delivered an amazing assortment of pitches with pinpoint control. He was funny to watch—unless you had a bat in your hand. In 1968 for Boston, he set an ML record for fewest hits allowed per nine innings—a remarkable 5.30.

10 BEST BREAKING PITCHES

BERT BLYLEVEN'S CURVE

BLYLEVEN'S big, looping bender was a textbook picture of how much a ball could break. No one of his time threw a better one. And with superb control, he rang up a lot of strikeouts and few walks. Of course, when his bender hung, it cost him in home runs. In 1986, he set the record by allowing 50 taters. Then to prove it was no fluke, he gave up 46 the next year.

THREE FINGER BROWN'S CURVE

A FARM ACCIDENT led to the amputation of young Brown's index finger and left him with a twisted middle finger and a crooked little finger. But it put a spin on the ball that no "normal" hand could. The ace of the potent Cubs of the early 20th century, Brown posted a 1.04 ERA in 1906—best ever for a 20-game winner.

STEVE CARLTON'S SLIDER

A MONG LEFTIES, only Warren Spahn won more games. Among all pitchers, only Nolan Ryan fanned more. Carlton was a good pitcher until he learned his remarkable slider, then he became a great one. He won four Cy Youngs, something nobody else had ever done. In 1972, he won 27 games for a Phils team that won only 59—the highest percentage of games won by one man this century.

CARL HUBBELL'S SCREWBALL

THE SCREWBALL is thrown by twisting the arm the opposite direction from the curve. Proof that Hubbell threw a zillion of them is that his arm was permanently twisted. But he dominated the National League in an era when big hitters were the rule. On July 2, 1933, he pitched an 18-inning shutout, striking out a dozen and allowing no walks.

SANDY KOUFAX'S CURVE

KOUFAX was the archetypal wild left-hander until a patient catcher told him to relax and rely on his curveball more. That curve became one of the deadliest weapons in Sandy's pitching arsenal. In his last five seasons (1962-66), he led the league in ERA every year; in wins, strikeouts, and shutouts three times; and in complete games twice.

CHRISTY MATHEWSON'S FADEAWAY

MATTY HAD ONE ESPECIALLY NASTY PITCH: the fadeaway, with its brutal opposite-direction break. (Today it would be known as a screwball.) He threw it rarely, perhaps a dozen times a game. In his book *Pitching in a Pinch*, he explained how he took it easy on most hitters; it was only "in the pinch" when he had to bear down.

CAMILO PASCUAL'S CURVE

PASCUAL ALWAYS HAD CONTROL, and a nifty fastball, but in his first five years (1954-58) he had just a 28-66 record. Then he learned how to fling a sensational sidearm curve that left batters flailing in futility or shaking their heads in dismay. He won an average of 17 games a year for the next six.

BRUCE SUTTER'S SPLITTER

THE SPLIT-FINGERED FASTBALL, gripped like a forkball but thrown so hard it could sink devilishly, was known as "the pitch of the 1970s," and Sutter's was probably the best one out there. He learned it after arm surgery threatened his career in 1973. Sutter used the nasty pitch to lead the NL in saves five of six years with the Cubs and Cards.

ED WALSH'S SPITTER

BEFORE 1920, the spitball wasn't dirty, sneaky, or illegal. It was simply a potent tool in the hands of a master like Ed Walsh. Walsh learned it from Elmer Stricklett, who learned it from the man who invented it. Walsh could throw it a lot without tiring. In fact, in 1908 he set the AL record by pitching 464 innings. He won 40 games that year too.

HOYT WILHELM'S KNUCKLER

WILHELM didn't make it to the majors till 1952 when he was almost 30 years old, but with that wildly dancing knuckleball of his, he stuck around until age 48. In Baltimore, the catcher wore an oversized glove to snag the thing. He won more games in relief than any other pitcher ever.

10 BEST CLOSERS

DENNIS ECKERSLEY

ALCOHOL PROBLEMS kept Eck from stardom in his first 12 years in the majors while a starter. But he put his demons behind him and moved into the bullpen, where he can lay claim to being the greatest closer ever. From 1988-92, his record was 24-9 with 220 saves, and he struck out 378 while walking only 38. In 1989-90, he had more saves (81) than hits (73) and walks allowed (seven).

ROLLIE FINGERS

FINGERS'S HANDLEBAR BECAME HIS TRADEMARK, along with his deadly efficiency. One of the first pitchers to refuse to pitch more than two innings (so he could be effective several days in a row), Rollie's regimen earned him a Cy Young Award, the ML record for saves upon his retirement (341), six World Series saves, and a spot in the Hall of Fame.

GOOSE GOSSAGE

NO ONE EVER SAID Gossage was "sneaky fast." He looked every inch the flamethrower, firing the ball with his powerful build and appearing as if every bone in his body would pop out of his skin. He was the captain of the Yankee bullpen during their 1978 world championship season, and he helped the Padres into the Series in 1984. He notched 310 saves.

TOM HENKE

HENKE QUIETLY WENT ABOUT his dominance year after year. He led the American League in saves in 1987 with 34; he reached the 20-save mark each year from 1986-93; and he hit the 30-save level in five of those seasons. Averaging more than a strikeout per inning, "The Terminator" employed a big fastball to set up a devastating forkball.

SPARKY LYLE

ONE OF JUST A HANDFUL of relief pitchers to win the Cy Young Award, Lyle used his sensational slider to top the 20-save mark five times (and lead the league twice). He is fifth all time in relief wins, and he was the dominant reliever in the game when his Yankees won the World Series in 1977.

FRED MARBERRY

FIRPO" WAS A TRUE IRON MAN, used both as a starter and a reliever. He led the American League in games pitched six times from 1924-32. Five times he topped the rest in saves (since the "save" was not an official statistic until 1960, this was determined retroactively). In 1929, he had 16 complete games and 11 saves.

DAN QUISENBERRY

WHEN QUISENBERRY was pitching in college, a tired arm forced him to drop down and throw sidearm. That became his legendary submarine delivery, low enough to be legal under 1880s rules. Quiz was noted for his exceptional control. *The Sporting News* named him Fireman of the Year five times, and he notched 161 saves from 1982-85.

LEE SMITH

LIKE 1960S CLOSER DICK RADATZ, Smith is one big dude. But unlike "The Monster," Smith has compiled a long and productive career. He is currently the lifetime leader in saves, and no one else is close. Smith throws hard and stares in at the batter even harder.

BRUCE SUTTER

WHEN SUTTER BEGAN THROWING his split-fingered fastball, every opposing manager was sure he was loading up. It just dropped too far too fast to be anything but a spitter, they reasoned. He led the Cardinals to the World Series in 1982 and rang up two saves there. He won one Cy Young Award and four Fireman of the Year Awards.

HOYT WILHELM

WILHELM TURNED 29 the first year he pitched in the big leagues, but he stuck around long enough after that to appear in more ML games than any pitcher ever (1,070). The secret was the dazzling dance of his knuckleball, so daunting that catchers turned to extra-large gloves to snag it. He had an ERA under 2.00 each year from 1964-68.

10 Best Hitting Pitchers

Jack Bentley

They were calling Bentley "the next Babe Ruth" in 1922, when he hit .349 in 153 games, finishing second in the International League for the Baltimore Orioles (Ruth's first team too). In 1923, he won 13 games for the pennant-winning Giants and hit .427 in 52 games. He also had two pinch hits in that year's World Series. In Game 5 of the 1924 Series, he slugged a two-run homer off Walter Johnson. His lifetime batting average was .291.

Ken Brett

With good-hitting pitchers a rarity in the modern game, Brett was a throwback. Brother of batting champion George, Ken was always certain to put the ball in play—a tremendous advantage for a pitcher. Along with his lifetime .262 average, he topped the .300 mark in three different seasons, and in 1973 he homered in four straight starts to set a record.

Doc Crandall

One of the first true relief pitchers in the game, Crandall's ability with the stick made him a valuable pinch-hitter. He swatted the ball at a .285 clip for his career. He had a sensational season in 1910, when he won 17 games, lost just four, and slugged his way to a .342 average.

WES FERRELL

FERRELL'S 38 HOMERS outdistance the career mark of any other pitcher, and his nine in 1931 is best for a single season. In 1935, he won back-to-back games with homers, one pinch-hitting and one for himself. Ferrell's hitting ability was a matter of hard work. He said, "A lot of guys could do it if they tried."

GEORGE MULLIN

MULLIN, a teammate of Ty Cobb, hit .262 for his career—and that was in the dead-ball era. He was used as a pinch-hitter 101 times and counted 23 triples among his 401 hits. In 1902, his rookie season, he cranked out a .325 average and scored 20 runs despite just 120 at-bats.

DON NEWCOMBE

IN 1955, Newcombe had quite a year. Not only was he 20-5 for the pennant-winning Dodgers, but he hit .359 and set an NL record for homers by a pitcher in a season with seven. Twice that season he hit two homers in one game. He even stole home once. His .271 lifetime average ranks among the best for pitchers in major-league history.

AL ORTH

THIS TURN-OF-THE-CENTURY PITCHER banged out 389 career hits as a hurler, and 78 times he was used to pinch-hit. His lifetime average of .273 is one of the best marks ever for a pitcher, and he hit .290 or better eight times. He also won 204 games.

SCHOOLBOY ROWE

ROWE WAS MORE THAN JUST A PITCHER who occasionally pinch-hit; he was counted on off the bench. In 1943, he led the National League in pinch hits, going 15-for-49. He is one of just five pitchers to slug a pinch-hit grand slam. He hit another grand slam to aid his own pitching cause.

JACK STIVETTS

IN 11 19TH-CENTURY SEASONS, Stivetts was a remarkably consistent batsman. His lifetime average of .297 as a pitcher compares favorably with that of Babe Ruth when the Bambino was a moundsman. His 21 homers as a hurler ranks him among the best.

GEORGE UHLE

IN 1923, slider pitcher Uhle tore the American League apart. He won 26 games, threw 29 complete games, and pitched 357 innings; all led the league. He also batted .361, one of the highest marks ever for a pitcher. He hit a grand slam off Dutch Leonard in 1921, and he holds the highest batting average (.289) of 20th-century pitchers (minimum 1,000 at-bats).

Note: Pitchers who played more than one-third of their major-league careers at other positions are not included.

10 Best Defensive Catchers

Johnny Bench

BENCH PUT IT ALL TOGETHER: size, strength, quickness, and a terrifying arm. He invented the art of one-handed catching, the perfect style for the newer and faster basestealers of his era. Twelve times Bench was an All-Star, and he won 10 consecutive Gold Gloves.

Yogi Berra

WHEN YOGI CAME TO THE MAJORS IN 1946, he was a miserable catcher. But he could hit so well, you couldn't keep him out of the lineup. With the aid of Yankee coach Bill Dickey, he made himself a quality backstop. Casey Stengel said, "He springs on a bunt like it was a dollar." Berra set two records with 148 consecutive errorless games, handling 950 chances.

Lou Criger

FROM 1897-1908, Criger had one job: Cy Young's personal catcher. When the winningest hurler of all time picks you out as the man he wants to throw to, your credentials as a first-rate backstop are indisputable. When Young changed teams, Criger had to come with him. Criger was not a big man, but a small and spry one.

BUCK EWING

ALTHOUGH HIS NAME is largely forgotten now, Ewing was considered one of the greatest players (not just catchers) of all time during his 1880-97 stint in the majors. Ewing was said to be the first catcher to throw from a crouch position and the first to back up other bases. He was blessed with a sensational arm.

GEORGE GIBSON

EVEN THOUGH HITTING WAS OUT OF HIS LEAGUE, Canadian-born Gibson was Mr. Reliable behind the plate for the Pirates from 1905-16. He still holds the Pirate record of catching 1,113 games. Three times he led the National League in fielding percentage. He once tallied 203 assists in a season.

GABBY HARTNETT

ALTHOUGH MOST PEOPLE THINK OF GABBY as a hitter, he was also the dominant defensive backstop in the National League in the 1920s and '30s. Four times he outpaced all other NL catchers in putouts, six times in assists, six times in double plays. He led in fielding average six times. Joe McCarthy called him "the perfect catcher."

JIM HEGAN

HEGAN'S SAVVY AT CALLING A GAME made him the man the Indians counted on from 1941-57. Six pitchers won 20 games a total of 18 different times with Hegan behind the plate. One opposing player said, "Hitters who strike out against the Indians cuss Hegan." He was especially skilled on pop-ups and balls in the dirt.

JOHNNY KLING

THE REMARKABLE CUB TEAMS OF 1906-10 had one of the best as their catcher. Ed Reulbach called Kling "one of the greatest catchers who ever wore a mask." In addition to leading the National League in fielding twice and putouts six times, Kling was spectacular in the World Series, setting several records that still haven't been broken.

SHERM LOLLAR

BIG, SLOW, INDOMITABLE, Lollar typified the catcher of the 1950s, and he was the best of the bunch. Five times Lollar was the best American League catcher in fielding percentage. His lifetime .992 fielding average places him sixth all time. In 1962, he tied the major-league record when he snagged six pop flies in one game.

RAY SCHALK

THE HONEST, aggressive Schalk was not asked to join in the plan to hand the 1919 World Series to the Reds. He topped the AL in fielding average and putouts eight times each. He still is the all-time leader in double plays (by 50) and AL leader in assists. He has the lowest batting average of any nonpitcher in the Hall of Fame.

10 BEST DEFENSIVE FIRST BASEMEN

HAL CHASE

SOME SAY THERE WAS NEVER A BETTER FIELDER at the initial sack. Smooth and handy, Chase was often able to charge a bunt, snatch the ball, tag the man heading to first, and then make a strong throw to third to nail the runner. He tied a single-game record with 22 putouts in 1906 that still stands.

KEITH HERNANDEZ

HERNANDEZ PUT TOGETHER a string of 11 consecutive Gold Glove titles (1978-88) because he was simply the best of his time. He holds the major-league record for most seasons leading first basemen in double plays (six) and is the National League lifetime assist leader. He was known to charge to the third base line on bunts.

GIL HODGES

HODGES'S SURE-HANDEDNESS was due to two things: 1) he came up through the Dodger organization in the mid-1940s as a catcher, and 2) his hands were huge (12 inches from thumb tip to pinky tip). Some folks said he didn't need a glove at all. In addition, his footwork around the base was so smooth that opposing managers often accused him of leaving the base before the ball got there.

ED KONETCHY

WHEN OTHER FIRST BASEMEN were content to stick close to the bag, Konetchy was ranging far afield. He was consistent and dependable. Konetchy led the National League in fielding seven times with four different teams, making only 224 errors in more than 21,000 chances.

DON MATTINGLY

THE YANKEE FIRST SACKER was a smooth enough fielder that occasionally he moved to second or third base for defensive reasons, even though he was a lefty. In 1994, he won his ninth Gold Glove, more than any first baseman other than Keith Hernandez. No one has a higher lifetime fielding percentage at first.

WES PARKER

PARKER ALWAYS THOUGHT he was playing out of position; he felt he should have been a center fielder. Yet the Dodger's lifetime .996 fielding average matches Don Mattingly's and Steve Garvey's for the best of all time. In 1968, Parker was charged with a controversial, bad-hop error—one of just two errors all season. Some said the official scorer who made the call had been drinking.

VIC POWER

THE PERSON WHO INVENTED the term "hot dog" may have been thinking of Power at the time.

He wasn't just a great fielder; he was a great showman, with flashy, snapping grabs of infielders' throws. Power won the first seven AL Gold Gloves in the late 1950s and early '60s.

GEORGE SCOTT

AN EIGHT-TIME GOLD GLOVE WINNER in the 1960s and '70s, "The Boomer" was a powerful hitter and fan favorite. A showboat in the Vic Power mold, although not blessed with Power's body type, Scott loved to scoop balls out of the dirt. When asked what his unusual necklace was made of, he answered with a grin: "Second basemen's teeth."

GEORGE SISLER

FOR SHEER GRACE AROUND THE BAG, Sisler reminded many people of Hal Chase. Sisler was the consummate professional, the artist at the base; finesse and unhurried smoothness were his calling cards. From 1919-27, he led the American League in assists six times.

BILL WHITE

WHITE WAS A BIG, TOUGH GUY, but he patroled the area around first like a whippet. From 1960-66, no other National League first sacker even smelled a Gold Glove. White served as one of the reliable masters on the highly defensive Cardinal teams. After his career, he kept moving up—to the broadcast booth and then to NL president.

10 BEST DEFENSIVE SECOND BASEMEN

EDDIE COLLINS

COLLINS WAS THE HEART of one of baseball's first great infields—the "$100,000 Infield" of Connie Mack's Philadelphia Athletics. Nine times he led the American League in fielding average. He's the all-time career leader in assists and chances by a second baseman.

FRED DUNLAP

IN THE 1880s, when it took a he-man just to play baseball (no one wore gloves), Dunlap was one of the best of them all. Known as "Sure Shot" for his exceptional throws, which he would make right- or left-handed as the situation dictated, he and teammate Jack Glasscock formed the "Stonewall Infield."

JOHNNY EVERS

EVERS WAS ONE OF THE GAME'S brightest and toughest players. His heads-up call on the Merkle baserunning blunder in 1908 effectively won his Cubs the pennant. A great player for the great Cubs teams, he was also the second baseman for the "Miracle Braves" of 1914. He won the National League's Most Valuable Player Award that year, even though he batted just .279.

CHARLIE GEHRINGER

THEY USED TO SAY OF GEHRINGER that he was the "Mechanical Man": just wind him up on Opening Day and let him go. In 16 full seasons (1926-41), he led all American League second basemen in fielding percentage and assists seven times, and he outpaced all others in putouts three times.

JOE GORDON

GORDON WAS A REMARKABLE SLUGGER for a second baseman, but he was also a wonderful and exciting fielder. His defensive exploits earned him the nickname "Flash." After being the Yankee second baseman for five pennant-winners, Gordon went to Cleveland and helped the Tribe win their first flag in 28 years in 1948.

BOBBY GRICH

GRICH INVITED COMPARISONS TO BILL MAZEROSKI for his fine defensive play. He set the major-league record for fielding percentage by a second baseman in 1973 (.995). Twelve years later, he reset the record, making just two errors all season on the way to a .997 mark.

BILL MAZEROSKI

THE BABE RUTH OF DEFENSE, Mazeroski holds more defensive records than any player who has ever played. He holds major-league records for double plays by a second baseman with 1,706 (nearly 100 more than the guy in second place) as well as double plays in a season with 161 in 1966. He led NL second sackers in double plays a record eight times, in chances a record eight times, and in assists a record nine times.

BID MCPHEE

EVEN WHEN OTHER PLAYERS started wearing gloves in the 1890s, Bid passed. He holds what may be the longest standing record still on the books: the record for putouts in a season by a second sacker, set in 1886. He led the league in double plays in 11 seasons and in fielding average nine times. He is No. 1 in career putouts.

SPINACH MELILLO

IN THE 1920S AND '30s, when big sluggers dominated baseball, the slick Oscar ("Ski" or "Spinach") Melillo was a genuine fielding superstar. Twice he led the American League in fielding percentage for second basemen. Three times he led in "fielding runs." He was underappreciated during his career and is almost forgotten now.

FRANK WHITE

NO SECOND BASEMAN IN AMERICAN LEAGUE HISTORY has ever matched Frank White's record of six consecutive Gold Gloves (he won two others also to hold the lifetime record). In 1977, the smooth White played in 62 consecutive games without being charged with an error.

10 BEST DEFENSIVE SHORTSTOPS

LUIS APARICIO

APARICIO DEFINED THE SHORTSTOP POSITION for slick glovework until Ozzie Smith came along. He still holds the American League lifetime records for assists (8,016) and double plays (1,553). When he first came to the big leagues, he played very shallow. When they asked him to move back, they were astonished at his arm.

GEORGE DAVIS

DAVIS WAS ONE OF THE UNSUNG HEROES of the 19th century. He started as an outfielder, but his hands and range were such that he was soon moved to third, and then to short. A political move (trying to sit out a season to get a better contract) led to his suspension from baseball.

RABBIT MARANVILLE

DESPITE LOW BATTING AVERAGES, Maranville was annually a heavy vote-getter for MVP honors. The basket catch was his trademark. After leading the NL in 10 defensive categories in a six-year span as a Brave, Rabbit went to Pittsburgh. There he led NL shortstops in fielding average in 1923 and NL *second basemen* in fielding in '24. He repeated the feat in 1930 (at shortstop) and '32 (at second).

Roy McMillan

THE BESPECTACLED McMILLAN was a small man, but he combined the art of scientific positioning with a durability that far outstripped his size. He won the first three Gold Gloves for shortstops (1957-59 with Cincy). His 584 consecutive games played at short are an NL record.

Everett Scott

SCOTT WAS A MASTER OF EFFICIENCY. Eight times in a row, Scott led the AL in fielding average at shortstop. During the 1916 World Series, opposing manager Wilbert Robinson bemoaned the fact that Scott's arm was flawless in throwing out his men at first, calling it "the trolley line."

Germany Smith

BEING A SHORTSTOP IN THE 1880s carried a much more dangerous job description than today. The fields were rugged, and the gloves were barely there. In this difficult atmosphere, Smith wasn't just good; he was superior, tracking down balls others couldn't reach. He led his league in shortstop assists four years in a row.

Ozzie Smith

THE WIZARD" was the flashiest, most exciting shortstop ever. And he didn't miss the easy ones, either. He leads all shortstops in career assists. No shortstop has ever led his league in assists (eight times) or chances (eight) more often. His 1980 record of 621 assists smashed by 20 what was thought to be an untouchable record.

OMAR VIZQUEL

AMERICA DISCOVERED VIZQUEL'S TALENTS in the 1995 postseason, when he helped Cleveland to the World Series. Baseball's greatest acrobat, Vizquel can dive for a ball, bounce up, and flip to first all in one fluid motion. Errors are rare with Vizquel, who's won four straight Gold Gloves.

HONUS WAGNER

WAGNER WAS SO GOOD every place he played that he didn't become a full-time shortstop until he was almost 30 years old. But he still ranks as the best overall shortstop of all time. Built more like a barrel than an infielder, he was still incredibly fast, and he had a powerful arm that could throw runners out from anywhere.

BOBBY WALLACE

WALLACE LIVES ON REPUTATION, because the fielding stats for 19th-century players are difficult to evaluate and compare to today's, given the playing conditions. But Wallace earned his spot in the Hall of Fame because his name often appeared among the league fielding leaders. Wallace was the first player who grabbed slow-hit grounders with his throwing hand to get off a quicker throw.

10 Best Defensive Third Basemen

Buddy Bell

When Bell came to the majors for the Indians in 1972, they already had a fine third baseman—Graig Nettles. So Bell spent a season in the outfield, where he made just three errors, and Tribe management knew it was time to swap Nettles. Bell shined with Cleveland and went on to win six consecutive Gold Gloves with Texas.

Clete Boyer

Even though his brother Ken won more Gold Gloves, Clete faced more competition, namely Brooks Robinson. The exceptionally slick-fielding Clete did win one Gold Glove late in his career. As the reliable third sacker for the Yankees, Clete set a World Series record for career assists.

Billy Cox

Cox's career wasn't long (1946-55), but he earned a reputation as an exceptional gloveman rapidly, and many historians feel he was the best until the arrival of Brooks Robinson. Originally a shortstop in Pittsburgh, he made his name at third with the Dodgers as a sure-handed and flamboyant star. Casey Stengel said of Cox, "That ain't a third baseman; that's a (bleeping) acrobat!"

Ray Dandridge

Because African-Americans were banned from playing in the major leagues, most fans never saw the artistry of Dandridge, a man with bowed legs, soft hands, and a superior arm. Roy Campanella once said, "I never saw anyone better as a fielder."

Willie Kamm

In his 13-year career (1923-35), Kamm outpaced all the third basemen in the American League in fielding percentage eight times. He combined superb hands with keen instincts and was helped by a White Sox pitching staff that induced grounders. Kamm was a master at pulling the hidden-ball trick on unsuspecting arrivals at third.

Don Money

As a Phillie in 1972, Money led National League third basemen in putouts, assists, and double plays. Then he was traded to Milwaukee and proceeded in 1974 to set the record for fielding percentage by an ML third baseman (.989). Only three players had a better lifetime fielding percentage.

Graig Nettles

In the 1978 World Series, the Yankees were down two games to none when Nettles made four brilliant grabs and throws in Game 3 to save as many as seven Dodger runs. The Yanks took that game as well as the next three. Nettles received two Gold Gloves during his career.

BROOKS ROBINSON

NOBODY EVER DID IT BETTER at third than Brooks. He holds the highest lifetime fielding percentage among third sackers (.971) and also is the all-time leader in putouts (2,697), assists (6,205), and double plays (618). No wonder he won 16 Gold Gloves and started in the All-Star Game 15 years in a row. His clinic of third base work in the 1970 Series is an absolute classic.

RON SANTO

SANTO WAS AN EXCEPTIONAL THIRD BASEMAN who got stuck with bad Cub teams in the 1960s and '70s. So he seldom gets his due. But he was the top third sacker in the National League for several years. He led the NL in putouts eight times, assists seven times, and double plays six times. He received five Gold Gloves.

MIKE SCHMIDT

UNDOUBTEDLY, Schmidt was the greatest third baseman of all time. In addition to his legendary slugging abilities, he was a remarkably consistent fielder with good range and a cannon arm. His leading total of 265 "fielding runs" (runs saved by defense) is nearly one-third higher than any other third baseman in history. He won 10 Gold Gloves.

10 BEST DEFENSIVE OUTFIELDERS

RICHIE ASHBURN

In the new stat of "fielding runs" (a measurement of how many runs a defensive player saved his team), Ashburn is second lifetime among outfielders. The Phillies' Ashburn was a true ballhawk with a fine arm who led the league in double plays three times.

PAUL BLAIR

Blair was very fast and was exceptionally good at going back for balls. So he played quite shallow, daring hitters to drop one in front of him. The strategy worked; he won eight Gold Gloves from 1967-75 and Baltimore pitchers won frequently. Blair made several memorable catches in postseason play.

ROBERTO CLEMENTE

The Pirate right fielder could get the ball and throw it as well as anyone had ever seen. And no one had ever seen it done with such ferocity, as though each ball hit his way was a personal threat. The list of great Clemente catches and throws is a long one. Particularly memorable was a play early in the 1971 World Series that turned the usually aggressive Orioles into timid baserunners.

JOE DIMAGGIO

HE WAS GRACE AND ELEGANCE PERSONIFIED, and although others put up better defensive stats, Joe DiMaggio patrolled the ominous spaces of Yankee Stadium with remarkable efficiency. DiMaggio was careful to position himself for hitters' tendencies, and his arm was excellent.

DWIGHT EVANS

EVANS'S ARM INTIMIDATED BASERUNNERS. He manned the odd-shaped right-field corner in Boston's Fenway Park and made it his own. His most dramatic catch took place in the highly dramatic 1975 World Series when, in Game 6, he took a potentially Series-winning clout by Joe Morgan and turned it into a double play.

MIKE GRIFFIN

GRIFFIN WAS CONSIDERED by the fans and players of his time to be the greatest outfielder of the 19th century. He led all the outfielders in his league in fielding average six times during the 1890s. In his single year with the Players' League, his 10 double plays were highest.

HARRY HOOPER

THE RED SOX RIGHT FIELDER INVENTED the sliding catch, whereby a ball he didn't snag would be stopped by his body. In the last game of the 1912 World Series, Hooper raced back for a long drive only to have it pop out of his mitt. He calmly snagged it with his bare hand and saved the game for Boston.

AL KALINE

THE WINNER OF 10 GOLD GLOVES from 1957-67, "Mr. Tiger" was so smooth in right field that he made the sensational look everyday. His arm was excellent; his knowledge of hitters and ballparks unsurpassed. And with his consistent hard work and dedication to perfection, Kaline was admired as well as skilled. He always gave his best.

WILLIE MAYS

PERHAPS THE MOST COMPLETE BASEBALL PLAYER EVER, Mays stood in center field and dared anyone to hit the ball to him. He could dive, leap, or slide for the tough ones, or use his trademark basket catch on the easy ones. His great catch in the 1954 World Series was less notable for the grab than for the unbelievable throw he released afterward.

TRIS SPEAKER

A LIFETIME .345 HITTER, "Spoke" played the best outfield anyone had ever seen. Playing a shallow center, he turned an unassisted double play from the outfield a record five times in his career. No major-league outfielder ever threw out more runners or took part in more double plays. Only Willie Mays caught more fly balls.

10 BEST PERSONALITIES

YOGI BERRA

THE MARVELOUS, sometimes uproarious, nearly Zen (but not quite) "Berra-isms" are inextricably intertwined with baseball lore, and they often show off a mind with a keen understanding of the game. The man who pronounced the deep truth about baseball—"It ain't over till it's over"—left the historic third game of the 1951 National League playoffs in the eighth inning.

DIZZY DEAN

NO BALLPLAYER ever had a more accurate nickname. Horrible English ("there is a lot of people in the United States who say 'isn't,' and they ain't eating") and a genuine boyish love of the game characterized Dizzy's personality. After a short but highly successful pitching career in the 1930s, he became a broadcaster for more than 20 years.

CHARLES FINLEY

THE A'S OWNER WAS WILDLY INNOVATIVE: Nighttime World Series games was his idea, but so too were mechanical ballboys and orange baseballs. With less money than his competitors, he tried to outwit them, and he succeeded in infuriating almost everyone. It is said his A's of the early '70s won three straight World Series because they were unified in hating Finley.

ARLIE LATHAM

THE FANS OF THE LATE 1800s loved Latham for his roaring enthusiasm. Latham would lead the fans in cheers and heckle the opposition without mercy. Then he'd somersault his way out to his position. In the off-season, fans would turn out around the country for his stage act.

BILL LEE

THE ACE FROM OUTER SPACE," Bill Lee marched to the beat of a different drummer—or two or three. The first time he saw Fenway Park's Green Monster, he asked, "Do they leave it up during games?" After Game 4 of the 1975 World Series, a reporter asked his impression of the Series so far. Lee answered, "Tied."

RABBIT MARANVILLE

IT MAY BE THAT NO ONE had more fun playing baseball than the Rabbit—the eternal puckish clown, the one with the funniest faces, the loudest pratfalls, and the highest consumption of goldfish. As a defensive player in the 1910s, '20s, and '30s, this longtime Brave was a superstar. As an on-the-field entertainer and practical joker, he was a genius.

BABE RUTH

THE ADJECTIVE "RUTHIAN" was coined to describe the outsized style of everything Babe Ruth did, but it was impossible to apply it to anything done by anyone else. Babe Ruth *lived* bigger than life: more food, more fun, more women, and more home runs than anyone had ever seen. Ruth put the roar into the Roaring '20s.

CASEY STENGEL

"STENGELESE" was the way this colorful manager dealt with the pestering questions of the press. "Best thing wrong with Jack Fisher is nothing," said Case. But Stengel was a beloved, fun-loving player long before he became a manager. In 1918, he tipped his cap to the crowd and a bird flew out.

BILL VEECK

VEECK BELIEVED THAT COMING TO A BASEBALL GAME meant you wanted to have fun, and no owner ever did more to assure that: from sending up a midget to pinch-hit, to moving the fences in and out between games, to letting the fans manage for a game, to exploding scoreboards, cow-milking contests, and bizarre giveaways. And of course, the other owners couldn't stand him.

RUBE WADDELL

A COLORFUL ODDBALL, Waddell possessed a child-like sense of life and baseball—an endearing trait attached to a sensational left arm. He loved fire trucks and fishing trips, he wrestled alligators, and his roommate had it written in his contract that Rube was forbidden to eat crackers in bed.

10 BEST UMPIRES

AL BARLICK

YOU ALWAYS KNEW WHERE YOU STOOD with Barlick, as his calls were loud and clear. No umpire has officiated at more All-Star Games than he did. In 1961, *The Sporting News* polled baseball writers to select the best umpire in the game. Barlick won easily but refused the award, saying in effect, "How can a writer judge how well I do my job?"

TOMMY CONNOLLY

CONNOLLY, born in England, never played baseball, but as batboy for a local nine he became fascinated with the rules. The first man to umpire an American League game, Tommy had a fierce temper and tossed 10 men in his first AL season. After that, he learned how to quell problems early and didn't have to heave anyone for 10 years. The last person he ousted was Babe Ruth.

BILLY EVANS

IN THE RUGGED EARLY DAYS of the 20th century, when umpires often had to use their fists, Evans stood above all that. Refined and dignified, he preferred being diplomatic (although he did have to meet Ty Cobb under the stands after one incident). In addition, he was one of the first umpires to write extensively about the game, adding the arbiter's insights to the literature.

JOHN GAFFNEY

THEY CALLED HIM "KING OF THE UMPIRES" because he was such a superb caller of balls and strikes, and "Honest John" because of his reliability. Gaffney was one of the greatest umpires of the 19th century, working countless World Series games. He was the first ump to move from behind the plate to behind the pitcher when a batter reached base.

DOUG HARVEY

THEY CALLED HARVEY "GOD." He looked the part: tall, white-haired, serious. And he acted it: always unflappable, certain and aware. In the 1980 NLCS, he made a call that confused baserunners and created a possible triple play. "God" quietly sorted it through and made the right call. He usually did.

STEAMBOAT JOHNSON

HARRY "STEAMBOAT" JOHNSON'S rich voice earned him his nickname. He was a major-league umpire for only one season (1914), as he was probably too colorful for the bigs. His book *Standing the Gaff* explains what life was like umpiring in the rowdy minors for most of his adult life. "Standing the gaff" means surviving all the abuse.

BILL KLEM

MOST PEOPLE AGREE THAT KLEM was the greatest umpire ever. In fact, he was so good at calling balls and strikes that for 16 seasons they wouldn't let him umpire the bases. For 37 years, he was simply the best. When he retired in 1941, they put him in charge of all the National League umps.

BILL MCGOWAN

FOR A PERIOD OF NEARLY 17 YEARS, McGowan umpired almost 2,541 games consecutively (missing just two). He had to be suspended twice for poor treatment of a pitcher in one instance and the press in another. But his toughness was always matched by his fairness: His early nickname of "Big Shot" was later changed to "Number One."

BILL MCLEAN

YOU HAD TO BE TOUGH to be an umpire in the 19th century. "Kill the ump" wasn't a slogan; it was a stratagem. McLean, a former professional boxer, was one of the toughest. The first true professional umpire, he combined honesty with toughness. His reputation was such that he was seldom challenged on the field.

CY RIGLER

THE NEXT TIME YOU SEE an umpire hold up his hands with his left indicating the number of balls and the right the number of strikes, you have Cy Rigler to thank, for he pioneered the use of hand signals. Rigler was a huge man, and because of it he was seldom truly challenged. If a scrap arose, he could often defuse it with humor.

10 BEST EXECUTIVES

ED BARROW

BARROW SAT AS GENERAL MANAGER or president during the Yankees' most potent years: 1921-44. As a successful minor-league manager and executive, he "discovered" Honus Wagner. As the Red Sox's manager, he began the process of turning Babe Ruth from a fabled pitcher into an everyday player. He also built the great Yankee farm system.

RUBE FOSTER

FOSTER WAS A HUGE MAN and as classy as he was large. A superb pitcher in black baseball, he helped form the Chicago American Giants and helped them stay a powerhouse for a dozen years. Then he began the Negro National League, and he was its first president as it expanded to eastern and western divisions. It enjoyed great success until the Depression brought it down.

WILLIAM HULBERT

IN 1875, Hulbert bought into the Chicago White Stockings of the National Association. But when cited for signing players illegally, he did what any proud, 19th-century captain of industry would do: He started his own league—the National League. With Al Spalding, he cleaned up the game (he even tossed New York and Philadelphia out) and established the NL's credibility and economic viability.

BAN JOHNSON

JOHNSON STARTED AS A SPORTS WRITER but found turning minor leagues around was more fun. So when he saw a chance, the dictatorial Johnson snatched up a load of ballplayers in 1901 and founded the American League—the only successful competition that the National League has ever had. Johnson had to be the boss in all respects.

KENESAW MOUNTAIN LANDIS

A FORMER JUDGE, Landis took the job as the game's first commissioner only because he received absolute power. He was a breathing symbol of fairness and unquestioned authority. He solidified the value of the World Series by swatting barnstormers and tossing out the "Black Sox."

LARRY MACPHAIL

MACPHAIL MOVED from Cincinnati's front office to Brooklyn's in 1938 and immediately ignored the New York ban on baseball broadcasting. Then he installed lights in Ebbets Field. New ideas were his strong suit. When he was hired to run the Yankees, he had his players flying via commercial planes instead of railroads.

MARVIN MILLER

MILLER WAS HIRED AS EXECUTIVE DIRECTOR of the players union in 1966. Under the domineering Miller, the players moved from being well-paid heroes to ridiculously overpaid "entertainers." With Miller-inspired arbitration and free agency, players now routinely earn 30 times what they would have earned 20 years ago.

BRANCH RICKEY

AN ELOQUENT MAN with the demeanor of a preacher who had just picked your pocket, Rickey instituted farm systems, modernized spring training, brought batting helmets to the majors, and signed Jackie Robinson. He was 77 years old when he tried to start a new league, which scared MLB into expanding for the first time in 60 years.

BILL VEECK

THERE WAS NEVER AN OWNER who had the fans' interests more at heart. Veeck learned the baseball business from the bottom up when he started as an office boy with the Cubs in 1933. Veeck developed wacky promotions, wild gimmicks. He sent a midget up to pinch-hit and installed an exploding scoreboard. And he developed winning teams (Indians and White Sox) in the process.

JOHN MONTGOMERY WARD

A STAR PITCHER, star shortstop, and trained attorney, Ward was an intense, natural-born leader. He became the founding father of the Players' League in 1890 when the owners instituted a salary cap. But then, as today, money and not principles did the talking, and his league failed.

10 Best Broadcasters

Mel Allen

POSSESSOR of one of the most marvelous baseball voices of all time—resonant and friendly, yet authoritative in a uniquely baseball way—Allen was the biggest deal in broadcasting for the biggest deal in baseball (the Yankees) for a quarter-century. He later became the voice of *This Week in Baseball*, where a new generation got to know him.

Red Barber

WHEN LARRY MACPHAIL brought Barber to Brooklyn in 1938, baseball broadcasting was brand-new to New York City. All Red did was set the standard for rigid professionalism and attention to detail. Some of the greatest broadcasters ever learned their trade as Red's assistants. The Southerner's many catch phrases became part of Brooklyn baseball history.

Jack Buck

DURING THE FIRST GREAT ERA of baseball on the air, men like Buck became local heroes for their consistent quality and genuine likability. Now they deserve to be recognized as national legends. For more than 40 years, Buck's voice was what ball fans all over the Midwest tuned in to hear, as he aired the Cardinal games over KMOX. He has worked National Football League games as well.

BOB COSTAS

COSTAS GREW UP listening to the great voices calling the game: Mel Allen, Red Barber, Lindsey Nelson, Vin Scully. But unlike most of his contemporaries, he followed his dream to become a highly respected broadcaster. He's best known for his superb work on baseball, but he's excelled at many sports for NBC.

ERNIE HARWELL

WHILE HARWELL WAS BROADCASTING Atlanta Cracker games, Brooklyn Dodgers owner Branch Rickey swapped the Crackers a player (Cliff Dapper) to get him. After working with Red Barber for several years, Harwell became the beloved and reliable voice of the Tigers. When new owners fired him, fan pressure brought him back.

RUSS HODGES

HODGES WAS BEHIND THE MIKE for the Bobby Thomson home run that shocked the baseball world, and his straight-ahead, love-them-Giants call was both a perfect emblem of his style and a piece of baseball history. Hodges worked for the Cubs, White Sox, Senators, and Yankees before joining the Giants for two decades.

WAITE HOYT

AFTER A HALL OF FAME CAREER as a Yankee pitcher during the Ruth era, Hoyt joined the Reds broadcast team in 1941 and became a beloved fixture in Cincinnati for nearly 25 years. Like a ballplayer, he had a fine sense of the art of storytelling.

AL MICHAELS

A S THE REDS AND GIANTS ANNOUNCER, Michaels's brutal honesty brought him national attention. He spent several years as the primary announcer on ABC's "Monday Night Baseball." His call in the 1980 Olympics of the U.S. hockey team's victory over the Russians is a classic.

BOB PRINCE

N O ONE EVER ROOTED for the home team more brazenly than "The Gunner," Pirate announcer for more than 25 years. He coined dozens of memorable phrases: "We need a bloop and a blast"; "Call up the Hoover"; "There's a bug loose on the rug"; "Call a *doc*-tor." Pittsburgh baseball began a long downhill slide when he was fired in 1975.

VIN SCULLY

R ED BARBER'S MOST ABLE PUPIL, Scully weaves words so poetically descriptive that listeners receive a much greater sense of the game than from anyone else. Some of his game calls have been transcribed and anthologized as classic efforts in baseball literature. His voice can be heard throughout Dodger Stadium on transistor radios.

10 BEST WRITERS

LEE ALLEN

ALLEN DIDN'T LEARN HIS TRADE in the press box or locker room. He held the post of historian at the Hall of Fame in Cooperstown for a decade. For years, he wrote a column for *The Sporting News* that led the way for a generation of SABR researchers. Among his best books are *The History of the World Series, The American League Story,* and *The National League Story.*

ROGER ANGELL

ANGELL UNITES the sensibility of the intelligent, curious fan with genuinely great writing. He is always a delight to read, and some of his reports for *The New Yorker* on each baseball season have become the definitive works for future researchers. Angell is able to create stunning word pictures that do much more than describe people and plays.

THOMAS BOSWELL

BOSWELL WRITES FOR A NEWSPAPER, but since his newspaper is in Washington, D.C.—where there is no major-league team—he is free to roam the countryside, and the results are splendid more often than not. Boswell's two best books, *How Life Imitates the World Series* and *Why Time Begins on Opening Day,* are compilations of his newspaper columns and tickle the edge of "reporting."

HENRY CHADWICK

CHADWICK PUSHED NEW YORK PAPERS to cover baseball games in the 1850s by writing the game accounts. Then he led the rules committee to make the game better, fairer, and more enjoyable. For nearly 30 years, he wrote the *Spalding Guides,* which summed up each season. Chadwick is the only writer enshrined in the Hall of Fame proper.

ROBERT CREAMER

CREAMER'S *Babe* was a breakthrough in baseball biography, perhaps the best baseball book ever written. Then he followed it up with *Stengel: His Life and Times,* a superb bio of the wonderful character Casey, and *Baseball in '41,* one of the best season histories.

BILL JAMES

OTHER PEOPLE were doing Sabermetric research when James started, but it was his crisp, insightful, and funny prose that brought the idea of "new stats" to the foreground of fans' (and some managers') thoughts. His "Baseball Abstracts" were big sellers, and his *Bill James Historical Baseball Abstract* is one of the best histories ever written.

ROGER KAHN

HIS *THE BOYS OF SUMMER* IS RATED by many as the best baseball book of all time, a bittersweet revisiting of the wonderful Dodger players of the

1950s after they had left the game. Kahn learned his trade in the hardscrabble world of daily New York sports journalism, but his use of language is far above the newspaper style.

RING LARDNER

LARDNER WROTE FUNNY. His classic tales of offbeat rookie Jack Keefe in *You Know Me, Al* is still marvelous to read. Lardner got his ideas from the most natural of sources: He was a baseball beat writer for years. Lardner had a keen eye for baseball drama. He was suspicious of the play of the White Sox early in the 1919 World Series.

GRANTLAND RICE

IT'S TOUGH TO WRITE ELEGANT, dramatic prose when you face the deadline gun every day. But Rice did it for decades. He is known for lines such as "It's not whether you win or lose; it's how you play the game," and (on Babe Ruth's death) "The Big Guy's left us with the night to face/And there is no one who can take his place."

FRANCIS RICHTER

A PIONEER in the field of sports journalism, Richter was the first editor of the sports page for several newspapers. In 1883, he founded *Sporting Life*, the first national sports publication. For the first quarter of the 20th century, Richter edited the popular *Reach's Guides*.

10 BEST FILMS

BANG THE DRUM SLOWLY

BASED ON MARK HARRIS'S NOVEL, this 1973 film stars two up-and-comers, Michael Moriarty and Robert De Niro, in the tale of two teammates—one a star, one a journeyman—who bond together in a sad, final season. Vincent Gardenia is great as a manager. And who could ever forget TEGWAR?

THE BINGO LONG TRAVELING ALL-STARS AND MOTOR KINGS

BLACK BASEBALL BARNSTORMING through small towns in the late 1930s has never looked like more fun than in this 1976 film. The players are intelligent, interesting showmen who play great ball and satisfy the customers too. It's a high-energy movie starring Billy Dee Williams, James Earl Jones, and Richard Pryor.

BULL DURHAM

WE NEVER KNEW MINOR-LEAGUE BASEBALL could be so sexy. Susan Sarandon makes aging catcher Kevin Costner and bizarre rookie pitcher Tim Robbins crazy. Unlike most of these other films, this one takes us down to the bushes, where players carry their own bags, rehearse what they'll say if they're ever interviewed, and dream of "the show."

EIGHT MEN OUT

WITH GREAT PRECISION, director John Sayles tells the tale of the 1919 Black Sox scandal. The historical basis for this film is both its greatest strength and its greatest flaw. There is fine acting from an ensemble cast that includes John Cusack, David Strathairn, D.B. Sweeney, and Charlie Sheen.

FEAR STRIKES OUT

TONY PERKINS'S PORTRAYAL of real-life outfielder Jimmy Piersall in this 1957 film moved him into the star circle. This is an unsettling movie as it depicts Piersall's difficulty in dealing with pressure from his father (a thoroughly believable Karl Malden). *Fear Strikes Out* is perhaps a little too dramatic in spots, but it's fascinating nonetheless.

FIELD OF DREAMS

FOR ALL OF ITS SENTIMENTAL SAPPINESS, this film still nudges open the tear ducts, as it links the idea of history to the concept of loss of the father. Kevin Costner is at his airheaded best, while James Earl Jones is merely along for the ride. If you build it, they will come.

IT HAPPENS EVERY SPRING

WHAT A HOOT! In this 1949 film, Ray Milland plays a meek college prof who invents a "wood repellent." Put it on a baseball and the thing will do incredible twists to avoid being hit by the bat. So Ray uses it to become the greatest rookie pitcher ever. Paul Douglas, who later would be in *Angels in the Outfield,* is Milland's catcher here.

MAJOR LEAGUE

THIS IS AN ALL-OUT, rude, crude, raucous farce about a down-in-the-dumps team (Cleveland Indians) that finds new life when an unscrupulous female owner comes up with an idea: If they finish last, she can move the club and dump all of the players. Of course, you know what they end up doing. And they use every possible baseball sight gag and cliche they can along the way.

PRIDE OF THE YANKEES

GARY COOPER and Teresa Wright were both nominated for Oscars for their acting in this film, easily the best baseball bio ever. But of course, what baseball story is more moving than that of Lou Gehrig? Babe Ruth plays himself and gives the only convincing performance of the Bambino any film has ever had. Other Yankee players are here too.

TAKE ME OUT TO THE BALLGAME

IT'S BASEBALL 1890S STYLE, with Frank Sinatra, Gene Kelly, and Jules Munshin teaming up as a short/second/first combination who also sing and do some fancy hoofing in vaudeville. With Esther Williams as the team owner, *Take Me Out* is the greatest MGM musical about baseball.

10 BEST BOOKS

BABE

BY ROBERT CREAMER. Creamer tackles the life of the youngster who became the legend with the seriousness of an historical biography, yet he never misses the fun that there was just being around the Babe. This is one of baseball's first truly adult biographies.

BASEBALL: THE EARLY YEARS
BASEBALL: THE GOLDEN AGE
BASEBALL: THE PEOPLE'S GAME

BY HAROLD SEYMOUR. Professor Seymour recounts the game's history in a manner serious yet pleasurable. The first two books, which track professional baseball from its beginnings through the late '20s, are indispensable; the third, a history of nonprofessional baseball, is merely breathtaking.

THE BILL JAMES ABSTRACTS AND HISTORICAL BASEBALL ABSTRACT

BY BILL JAMES. These books are noteworthy not because of their stats, but rather for the insights they offer into the game. Written in a delightfully nonacademic style, these works move James into the first rank of baseball historians along with Harold Seymour and David Voigt.

THE BOYS OF SUMMER

By ROGER KAHN. This remarkable book offers a bittersweet look at what happened to the Dodgers of the late 1940s and early '50s when they left baseball to face the often harsh realities of the world. Their essential nobility seldom leaves them. They deserve to be adored. This book makes every baseball literary Hall of Fame list.

THE GLORY OF THEIR TIMES

By LAWRENCE RITTER. Oral history was a new thing to baseball when Professor Ritter sat down with these players from the earliest years of the century. The result is an insight into that era that we couldn't have gotten any other way. In some ways, it's the foundation for all baseball oral history since.

THE HOT STOVE LEAGUE

By LEE ALLEN. When most baseball writing was pedestrian "sports reporting," Allen was a master of the clever phrase and telling metaphor. The combination of those writing skills with his encyclopedic knowledge of the game make for delightful, insightful literature.

THE LONG SEASON

By JIM BROSNAN. It's hard to understand now what a stink this book stirred up in the early '60s. A real diary about baseball players as real people with faults, problems, and bad habits, it was a revelation of the time. Remarkably, it still holds up today because of its honesty and clarity.

THE (MACMILLAN) BASEBALL ENCYCLOPEDIA

EDITED BY JOE REICHLER. When this tome made its first appearance to celebrate baseball's centennial in 1969, it took everyone's breath away. All those numbers! All those players! We all figured we had reached the Holy Grail of baseball information. We didn't realize we were just taking the first steps on a brand-new (and ongoing) adventure.

NICE GUYS FINISH LAST

BY LEO DUROCHER AND ED LINN. This book is full of the giants Leo played and managed with and against, which makes it that rare item: a significant baseball history disguised as a memoir. Branch Rickey, Babe Ruth, Rabbit Maranville, Jackie Robinson, Willie Mays, Bobby Thomson—who do you want to know about?

TOTAL BASEBALL

EDITED BY JOHN THORN AND PETE PALMER. The ongoing competition between this book and the Macmillan encyclopedia is a boon for baseball lovers of all kinds. *Total Baseball* includes the "new stats" and also features articles on other baseball subjects, such as "Scandals and Controversies" and "Phantom Ballplayers."

10 BEST FANS

HILDA CHESTER

FAMOUS FOR RINGING her cowbell from the center-field bleachers in Ebbets Field, Chester was the epitome of the raucous Dodger fan. She carried not just one cowbell but two, to ring out in celebration or in mourning. (One of the bells is now in Cooperstown.) She also carried a large sign that let everyone know that "Hilda Is Here."

HI DIXWELL

SOME CALLED HIM "GENERAL," which was not an official title, but he was a well-known figure in Boston in the late 19th century. *The Sporting News* said, "He lives for the national game." He also got himself invited along on road trips, perhaps because he was known to pass out cigars to the Red Stocking players.

WILD BILL HAGY

IN SECTION 34 of Baltimore's Memorial Stadium in the late 1970s rose up a large, long-haired, full-bearded, well-beered cab driver who spelled out O-R-I-O-L-E-S with his body, and the crowd went bonkers. One writer said Hagy had "a voice that sounds like a cement mixer in action." When told he was "amazing," Wild Bill responded, "There ain't nothing amazing about it. They could do the same thing if they drank a case of beer every night."

LOLLIE HOPKINS

UNLIKE THE OTHER FAMOUS FANS, Lollie was a Boston fan of the pre-World War II era who would never think of hollering. She used a megaphone. And, in polite New England style, she was perfectly willing to cheer for good play on the part of either team.

BRUCE "SCREECH OWL" MCALLISTER

IT WASN'T A PLEASANT SOUND, but it was memorable. When Bruce McAllister let go one of his patented screams back in the 1930s, no one sitting in Forbes Field could miss it. Of course, with KDKA beaming Pirate games all over the East and Midwest, Bruce would often be heard in Missouri and Connecticut too.

MIKE "'NUF CED" MCGREEVY

THE MAN'S MONIKER came about because he was the ultimate authority on any sports question you threw at him. Bartender McGreevy headed the Royal Rooters, a most raucous group of Boston fans. In 1912, when a front-office blunder shut the Rooters out of Game 7 of the World Series, they just broke down the gates and marched around the field.

GUS MILLER

HE OWNED THE NEWSSTAND next to Forbes Field and worked as an usher in the very first game played in Forbes in 1909. Miller was such an identifiable figure on the Pittsburgh sports scene that—like Pele, Madonna, and Elvis—he was referred to by just his first name. The official Pirate fan club named itself after him: "The Gus Fan Club."

MARY OTT

ONE WRITER CALLED OTT'S VOICE "a neigh known to cause stampedes in Kansas City stockyards." That's particularly impressive when you realize Mary lived in St. Louis! The "Horse Lady of St. Louis" first came to national attention when revered umpire Bill Klem threatened to throw her out of a game in 1926.

PATSY O'TOOLE

IN DETROIT IN THE 1930s, the fan who made the most noise was Patsy, who rightfully earned his nickname as "the All-American earache." Opposing players got the full brunt of a Patsy attack, and he was especially tough on the hated Yankees.

JACK PIERCE

PIERCE'S FANDOM BORDERED ON OBSESSION. He was sure that Dodger infielder Cookie Lavagetto was the greatest player ever. So to honor his idol, Pierce showed up at Ebbets Field every day, bought 10 seats, and—using the containers of gas he brought along—blew up dozens of balloons with "Cookie" on them and released them throughout the game.

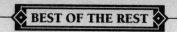

BEST QUOTES

"A couple of years ago, they told me I was too young to be President and you were too old to be playing baseball. But we fooled them."
—45-YEAR-OLD JOHN F. KENNEDY TO 41-YEAR-OLD STAN MUSIAL AT THE 1962 ALL-STAR GAME

"A rabbit didn't have to think to know what to do to dodge a dog.... The same kind of instinct told Babe Ruth what to do and where to be."
—YANKEE OUTFIELDER SAMMY VICK ON THE MAN WHO REPLACED HIM

"All I want out of life is that when I walk down the street people will say, 'There goes the greatest hitter who ever lived.'"
—RED SOX ROOKIE TED WILLIAMS

"Any ballplayer that don't sign autographs for little kids ain't an American. He's a Communist."
—ROGERS HORNSBY, *THE SATURDAY EVENING POST*, JUNE 12, 1963

"Anybody with ability can play in the major leagues. To last as long as I did with the skills I had, with the numbers I produced, was a triumph of the human spirit."
—BOB UECKER, WHO HIT .200 OVER SIX BIG-LEAGUE SEASONS, *CATCHER IN THE WRY*

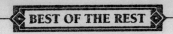

"Baseball is pitching, fundamentals, and three-run homers."
—EARL WEAVER, *HOW LIFE IMITATES THE WORLD SERIES*

"Baseball is the most intellectual game because most of the action goes on in your head."
—HENRY KISSINGER

"Baseball is a game where a curve is an optical illusion, a screwball can be a pitch or a person, stealing is legal, and you can spit anywhere you like except in the umpire's eye or on the ball."
—JIM MURRAY, *THE BEST OF JIM MURRAY*

"Baseball is the very symbol, the outward and visible expression of the drive and push and rush and struggle of the raging, tearing, booming nineteenth century."
—MARK TWAIN, APRIL 8, 1889

"Baseball is 90 percent mental; the other half is physical."
—YOGI BERRA

"Can I throw harder than Joe Wood? Listen, my friend, there's no man alive who can throw harder than Smokey Joe Wood."
—WALTER JOHNSON

"Can't anybody here play this game?"
—MANAGER CASEY STENGEL ON HIS 1962 METS TEAM, WHICH WENT 40-120

"Don Buddin should have 'E6' on his license plate."
—SPORTS WRITER CLIFF KEANE ON THE ERROR-PRONE RED
SOX SHORTSTOP, *THE PICTURE HISTORY OF THE
BOSTON RED SOX*

"Don't quit until every base is uphill."
—BABE RUTH, *THE BABE RUTH STORY*

"Don't look back. Something might be gaining on
you."
—SATCHEL PAIGE, *COLLIER'S*, JUNE 13, 1953

"Errors are part of my image. One night in Pittsburgh, 30,000 fans gave me a standing ovation
when I caught a hot dog wrapper on the fly."
—FIRST BASEMAN DICK STUART, KNOWN AS "DR.
STRANGEGLOVE," *PLAYING THE FIELD*

"Fans, for the past two weeks you have been reading about the bad break I got. Yet today I consider
myself the luckiest man on the face of the Earth."
—OPENING OF LOU GEHRIG'S FAREWELL ADDRESS AT
YANKEE STADIUM, JULY 4, 1939

"Fenway Park in Boston is a lyric little bandbox of
a ballpark. Everything is painted green and seems
in curiously sharp focus, like the inside of an oldfashioned peeping-type Easter egg."
—JOHN UPDIKE, *THE NEW YORKER*

"Having Willie Stargell on your team is like having a diamond ring on your finger."
—PITTSBURGH MANAGER CHUCK TANNER, *TIME*, OCTOBER 29, 1979

"He sometimes throws and catches a ball for hours with his aide-de-camp."
—AMERICAN SOLDIER UNDER GENERAL GEORGE WASHINGTON

"He says hello on Opening Day and good-bye on Closing Day, and in between he hits .350."
—MICKEY COCHRANE ON CHARLIE GEHRINGER

"He went from Cy Young to sayonara in a year."
—GRAIG NETTLES ON YANKEE TEAMMATE SPARKY LYLE, *BRONX ZOO*

"He had larceny in his heart but his feet were honest."
—SPORTS WRITER BUGS BAER ON SLOW-FOOTED PING BODIE

"He's a remarkable catch, that Canzoneri. He's the only defensive catcher in baseball who can't catch."
—CASEY STENGEL ON MET RECEIVER CHRIS CANNIZZARO, WHOSE NAME HE COULD NEVER REMEMBER, *NEWSDAY*, AUGUST 31, 1965

"Heck, if I'd a known it was going to be a famous record, I'd a stuck it in his ear."
—TOM ZACHARY AFTER ALLOWING BABE RUTH'S 60TH HOMER OF THE 1927 SEASON, *RAIN DELAYS*

"Hitting is timing. Pitching is upsetting timing."
—WARREN SPAHN

"I know, but I had a better year than Hoover."
—BABE RUTH'S RESPONSE WHEN A REPORTER POINTED OUT
HIS 1930 SALARY DEMAND OF $80,000 TOPPED THAT OF THE
PRESIDENT'S $75,000 SALARY

"I don't room with him; I room with his suitcase."
—YANKEE BIG BODIE ON HIS MISCHIEVOUS
TEAMMATE/ROOMMATE BABE RUTH,
BABE: THE LEGEND COMES TO LIFE

"I would be the laughingstock of the league if I
took the best left-handed pitcher in the league and
put him in the outfield."
—RED SOX MANAGER ED BARROW IN 1918 ON MOVING
BABE RUTH FROM THE MOUND TO A FULL-TIME POSITION,
THE SPORTING NEWS, JANUARY 16, 1965

"I am glad to hear of their coming, but they will
have to wait a few minutes till I get my turn at bat."
—ABRAHAM LINCOLN, ON BEING INFORMED OF HIS
NOMINATION FOR PRESIDENT, 1860

"I don't know a lot about politics, but I know a lot
about baseball."
—RICHARD NIXON, 1981

"I hit with a bat, not with my face."
—YOGI BERRA, RESPONDING TO NEEDLES ABOUT HIS HOMELY
COMPLEXION

"I can remember a reporter asking for a quote, and I didn't know what a quote was. I thought it was some kind of soft drink."

—JOE DIMAGGIO

"I like the job I have now, but if I had my life to live over again, I'd like to have ended up a sports writer."

—RICHARD NIXON, PRESIDENT OF THE UNITED STATES AT THE TIME

"I want to be remembered as a ballplayer who gave all he had to give."

—ROBERTO CLEMENTE

"I don't care if half the league strikes. This is the United States of America and one citizen has as much right to play as another."

—COMMISSIONER FORD FRICK TO CARDINALS PLAYERS, WHO HAD BEEN PLANNING TO STRIKE WHEN THE DODGERS AND JACKIE ROBINSON CAME TO ST. LOUIS IN 1947, *THE SUMMER GAME*

"I don't know that it's so important to have Tug McGraw's autograph. It's not like he's Donald Duck or something."

—ELEMENTARY SCHOOL GIRL ON MEETING TUG MCGRAW AT HIS CHILDREN'S SCHOOL, *SPORTS ILLUSTRATED*, NOVEMBER 20, 1978

"I never questioned the integrity of an umpire. Their eyesight, yes."
—LEO DUROCHER, *NICE GUYS FINISH LAST*

"If I'd known I was gonna pitch a no-hitter today, I would have gotten a haircut."
—BO BELINSKY, *THE SUITORS OF SPRING*

"If they came to Josh Gibson today and he were 17 years old, they would have a blank spot on the contract and they'd say, 'Fill the amount in.' That's how good Josh Gibson was."
—JUNIOR GILLIAM, *BASEBALL DIGEST*, JUNE 1969

"If a black boy can make it on Okinawa and Guadalcanal, hell, he can make it in baseball."
—BASEBALL COMMISSIONER HAPPY CHANDLER ON THE BREAKING OF THE MAJOR-LEAGUE COLOR LINE

"If I wasn't expected to drive the ball out of the lot every time I come up there to the plate, I'd change my batting form tomorrow. I'd copy [Ty] Cobb's style in every single thing he does."
—BABE RUTH, *BABE RUTH'S OWN BOOK OF BASEBALL*

"In baseball, you don't know nothing."
—YOGI BERRA, *BASEBALL: AN ILLUSTRATED HISTORY*

"Is that the best game you ever pitched?"
—QUESTION POSED BY AN ANONYMOUS REPORTER TO DON LARSEN FOLLOWING HIS PERFECT WORLD SERIES GAME IN 1956

"It took eight hours...seven and a half to find the heart."
—STEVE MCCATTY ON HEARING OF CHARLIE O. FINLEY'S
HEART SURGERY, *TEMPORARY INSANITY*

"It was so wonderful, Joe. You never heard such cheering."

"Yes, I have."
—EXCHANGE BETWEEN NEWLYWEDS MARILYN MONROE AND
JOE DIMAGGIO ON MONROE'S RETURN FROM KOREA, WHERE
SHE HAD ENTERTAINED SOME 100,000 ARMY TROOPS

"It ain't over till it's over."
—YOGI BERRA

"It gets late early out there."
—YOGI BERRA ON THE TOUGH LATE-INNING SHADOWS IN
YANKEE STADIUM'S LEFT FIELD

"It's a great day for baseball. Let's play two."
—ERNIE BANKS

"Keep your eye clear and hit 'em where they ain't."
—WEE WILLIE KEELER

"Keep it low."
—TIGER CATCHER BOB SWIFT GIVING HIS PITCHER LES CAIN
ADVICE ON HOW TO PITCH TO 3'7" BROWNS BATTER
EDDIE GAEDEL, *RAIN DELAYS*

"Most important of all—and this goes not alone for baseball but every other profession—save your money! If I had saved from the start of my career, I might have had a million dollars today."
—BABE RUTH, *BABE RUTH'S OWN BOOK FOR BASEBALL*

"Mr. Rickey, do you want a ballplayer who's afraid to fight back?"

"I want a ballplayer with guts enough *not* to fight back!"
—EXCHANGE BETWEEN JACKIE ROBINSON AND BRANCH RICKEY ON AUGUST 28, 1945, THE DAY ROBINSON SIGNED A BROOKLYN CONTRACT

"Nobody ever says anything nice about an umpire, unless it's when he dies and then somebody writes in the paper, 'He was a good umpire.'"
—UMPIRE TOM GORMAN, *CATCHER IN THE WRY*

"Nolan says throw it high because amateurs get out there, no matter how good they are, and throw it in the dirt. You get more of an 'ooooh' [from the crowd] if you heave it over the [catcher's] head instead of going with the fast-breaking deuce into the dirt."
—GEORGE BUSH ON ADVICE NOLAN RYAN GAVE HIM ON THROWING OUT THE FIRST BALL WHILE PRESIDENT

"Show me a good loser, and I'll show you an idiot."
— LEO DUROCHER

"Sixty. Count 'em. Sixty! Let's see some other SOB match that!"
—BABE RUTH IN THE YANKEE LOCKER ROOM AFTER HITTING HIS 60TH HOMER OF THE SEASON, SEPTEMBER 30, 1927, *CLOUT! THE TOP HOME RUNS IN BASEBALL HISTORY*

"Son, I won more games than you'll ever see."
—CY YOUNG, RESPONDING TO A YOUTHFUL REPORTER

"Spahn and Sain and pray for rain."
—JINGLE COINED DURING THE 1948 SEASON, WHEN BRAVES PITCHERS WARREN SPAHN AND JOHNNY SAIN WON NINE GAMES IN A 21-DAY STRETCH IN SEPTEMBER

"Sure, I believe he has arthritis. But it doesn't hurt from the first to the ninth inning. I know that."
—ROBERTO CLEMENTE ON SANDY KOUFAX, *THE BASEBALL LIFE OF SANDY KOUFAX*

"The saddest words of all to a pitcher are three: 'Take him out.'"
—CHRISTY MATHEWSON, *PITCHING IN A PINCH*

"The secret of my success was clean living and a fast-moving outfield."
—PITCHER LEFTY GOMEZ, *THE NEW YORK TIMES*, APRIL 25, 1976

"The more I see of Babe, the more he seems a figure out of mythology."
—BOSTON SPORTS WRITER BURT WHITMAN ON YOUNG RED SOX PHENOM BABE RUTH

"There is always some kid who may be seeing me for the first or last time. I owe him my best."
—JOE DiMAGGIO

"There's never been anyone like this kid which we got from Joplin. He has more speed than any slugger and more slug than speedster—and nobody has ever had more of both of them together."
—ON A YOUNG MICKEY MANTLE, QUOTED BY BOB DEINDORFER IN BASEBALL STARS OF 1963

"To Johnny Bench, a Hall of Famer for sure."
—INSCRIPTION ON BALL SIGNED BY TED WILLIAMS FOR CINCINNATI'S 20-YEAR-OLD ROOKIE CATCHER, SPRING TRAINING 1968

"Washington—first in war, first in peace, last in the American League."
—CHARLES DRYDEN ON THE LOWLY SENATORS

"We had a lot of triple-threat guys—slip, fumble, and fall."
—PITTSBURGH CATCHER JOE GARAGIOLA ON THE AWFUL PIRATE TEAMS OF THE EARLY 1950S, BASEBALL DIGEST, OCTOBER 1963

"When Steve and I die, we're going to be buried 60 feet, six inches apart."
—TIM McCARVER, STEVE CARLTON'S "PERSONAL" CATCHER MUCH OF HIS CAREER, THE PITCHER

"Whoever wants to know the heart and mind of America had better learn baseball, the rules and realities of the game."
—JACQUES BARZUN, PHILOSOPHY PROFESSOR, COLUMBIA UNIVERSITY, 1954

"You can't tell the players without a scorecard."
—CONCESSIONAIRE HARRY M. STEVENS, LATE 19TH CENTURY

"You spend a good piece of your life gripping a baseball and in the end it turns out that it was the other way around all the time."
—JIM BOUTON, *BALL FOUR*

"You can have it. It wouldn't do me any good."
—RAY CHAPMAN TO UMPIRE BILLY EVANS AFTER TAKING TWO STRIKES FROM WALTER JOHNSON IN 1915; HE HAD ALREADY BEEN ON HIS WAY TO THE DUGOUT WHEN EVANS INFORMED HIM HE STILL HAD ONE STRIKE

"You gotta be a man to play baseball for a living, but you gotta have a lot of little boy in you, too."
—ROY CAMPANELLA, *NEW YORK JOURNAL-AMERICAN*, APRIL 12, 1957

"You can see a lot just by observing."
—YOGI BERRA

"You don't save a pitcher for tomorrow. Tomorrow it might rain."
—LEO DUROCHER

BEST NICKNAMES

John "Terrible Swede" Anderson

Luke "Old Aches and Pains" Appling

Hank "Bow Wow" Arft

Luis "Yo-Yo" Arroyo

Abraham Lincoln "Sweetbreads" Bailey

Steve "Bye-Bye" Balboni

Lady Baldwin

Jimmy "Foxy Grandpa" Bannon

Bald Billy Barnie

Boom-Boom Beck

Bill "Ding Dong" Bell

Joe "Bananas" Benes

Jittery Joe Berry

Don "The Weasel" Bessent

Emil "Hill Billy" Bildilli

Bingo Binks

Ewell "The Whip" Blackwell

Paul "Motormouth" Blair

Bob "Butterball" Botz

Oil Can Boyd

Bunny Brief

Frank "Turkeyfoot" Brower

Downtown Ollie Brown

Mordecai "Three Finger" Brown

Pee Wee Butts

Sammy "Babe Ruth's Legs" Byrd

Ron "The Penguin" Cey

Pearce "What's the Use" Chiles

Boileryard Clark

Jack "The Ripper" Clark

Will "The Thrill" Clark

Dain "Ding-a-Ling" Clay

Fidgety Phil Collins

Frank "Runt" Cox

Nick "Old Tomato Face" Cullop

Jack "Sour Mash" Daniels

Yo-Yo Davalillo

Pickles Dillhoefer

Spittin' Bill Doak

Joe "Burrhead" Dobson

Shufflin' Phil Douglas

Buttermilk Tommy Dowd

George "Pea Soup" Dumont

Shawon "Thunder Pup" Dunston

Leo "The Lip" Durocher

Fred "Moonlight Ace" Fussell

Pud "The Little Steam Engine" Galvin

Phil "Scrap Iron" Garner

Pebbly Jack Glasscock

Burleigh "Stubblebeard" Grimes

Ron "Louisiana Lightning" Guidry

Doug "Eyechart" Gwosdz

Jack "Do-Little" Hardy

Mike "The Human Rain Delay" Hargrove

Egyptian Healy

George "Old Wax Figger" Hemming

Piano Legs Hickman

Handy Andy High

Still Bill Hill

Johnny "Hippity" Hopp

Elmer "Herky Jerky" Horton

Al "The Mad Hungarian" Hrabosky

Joe "Poodles" Hutcheson

Happy "Dimples" Iott

Reggie "Mr. October" Jackson

Shoeless Joe Jackson

Baby Doll Jacobson

Al "Bear Tracks" Javery

Hughie "Ee-Yah" Jennings

Oscar "Flip Flap" Jones

Willie "Puddin' Head" Jones

Wee Willie Keeler

George "Highpockets" Kelly

John "Chickenhearted" Kirby

Gene "Rubber" Krapp

Tobacco Chewin' Johnny Lanning

Slothful Bill Lattimore

Tony "Poosh 'Em Up" Lazzeri

Aurelio "Señor Smoke" Lopez

Bris "The Human Eyeball" Lord

Sal "The Barber" Maglie

Willie "The Say Hey Kid" Mays

Sudden Sam McDowell

Cliff "Mountain Music" Melton

Benny "Earache" Meyer

Russ "The Mad Monk" Meyer

Roscoe "Rubberlegs" Miller

Earl "Steam Engine in Boots" Moore

Hugh "Losing Pitcher" Mulcahy

Johnny "Grandma" Murphy

Yale "Tot Midget" Murphy

Julio "Whiplash" Navarro

The Only Nolan

Lou "The Mad Russian" Novikoff

Jack "Peach Pie" O'Connor

Blue Moon Odom

Al "The Curveless Wonder" Orth

Charlie "The Old Woman in the Red Cap" Pabor

Camilo "Little Potato" Pascual

Mark "Humpty Dumpty" Polhemus

Phil "Grandmother" Powers

Claude "Little All Right" Ritchey

Raw Meat Bill Rodgers

Babe "The Sultan of Swat" Ruth

Joe "Horse Belly" Sargent

George "Twinkletoes" Selkirk

Bucketfoot Al Simmons

Harry "Suitcase" Simpson

Lou "The Nervous Greek" Skizas

Jimmy "The Human Mosquito" Slagle

Frank "Piano Mover" Smith

Moe "The Rabbi of Swat" Solomon

Dick "Dr. Strangelove" Stuart

Ed "Kickapoo Chief" Summers

Jim "Abba Dabba" Tobin

Specs Toporcer

Bill "Mumbles" Tremel

Frank "Sweet Music" Viola

Dixie "The People's Cherce" Walker

Walt "No-Neck" Williams

Charlie "Swamp Baby" Wilson

Jimmy "The Toy Cannon" Wynn

Rollie "Bunions" Zeide

INDEX

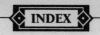